YOUR RESTAURANT STILL SUCKS!

STOP PLAYING SMALL.
GET WHAT YOU WANT.
BECOME A BADASS.

DONALD BURNS
THE RESTAURANT COACH™

Testimonials

Praise for Your Restaurant STILL Sucks!

" *'Those who can do, those who can't teach' (George Bernard Shaw).* Donald is one of those rare breeds who CAN do, and has time and time again, but has focused his efforts on how to teach and coach, to get others to improve by showing the simple, unique steps to achieve CAN do. This book is one more step in that direction."

-Chef Jay McCarthy, Director of Operations,
Richard Sandoval Hospitality

"Donald Burns aka 'The Restaurant Coach™' is a highly sought after and respected hospitality industry speaker, consultant, and author. He has penned yet another blockbuster follow-up book entitled, 'Your Restaurant STILL Sucks!'. This proves that wisdom comes in sequels! Donald's trademark no-nonsense, no compromise, and transformational methods have earned him countless accolades and international reputation as a top industry expert and leader. Wisdom dictates adding this treasure to any restaurant's recipes for success!"

-Brian Duncan, Founder, Down
to Earth Wine Concepts

"In life, you can have many coaches, but there's only one that I know that will jump out of planes with you, make you more money, break your ego, and answer your phone calls all hours of the night, and that's Donald Burns 'THE' Restaurant Coach™!"

-Peter Barlow, Executive Chef & Co-Founder,
Niteshade Chef Collaborative

"Everyone should pick up a copy of this book. It's that good!!!"

-John Maier, Enterprise Business
Consultant, Shamrock Foods

"Donald explains things honestly and candidly. There is no sugar coating, and this is what makes Donald real. Because he tells it like it is. He isn't going BS you, or tell you something nice so not to hurt your feelings. He'd rather see you succeed, prosper, and thrive than to let your excesses be your downfall. This is what separates him from others in his industry. You'll find new techniques or familiar ones you may have forgotten about. New ideas and thoughts around the subject of time and many more hidden gems. This is a must for anyone in the restaurant business."

-Brian Alcorn, Owner, Paleo Brio

"Donald has enabled me, coached me, and given me the confidence to reach high levels of success within the restaurant industry. As a pastry chef who can relate to what Donald has written about, this book is engaging for not only chefs like me but all industry and restaurateurs alike; bringing business individuals and companies great results. This book is a game changer -- why wouldn't you want to unlock your potential?!"

-Casey Nicole, Executive Pastry
Chef, Dallas Country Club

"Improving your bar or restaurant means going on a daily journey toward bettering yourself and your attitude. Donald Burns' 'Your Restaurant STILL Sucks!' is your roadmap to becoming a more successful operator."

-David Klemt, Editor, Nightclub & Bar

"Finding Donald was the best thing that could have happened to our restaurant and us, we were in a desperate situation not knowing why sales had dropped down, the atmosphere had faded away and the excitement we had at the beginning was just a memory. We started working through the roadmap to success that Donald designed, and within two months we started seeing amazing changes, the culture was defined, the concept and communication aligned, the team was motivated, and sales were increasing!! We now have a plan, and what's better we have clarity on how to achieve it. I won't ever have enough words to thank Donald for saving our investment and for showing us the path to being a successful restaurant. Thank YOU!!!"

-Andres M Cardona, Owner, Instinto
GastroBar, Bogota, Colombia

BY THE SAME AUTHOR
Outstanding Mindset: *How to Set Yourself and Your Restaurant Up for Success Each Day!* (2019)

Your Restaurant Sucks! *Embrace The Suck.*
Unleash Your Restaurant. Become Outstanding. (2017)*

**Winner: 2019 Industry Book & Author of the Year by Nightclub & Bar*

Dedication

To my Children:
Morgan Lee and James Alexander
I am proud of you both more than words could ever say.

To my Closest Friends:
Thax & Donna Turner, Jay McCarthy, Bryon Kelly, John Trevor-Smith, Eva Ballarin, Kelly Musselman, and Brian Duncan.

> *They say the difference between a friend and a true friend is this:*
> *A friend will help you move;* **a true friend will help you move a body!**

To my Restaurant Coaching Clients and Fans of The Restaurant Coach™ Brand:
Thank you for your support and for sharing my message around the globe.
I am honored to serve and coach you.
To The Restaurant Coach™ Nation:

> *Thank you for being a part of a global tribe where sisters and brothers from the restaurant industry fight against the forces of mediocrity.*

To Members of Restaurant Masterminds™:

For those that walk a different path. "Two roads diverged in a wood, and I— I took the one less traveled by, And that has made all the difference."-Robert Frost

Table of Contents

*"If everything seems under control,
you're not going fast enough."*

-Mario Andretti

EXPLICIT LANGUAGE AHEAD

AUTHOR'S NOTE:

As you read these words on the following pages, please remember that they are merely words and they lack two of the three critical elements of effective communication: tone and non-verbal body language.

If you have seen me at a workshop, keynote event, or attended one of my workshops, you'll have a greater sense of the positive nature of my tone and the accompanying enthusiastic non-verbals. **Please know that my only intention is to help you reach your true potential.** If the words ahead offend you or piss you off, remember they are only words on paper, and *you* are adding *your* tone to them.

Relax, embrace the suck, take the lessons, and just let that negative shit go.

If you are sensitive to language, you might want to **stop** reading here. The material in this book is written in real-world terms and uses language that occurs in restaurants.

Please note that I don't use profanity to offend anyone. I use strong language to break your thinking patterns and make you uncomfortable. When you get to that place, then (and only then) will you start taking action to make changes.

That being said, I have worked in restaurants and kitchens for nearly four decades, and yes, I do drop the F-Bomb quite often. Let's have a fucking great time getting you the restaurant and life you know you want, deep down.

See, I warned you.

How to effectively use this book.

I'm not telling you how to read, I want to be clear and throw a few tips out there for you so you can get the most out of this book.

1. This book is not your typical start at the front and read through to the end kind of book. The chapters are arranged by topic, and you can jump around however, you wish.

2. Whatever you are struggling with (whether it's culture, leadership, teamwork, mindset, marketing, menus, etc.) THAT is the best place to start.

3. Share what you learn with others on your team while it's fresh in your mind. Each section is concise and to the point, so you can get to work building the restaurant and life you want.

4. Lastly, to read and do nothing with this information is a waste of your potential and time (*and a damn good book!*). We don't improve unless we challenge ourselves to do new things. In the pages ahead, you will find hundreds of tools, ideas, and questions that you can apply immediately to become better. Becoming better was my inspiration when writing this book. ***I want you to stop playing small in the world.*** If you ever think that you can't do it or do not know how to apply these tools, then perhaps it's time we speak about getting you a coach.

The greatest honor you can bestow upon me is to be your coach.

Introduction

Foreword

"You run the restaurant, don't let the restaurant run you!"

That's a quote a former boss and mentor would often sound-off during a shift that was going south. Like many restaurateurs, we plan to run the elusive perfect shift, but it never happens. Running a restaurant is controlled chaos at its finest, and the best of the best can run a shift with a smile, no matter how much adversity they face. The truth is, the only thing you can control in a restaurant is your own emotion and reaction. Either you or one of your managers will crack almost every shift. The vendors, guests, or even worse, your team members, will be the recipients of your negative emotion and destructive behavior. As Maya Angelou so eloquently stated, *"People will forget what you said, they will forget what you did, but people will never forget how you made them feel."*

For the last 20 years, my team and I have been building an amazing business, and we proudly serve over 2,800 restaurant brands in over 56 countries, from independents to global restaurant chains. I've dedicated 30 years of my life to this beautifully complex industry, and I've learned that the best leaders live their company core values, are constantly investing in team member development, and are truly humble. I suppose you've been humbled, and that's why you're reading *this* book.

No one wants to hear his or her restaurants sucks, because the truth bites. Donald masterfully created this book to share digestible daily readings to inspire you to reach your full potential as a leader, so you can, in turn, inspire others to reach operational excellence. Who knows, after reading this book, you just might find yourself running the perfect shift someday. If embraced and applied, Donald's years of wisdom and coaching can help you bring hospitality to the world, education, and pride to the next generation of restaurateurs, and the sizable profits you truly deserve.

David Cantu
Co-Founder, HotSchedules®

Déjà Vu

How the hell have you been?

I can't believe it's been a year since my first book (*Your Restaurant Sucks! Embrace the suck. Unleash your restaurant. Become outstanding.*) was released and started a real storm in the restaurant world about what makes one restaurant good, one great, and one outstanding. It surely has stirred up some interesting "haters" on the internet who love to throw shade our way. It's been awesome, and I appreciate all of it! ***The good, the bad, and the ugly!***

You should appreciate it as well. If you read my first book, you probably haven't changed as much as you wanted, or changed at all. How do I know this? Because here you are, reading book number 2 and still looking for the damn magic formula that will finally get you the restaurant and the life you want. ***Is it just me or do you have déjà vu, too?***

Maybe it's my fault for not giving you a detailed action plan in my first book. Maybe I needed to be more direct like I am with my coaching clients. Maybe you need an old school ass-kicking? Okay, perhaps that was crossing the line—no one is going to show up at your restaurant and kick your ass today. *Even if you might need it, or want it! LOL*

What I want for you to do is to kick your own ass this time. I want you to dig deep down and pull out whatever the fuck is inside you that's holding you back from having it all, everything you desire. For once, step the fuck up and claim the life you want! Do you say it can't be done? **Bullshit**—I do it every damn day with my clients. If you really take the words in this book to heart and use it as your bible to run your restaurant and your life, you *will* see the Promised Land!

So, why are you still here in Déjà Vu-land thinking that a new book is going to change your life? Granted, this book has the **potential** to change your life if you follow through and apply the lessons in it **today**. Not tomorrow, not next week, not come New Year's; **now.** Like right NOW. Stop the whining.

Stop telling yourself all the excuses why you can't. Start finding out why **you can**. That comes from one place: **your heart**.

You have to want change more than anything. No one likes change. It's scary. It's the unknown. It's outside your comfort zone. But that's **exactly** why change is amazing. All the good stuff in life is out there. If the good stuff was already here, in front of your face, you wouldn't be wanting more because you'd already have what you want. Boats are safe in the harbor, but that's not what boats are built for; you must get out into uncharted territory if you want what you truly seek.

"What you seek is seeking you." ~Rumi

It baffles me how many people fight against the universe. They struggle and rage against the very energy that's created to get them exactly what they want. I didn't realize this until late in my life. I was one of those who screamed at the heavens and asked when it was going to be my turn for a damn break. I blamed others for low salaries, labeling owners and general managers as "cheap" for not paying me big money. The truth is I didn't see my true potential, a potential that goes beyond money, and I had low self-esteem. In those days, I fought what I thought was the good fight, rallying: **Me against the world! I'll show them! Get out of my way!**

Does any of that sound like something you might have said? *Be honest.*

If you have, great—*this is the book you need!*

A funny thing happens when you find clarity and, perhaps, grow a little older: you give less fucks about what others think. It's quite liberating. Freedom comes from being your authentic self. Don't worry, we're going to really dig into what makes you tick in the chapters ahead. Now, before we get started, I want you to take that emotional baggage you have and leave it outside the door. Yes, I know you have some baggage because we all do, even me. It's just that over the years I have continuously downsized mine to more of a convenient travel size. *It's time you did the same.*

Restaurant success is really about personal success. My coaching clients realize that shortly after they start their program with me. Yes, I want to see your Profit and Loss (P&L) each week. Yes, we are going to discuss your menu and how to optimize it. I'll give you ways to improve your marketing. Yes, I can give you checklists and templates to streamline and standardize your systems.

However, the main thing I'm going to do as your coach is push you to become a better person.

Restaurants only become better when the people in them become better. It's really that simple. All the problems and drama that plague most restaurants come from the people who work in them. Fix the people problems and those business problems will vanish.

In this second book I'm going to take you on a trip into the mindset of peak performance. Along the way you're going to discover some things about yourself you like…and a few things you don't. This isn't a book to judge you and make you feel bad; it's intended to provide you self-awareness and help you become a better human being. It's about stepping up and not settling for a life that's below the level you deserve. The parallels between your restaurant life and your personal life are strongly linked; improve one, and the other naturally improves.

I WANT YOU TO HAVE IT ALL.

Starting now...

Donald Burns
The Restaurant Coach™
January 2019

Why Your Restaurant STILL Sucks!

"The definition of insanity is doing the same thing over and over again, but expecting different results."

—Attribution unknown

Green Feet and Emotional Triggers

"You want it where?" the tattoo artist asks me.
"On my right ass cheek," I reply.

Pararescue has a long-standing history that is steeped in tradition. Symbols become a rite of passage, and they also serve as a bond of brotherhood. Think of some traditions that are handed down in your family or among friends. We form closer bonds and trust when we share experiences, and this can go a long way to building a richer culture in your restaurant.

Traditions have always been in my life even if I never really thought about them as such. My Kempo Karate Instructor, Terry Bryan, gives you a silver dollar when you get your black belt, and another for every degree you attain after that (I have five from him). They serve as triggers to the moment when I received them; they trigger the peak emotions I was experiencing at that time. In Neuro-Linguistic Programming (NLP), a trigger is known as an anchor.

Triggers activate the emotions at the time the anchor was set. You have anchors already, some good and some bad. Driving down the road and you hear *that* song from high school, and you're automatically transported back to *that* time and those emotions. Conversely, maybe there are words that trigger a negative anchor in you. Someone says you're an idiot and you're taken back to an experience, resulting in all those negative emotions flooding back.

The goal is to create more positive anchors in your life so you can activate them to reach a peak emotional state on demand.

My father was an incredible chef. He was also hell on wheels in the kitchen. His nickname by the staff was "Wild Bill." He understood triggers in everyone around him and could use them as buttons to push when he felt like it. But, for all his exterior toughness, he could also be kind and compassionate.

I remember when I was around 16 and just starting to work more on the kitchen line and not just doing dishes or peeling vegetables. I was standing in the back once, peeling potatoes, and he walked up and threw a copy of *The Professional Chef* by The Culinary Institute of America (known as the CIA) at me. He barked, "If you're going to be a chef one day, you need to know everything in this book. Read a chapter each week, and I'll quiz you. If you pass, I'll teach you new techniques. If you fail a test, you'll be back here peeling potatoes."

He went to his office and came back a minute later. He laid a Wüsthof chef's knife on my cutting board. Then he said, "If you're going to cook, you need professional tools. This is one of my favorite knives, and I want you to have it." He looked down for a second like he wanted to say something else, then he walked back to his office.

That knife is one of my most valuable possessions. Every time I see it, I'm transported right back to that exact moment. It fills me with joy, pride, and love. My father had a hard time telling people he loved them—it wasn't his style. Giving me that knife was his way.

At Wolfgang Puck, all chefs were given a plating spoon by Chef himself. It was a rite of passage, and you carried that damn thing in your back pocket if you were in the kitchen working. It was part of your uniform. He wanted his chefs to taste everything! Tasting everything is part of the culture there.

I would take that spoon and make a challenge game out of it. The "Spoon Check" became a fun way for the team to bond, and it could get you some free drinks after work. It worked similarly to my Pararescueman (PJ) days. When I graduated as a PJ, I received a Pararescue Coin that I still have to this day. If another PJ pulled out their coin and challenged me, but I didn't have it on me, I lost the challenge. That meant I was buying drinks at the local bar. Now, if they challenged me and I *did* have my coin, they owed me a drink. It can get a little expensive if you do a coin challenge in a group of PJs, trust me.

Back to the tattoo.

Part of the Pararescue tradition is to get the symbol of a PJ tattooed on your right butt cheek. Back in the days, the preferred transportation was either the HC-130 or the HH-53 helicopter, the latter was nicknamed the Jolly Green Giant, and the symbol of two green feet became the stuff of PJ tradition. We would spray paint it in some crazy places as a calling card we had been there. Many a PJ has repelled down the side of a water tower or barracks to tag it with our sign. The green feet are a part of the brotherhood.

So, there I was in Ipswich, Great Britain, lying face down on the table with the tattoo artist getting ready to brand me as a PJ for life! Now, getting just the green feet would be the easy thing to do. If you know me at all, I always say, "Fuck easy." I went for a statement. My tattoo is a capitalized "P" with a "J" going through the middle. A maroon beret (worn by PJs) hangs off the corner of the "P," and there are two green feet under the "J."

"Yeah, that will do."

"You sure?" the tattoo artist asked in a heavy East Anglian accent.

"Fuck yeah!" I replied.

If you've never gotten a tattoo, I will describe it as having someone take a knife and carve on you. Of course, I had to act tough because I was there with two fellow Pararescuemen who were also being tattooed that day (both classmates of mine throughout Pararescue School: Steven Smith and Scott Shepard). Shepard, of course, had to one-up everyone and got this monster Pararescue tattoo that pretty much covered his entire right cheek! To say PJs aren't competitive would be a lie. We live to push each other past any perceived limits. *We push ourselves even more.* To a PJ, there are no limits, only obstacles that need to be navigated. There is strength in the team, complemented by the individual strengths everyone on your team brings.

> Those anchors are set deep in my mind, and whenever I need to change my energy. I have a wide range of triggers I've collected over the years that I can use to get me into a peak emotional state. You need to think about some simple triggers you could anchor to change your energy.

Music is a big one for many people, including me. Have you ever had a bad breakup with someone and you're driving down the road and "your song" comes on? You could be in a great mood and when that song comes on you head right back to the emotional Heartbreak Hotel! Make a playlist that can trigger those positive-energy emotions you want to activate. Songs are an amplifier of moods.

Symbols, anchors, and triggers are the way to rewire your brain to achieve peak performance levels more consistently. Bad shit is going to come at you from time to time—that's just life. You can't have all-sunshine every day because you need the rainy days for growth, and to appreciate those sunny days. Peak performers learn to appreciate the rainy days as much as the sunny days. This book has a lot of tools that you can add to your mental toolbox to get more from yourself. When you do that, you will see that others want to know how you did it, and then you can share your tools with them. ***Here's the catch: start with changing yourself first.***

I get asked often to come in and "fix" someone. First, I don't fix people. We are human beings, and all humans have flaws. *What I do is fix the thinking that causes the problems.*

Once I do that, the problems tend to fix themselves.

What to Do If Your Restaurant STILL Sucks (And It Might!)

Wait a minute—*sucks?* That sounds harsh. Okay, maybe *sucks* is a little dramatic. Surely you have some positive things going on in your restaurant. Maybe, though, you'd like even more. To get you more, we need to look at your business as a whole. Especially the things that might suck.

"The fears you run from, run to you." – Robin Sharma

Now, if things in your restaurant are not 100 percent the way you want them, there's room for improvement. Here's the real secret: you can always improve something. Remember that "good enough" is the battle cry for restaurants stuck in a never-ending version of their own *Groundhog Day* movie (yeah, the one with Bill Murray). You keep doing the same thing over and over, getting the same results. That might be okay, for now. However, you must be aware that markets change. Guests tastes and wants change. More competition will come to your town, and while you're happy doing things the same way, you'll soon find yourself behind the times. Your once shining brand will become dull in your guests' eyes. You have succumbed to the first sign on the road to mediocrity: complacency.

Complacency sucks.

OWN IT AND STOP IT

The first step is to take ownership of the situation. Stop using softener phrases like:

"*It's not that bad."*
"*It could be worse."*
"*It is what it is."*

If it's not how you want it, be honest about it. The beauty of this situation is that if you got your restaurant into the pit of complacency, you could get it out! The first thing to do when you find yourself in a hole is to stop digging.

Once you own it and stop sitting on the sidelines coming up with excuses as to why you can't change and improve things, you break free from the chains that are holding you down. Self-awareness is liberating. Painful at times but liberating long-term. As the owner or leader, you're the one who got your restaurant into this situation. The actions you did or did not take *put your brand here.*

Don't beat yourself up too badly. The world of 'coulda' and 'shoulda' is a mindset that belittles you and breaks down your self-confidence. **Own the fact that you're responsible and let's move forward.**

GET HELP

Asking for help is not high on the list of most restaurant leaders and owners. Many feel it's a sign of weakness. Let's be clear; it's not: it's smart business to ask for help.

Often, if you look within your team, you'll find you have untapped resources that are more than willing to give you a hand. If you're not a computer wizard and the thought of creating a spreadsheet would take you days, then why kill yourself wasting time? You might have someone on your team who's an Excel badass, someone who would love to take on the project. Not comfortable with Snapchat yet you know it would be great to use to market to Millennials? Why not ask a Millennial on your team to jump in?

Remember that proverbial hole you dug yourself into earlier? The three things that keep people stuck in their holes are the ghosts of dead restaurants also knows as the three Cardinal Sins of Leadership: **ego, pride,** and **denial**. They're so focused on the problems that they see nothing else. If they would look up, they might see there are a lot of people reaching down with an open hand to pull them out of the pit of complacency. They need to be willing to reach up and accept help. Don't let those three ghosts keep you a prisoner in your hole.

UNDERSTAND YOUR GAP

The habits and mindset that got you to the level of success you're at now likely won't be the same needed to get you to the next level. There's usually a "habit gap." You probably have some habits that served you well in the past, but now they're holding you back. As your business grows, you must grow with it. You can't expect things to change around you without changing yourself. I mean, you can, it just doesn't work. Every level of business success requires a new level of skills. Invest in yourself, adjust, and add new habits to reach this new level.

Going from operating one restaurant to two requires different habits and a different mindset, just like the habits and mindset to go from two to four locations are different. As the stakes go up (either in sales volume or number of locations), so does what you need to become a better leader. This is seen clearly in people with highly dominant habits of wanting to control things. Being on top of everything and everyone might have served you well when you had one busy location, but now you have three locations, and that previously successful habit is now seen by the team as micromanaging. People want to be trusted and allowed to do what you hired them to do. If you take those things away from them, they might stay for a while and then leave. Worse, they may stay but become disengaged and just go through the motions. This creates a vicious cycle that keeps your business stuck deep down in the pit of complacency. You micromanage, they disengage. Then they don't do their job, which makes you micromanage more, which creates a never-ending cycle of blame and shame. You can stop this cycle by trusting your team and allowing them to do what you pay them to do.

Now, if you want to throw out that they don't do what they're supposed to do and that's why you need to stay on top of things, ask yourself this question: Have you ever had a crystal-clear conversation about what their job truly is and what you expect from them day to day? There is power in clarity. Many restaurant problems are due to undeclared or unspoken expectations. You *assume* they know what to do, and *assumptions* are never a good thing when running a successful business. You want to make sure your team knows your standards, expectations, and absorbs what you tell them.

People can be blind to their "habit gap," and that's why getting a mentor or coach* is critical.

> *"Every famous athlete, every famous performer has somebody who's a coach. Somebody who can watch what they're doing and give them perspective. The one thing people are never good at is seeing themselves as others see them. A coach really, really helps."*
> —*Eric Schmidt, former CEO of Google*

A mentor or coach will help you tap into your natural strengths and see where your shadow habits are hiding. What are shadow habits? Those things that most people see you do, except you. Not too many on your team are going to call you on your bullshit. A good coach will point out those shadow habits; a great coach will guide you to discover the truth for yourself. My job as a coach is not to give you a pass on your bullshit; it's to make you deal with it! Awareness precedes choice; choice precedes change.

The number one shadow habit is integrity. The word evolved from the Latin adjective "*integer*," meaning "whole" or "complete." When you have integrity, you're one with your thoughts, words, and actions. People who are one way on the inside and another way on the outside lack integrity. They struggle with internal/external duality. People with a lack of integrity become conflicted and lose connection with their core values (what they stand for). They are generally unhappy and can find themselves trapped in the pit of complacency. They're at conflict with themselves. Integrity requires self-reflection. Self-reflection is not easy. However, it is a necessity if you want to elevate your game.

So, if your restaurant is not exactly where you want it to be, then stop and be honest. If things suck, then own it. Only then can you take the action needed to free yourself from complacency before it turns into mediocrity. Once *that* happens, that's it: game over.

* shameless plug to be your coach!

3 Things About Restaurant Profits You Need to Hear NOW

How are the profits in your restaurant? Great? Amazing? Is it your best year ever or are your profits on life support? Wherever you are now, it can be assumed that you want more. It's human nature to climb to the top.

The restaurant business can be very brutal on people at times, particularly when it comes to the area of making money. How do you beat the odds and maximize your profit potential?

Here are three things that are getting in the way of you and your profits:

1. YOU DON'T KNOW YOUR NUMBERS

Sure, you've played around on Excel, and maybe you roughly know some of the costs associated with items on your menu. That's what the average restaurant does. The problem with average is that it just sucks. Time to get in there and become a profit seeker by understanding your spreadsheets!

Is digging into the numbers fun? For some people, yes. For the vast majority, that would be a *no*. Here's the thing that many forget: if you don't like the numbers side of the business, hire someone who does. You must know your numbers, and you must know them every day because things change quickly. Sometimes *very* quickly! No one said you had to do it yourself. However, you do need to be aware of where the money goes.

Study the reports from your POS system religiously and consistently. Look at your check average. Is there something you could offer or train your team to prompt that might add a few extra dollars to increase the check average?

How much are you spending on paper goods? This can become a very costly line item if you have a big delivery and take-out business. How about linen costs? What about managing the overtime of the team? Little things make a big impact when looking for a few percentage points to add to the bottom line. Just imagine if you dropped your turnover rate 10 percent? That can be a game changer for some restaurants, and it's not very hard to do.

2. YOU DON'T KNOW YOUR TEAM

Speaking of turnover, you've probably heard the line that people don't leave restaurants; they leave managers. Well, that's fairly accurate. People are motivated by different reasons, and the key is to understand what motivates each person on your team. Most managers assume that what inspires them to go to work is the same thing that drives others on their team. Sorry, that's a gross generalization and not accurate.

Getting to know your team and what is important to them will enrich your company culture. An amazing culture is like having the world's most powerful magnet: it attracts top talent and compels them to stay. If your turnover is high, you must take a hard look at your culture and ask why. You might not like the answer you find, but you need to face the truth. If your culture is rotten, it will impact your profits. Turnover isn't cheap [Cornell reports around $5,200 per hourly employee (Tracey and Hinkin, 2006); and Otto (2017) reports up to 33% of the employee's salary] and that revolving door of people coming and going is slowly bleeding the profits away. Get control by understanding what your current turnover rate is and act to reduce your turnover immediately.

3. YOU DON'T KNOW YOUR GUESTS

Lastly, if you don't have your finger on the pulse of your guests, you're ignoring the most powerful way to increase your profits. Your guests tell you every day what they want through their buying habits. Once again, there's gold in your POS reports if you take the time to examine them and ask yourself questions:

What's your best seller?
What beverages are most popular?
What's the average table turn time?

Once you analyze the data, put your ego aside (yes, this is the hard part) and just give them more of what they want! Not exactly rocket science, yet it's fundamental to marketing. Too many restaurants create their menus based on their egos and what they *think* guests want. They might have a few good sellers but most of the menu limps along, sucking profits. Better to have a solid menu of hits that sells than one item that needs to carry the load because you're too proud to take the other loser menu items off.

Being a smart restaurateur means doing what is best for the brand. That means giving the market what they want, not what you want. Restaurant brands do well when they find a need within a niche market and fulfill that need. Creating a niche and trying to find guests to come to your new concept requires a lot of marketing and sometimes good timing in the market.

Finding profits is not that hard if you're willing to swallow your pride a little and admit that you need to work at it. Commit to nail down your numbers and know them like the back of your hand. Knowing your numbers will help you make better decisions every day, and that allows you to make adjustments that can add more to your bottom line.

Talk to your team and open yourself up to get to know them. Know their families (kids' names, etc.), birthdays, and work anniversaries, and make a big deal out of them. Show your team you appreciate them by thanking them. "Thank you" might be the most under-used and under-appreciated sentence on the planet, yet is appropriate in nearly every situation. Use it.

Understand your guests by talking to them and knowing what the data tells you about how they spend their money in your restaurant. Recently, an upscale restaurant was struggling with a depressed economy in its market as oil prices were hit hard. They decided to start a prix fixe menu to ease the burden and show the locals that they understood and wanted to provide a way for people to come in still and enjoy their restaurant even during down times. The restaurant saw a rise in sales due to their new menu and, surprisingly, an increase in wine sales as people had a little extra money to spend on wine since the menu was priced to support the local guests.

If your profits are not where you want them, all you need to do is change a few things and take new action to get new results.

Insanity is doing the same thing you are doing now and expecting different results— stop that.

7 Horrible Mistakes You're Making in Your Restaurant

This year could be your best. The restaurant industry is approaching epic market growth, and that's the sign of a healthy economy. The downside is that the market can only support so many restaurants before the bubble bursts; many will close their doors in the wake of the coming restaurant apocalypse. It truly is Darwinian Theory at work: the strong will survive, and the weak (or average) will perish.

How do you ensure your restaurant will survive? By being honest and avoiding the seven catastrophic mistakes that restaurants make in their operations.

The seven signs of the impending restaurant apocalypse (take them to heart):

1. LYING TO YOURSELF

Denial is a powerful emotional drug that tempts us to stay where we are. It comes from that place inside all of us that doesn't want to know the truth. It's the byproduct of the infamous comfort zone, the place we retreat to escape the world and, well, feel comfortable.

We avoid the truth because sometimes it can be both painful and fearful (a double whammy). Your options: make the changes you know you must or stay "safe" in your comfort zone. You probably know what most people choose, and they justify that decision by using what is known as "verbal softeners." These little white lies are designed to make you feel good for now. Maybe you've heard or said some of these:

- They're not that bad.
- It could be worse.
- They will change.
- It's just a rut.

All those statements are fear dressed up as optimistic banter. You can convince yourself of pretty much anything, including how bad you're supposedly *not* doing.

Solution: Stop lying to yourself! If things are not 100 percent the way you want them, stop coming up with excuses and lies. You'll never get what you want from your restaurant or yourself until you admit that things suck.

2. NOT KNOWING YOUR NUMBERS

Now that you're going to face the facts and the truth, it's time to get your bottom line in shape. If you've ever gone back to the gym after a lazy winter of eating whatever you wanted and experienced the struggle of getting fit again, this is how your financial fitness is going to be as well.

The sad thing is many restaurateurs have let the bottom line become a secondary focus. When sales boom and cash flow is strong, we tend to think everything is fine. Then the market tightens up, and your bank account becomes less happy than it once was, and the bottom line is sagging.

Time to hit the accounting gym.

It's easy to take your eyes off the numbers or not even worry about them when cash flows freely. It's not an excuse; it's normal to lose sight of an activity that many do not like. The numbers side of the business, after all, isn't sexy to every entrepreneur. Restaurant openers and operators love the creative, fun, people side. However, you must have balance in everything for long-term success.

Solution: Take control of your business by digging in and knowing your numbers. You can hire someone to do the work if you aren't good at this task, but you must be included and understand where every penny goes. Ignorance is not bliss; *it's just ignorance.*

Where to start:

- Food and beverage costs (update all your recipe and costing sheets).
- Cost out your weekly labor schedule so you can see where your labor dollar is going.
- Use a budget. If you fail to plan, you're planning to fail. Set sales projections and targets for your team to hit. Set up spending budgets for food, beverage, and labor to control these potentially high-dollar spending categories.

3. TOLERATING POOR PERFORMANCE

This circles back to sign number one, lying to yourself. You most likely have a few poor performers on your team that you've been holding onto out of fear. These "C-list" players are just dead weight that your "A" players are dragging around. They do only the minimum amount of work to avoid getting fired and don't truly contribute to the growth of the brand. They also annoy the shit out of your "A" players.

Think of them like the entourage that hangs around big celebrities. They take the free stuff and hang around, never adding anything of value. As an operator, keeping these types of employees around means, you're just paying for the privilege of their company — time to stop picking up the tab on those who don't produce results.

Solution: Come to the reality that if you have people on your team who aren't lifting your brand, they're holding it down. You may have a sense of loyalty to them because they've been with you from the beginning, and you feel an obligation to take care of them—stop it. If they're not actively growing personally and professionally, they're dead weight, dragging down your business. Truthfully, you're hurting their growth by not being honest and giving them feedback that could help them become better.

This is very common in brands that are making the leap from small operations (one to two locations) to an emerging restaurant group (three or more locations). They drag along these negative people wondering why they're struggling to grow and break through the big-time growth barrier. You must take an honest, hard look at the people with whom you surround yourself. It's also time to make some tough decisions. Remember, not everyone is a good fit for your brand.

4. PLAYING IT SAFE WITH YOUR MARKETING

With the rise of the internet, there has never been a better time to market your restaurant. So many play small in the online world, and that's truly sad. The entire world is accessible from your phone, why not show them who you are and what you stand for?

Once again, this comes back to fear and your comfort zone. That comfort zone loves to keep you stuck in mediocrity (or worse). Time to break free from its grips and claim your market share. That requires you to do things differently and, in some cases, maybe even become a little edgy.

Solution: Take your social media game up to the level of the big dogs. Here's how:

- *Get on multiple social media platforms.* You should be on Facebook, Twitter, Instagram, LinkedIn, and possibly Snapchat.
- *Double-down on your posts.* Chances are you're only posting a few times per week. To have an impact on social media means keeping your brand top of mind. That requires posting every day (sometimes multiple times a day).
- *Jump into video.* Video is the best and most effective way to stand out in a crowded market. Years ago, you needed to hire a professional video production team to shoot a video for your brand. Today you need a smartphone and a few apps. There are no excuses for failing to embrace the digital age with video posts or live streaming events.

5. OVERREACTING TO NEGATIVE ONLINE REVIEWS

The flip side of having the World Wide Web to broadcast your brand to the globe is that you'll also attract people who want to voice their negative opinion of your restaurant. True or not, these people will feel compelled to tell everyone how bad their experience was. The last thing you want to do is react emotionally to bad online reviews.

Is it easy to read someone's crude and sometimes rude comments about your brand? Of course not! Your restaurant is your child, and any parent would go out of their way to protect their kid. Just don't let the heat of the moment drag you into an online argument during which your reply can be easily taken out of context and cause more harm than good.

Solution: Take a deep breath and examine the facts. You must separate fact from fiction.

- Write out a reply on a piece of paper and let it all out. Release the emotions that you're feeling (anger, frustration, disgust). Read through it and make sure all those nasty feelings are free. Now, tear it up or burn it and release those negative feelings.
- Write a reply that is empathetic (understanding of *their* feelings) and not judgmental. Will it take you a few times to get it right? Probably. Just be open to the idea that they had a bad experience and you're thankful they wrote the review, so you have the opportunity to correct any issues.
- Keep track of common topics. If you're getting more than your fair share of negative reviews, then you might have a real problem that you need to address. Slow ticket times, cold food, and rude staff members are symptoms to deeper problems within your culture

and training. Don't go back to number one and be in denial about this—search for the truth.

6. POOR COMMUNICATION

All business problems are people problems at their core. Nine times out of ten, those people problems are communication problems. We fear talking to our team because they might take it the wrong way. We fear being critical to avoid hurting people's feelings. We fear transparency and being true to ourselves.

Fear, in general, is what stops you from getting the restaurant you want deep down. You had a grand vision and built a brand. When you were building that brand, you were fearless because you had nothing to lose. Now your stakes have increased, and you hesitate to state the truth. You side step issues that need to be talked about. You've become weak due to poor communication. That weakness threatens everything you took the time to build, yet you don't speak up.

Stop being afraid to be authentic. Stop being afraid, to be honest. Step up and become the leader your team wants and needs. They want someone to lead them. They need someone to challenge them. They want someone who inspires them to become better. That can be you if you dare to open your mouth and be authentic.

Solution: Time to step forward and become the leader:

1. *Talk clearly about your expectations.* State exactly what you want from your team as far as performance and standards. Never assume they know—you need to make sure they know. Ask them to explain it to you without being condescending.

2. *Don't be a jerk.* Finding your true voice as a leader is about being open and honest, not talking down to people. Always communicate respectfully with everyone. That includes people in your personal life, too. You can't be one way outside of your business and a different way around your staff. You must commit to being authentic and genuine, or your employees will think you're dishonest and untrustworthy.

3. *Watch your self-talk.* Yeah, you're probably harder on yourself than you should be. Compassion for others starts with compassion for ourselves.

7. NOT HAVING AN EXIT PLAN

All goals need a target. You can say you want to lose weight, but what does that mean? When will you know you've reached your goal? If you can't measure it, you can't manage it. Without an end goal, you don't have anything pulling you toward a compelling future. The days will become longer, and the pressure of everyday operations will turn into stress that slowly sucks the life out of you. You'll start to question whether any of what you're doing is worth it.

You need an exit plan. Now, an exit plan might not be to sell—it might mean to build up the first location to a certain level, then open more locations. It could mean building the brand with the intention of your children taking the reins someday (a legacy brand like Lettuce Entertain You®). Maybe you want to build up to 6 locations and start franchising. Wherever you see yourself in 5, 10, or 20 years, you need to write it down because that's your target.

Once you have your exit plan (or growth plan if you like that term better), you have to reverse engineer it into actionable steps. If your plan is a five-year plan, for example, break down the key milestones required between now and then by year until you see the path you must take. Having a plan is one thing—executing a plan is the real challenge.

Solution: Create and execute your plan.

- Know that people will have a hard time buying into a big vision. It's not that they don't believe you, it's just that most don't dream big. It'll be like you're one of the Wright brothers trying to tell someone that one day "flying machines" will fill the air.
- Get someone to hold you accountable. You need an outside person who isn't emotionally attached to you and who doesn't have an agenda to keep you on track. Accountability is the key element for those who reach their goals consistently.
- You'll need faith—a lot of faith. There will be times when you'll question yourself. Others will question you. Your comfort zone devil will try to tempt you to settle for what you have. Don't falter, have faith in yourself.

Look at the horizon of the restaurant industry, and you'll see storm clouds growing in the distance. The market can only sustain so many restaurants until the bubble bursts. Smart operators take advantage of the storm before it hits.

They double check to ensure their financials and numbers are right. They constantly recruit to attract top talent. They build a culture of transparency through communication with their team and their guests. They market consistently and constantly. They don't focus on the competition; they focus on improving themselves, so the competition becomes distracted by what they're doing.

In an ultra-competitive market, there are lions, and there are gazelles. One gets dinner, and the other is dinner. Which would you rather be?

6 Unwritten Rules Anyone Working in a Restaurant Should Know

You've been in the business awhile. Maybe you've seen a few things that are sure to be included in your memoirs one day that'll turn into the next *Kitchen Confidential*. That A-List celebrity is dragging his foulmouthed girlfriend through the kitchen to escape out the back door to avoid the paparazzi.

That Hollywood socialite who made you stop cooking a five-course meal because she wanted Cocoa Puffs. Yeah, it's a wild ride at times.

Just remember that like any industry, there are certain unwritten rules of conduct. Call it a code. There are many of these unspoken rules in our business. You might be a little shocked that we're even talking about them. Well, it's time to let the cat out of the bag! Actually, I'm not sure why people would want to put a cat in a bag in the first place, but work with me here—I'm on a roll.

1. NEVER TOUCH ANOTHER PERSON'S *MISE*

Of all that is holy in the world of culinary gods, this is at the top of the list! Your *mise en place* is so personally a part of your pride as a cook that having someone take your prep without asking is like Loki betraying Thor. You can't trust them after that, no matter how many times they say they'll change.

The only other violation more severe than raiding another person's mise is using one of their knives without permission. Hey, chefs have a very personal relationship with their tools, much like a samurai has with his sword. Take a knife without asking, and you're pretty much dead in the eyes of the person whose blade you took. You took their soul, so be prepared for Hell.

2. MOVE WITH A SENSE OF URGENCY

You must realize that restaurant work is a race against time. When guests walk through a restaurant's front door, their imaginary time clock starts. You must stay focused and alert to win the time game, and that means picking up the pace. Having food come together from multiple stations to compose a plate is one challenge. Having all the plates for a table up in the pass-through at the same time is another.

Moving with a sense of urgency doesn't mean running around like a chicken with its head cut off, it's about moving efficiently and with purpose. Stay focused on the task at hand. Distractions are the enemy when it comes to getting things done in the restaurant business.

3. IF YOU'RE NOT A COOK, DON'T WALK BEHIND THE LINE

Wandering around a cooking line can be dangerous. The last thing you want is to be back on the line where there are things that can leave a mark: hot equipment, hot pans, and sharp objects are scattered around the kitchen just waiting for someone who isn't paying attention. A second-degree burn or a deep cut can become a quick trip to the E.R., and that isn't a fun way to spend your evening.

Its part of unwritten etiquette that many would say is just common sense. The funny thing about common sense is that, at times, it's not so common. Stay away from things that can burn or cut you if it's not in your job description. Sure, venturing behind the line can give you an interesting story to tell your friends, but it's a painful place to go exploring.

Besides, cooks know things that might not be obvious to the average bystander: assume everything is hot! Do you think they walk around with a kitchen towel in their hand to look cool? No. They assume that everything handed to them is blistering hot. A lesson a young Sous Chef working for me forgot one day as I reached into the oven to grab a sauté pan (using a towel) that I placed on his station. He grabbed the handle without a towel, and it left a very nice brand on the palm of his hand. Ouch. That left a mark.

4. FULL HANDS IN, FULL HANDS OUT

Also known as "working both ways." Restaurant work can take its toll on you if you don't work smart. It involves open communication and team members looking out for each other.

For cooks, this means asking if anyone needs anything whenever they head to the walk-in for something. For the service team, this means bringing back dirty plates or finding ways to assist the team on their way back through the dining room after taking something out of the kitchen to deliver to a table. Remember, for a restaurant to truly succeed; all work involves working together as a team.

5. CLEAN AS YOU GO

When dealing with food and the potential for foodborne illnesses, you must work with a clean station. That is the mark of a true professional, one who can handle the pressure while maintaining a clean work station. Many say they can cook; most can't cook and clean as they go.

As I mentioned earlier, my father was hell on wheels as a chef, and his nickname was "Wild Bill" for a good reason. He ruled the kitchen with an iron fist, and if you failed to keep your station clean during your shift, he would have you chant out loud, "Clean as you go. Clean as you go. Clean as you go," over and over again until it sunk into your head. Today that might be considered hazing but back in the early '80s that was how chefs ran their kitchens. I use a subtler approach these days by helping the team member find their own "why."

Remember, people are only motivated by *their* reasons, not *your* reasons. The first gets them to commit and the second to comply. My way is more Jedi Mind Trick. I calmly say, "Your work station is a reflection of your mind. I will teach you more advanced techniques when you show me your mind is ready."

6. ALWAYS SAY _____

A restaurant moves at a fast pace, and accidents can happen if there is no communication. A couple of key words are said and expected to be said often:

"Corner"

The trademark word called out whenever you're coming around—you guessed it—a corner. Many loud crashes heard in the dining room are a result of people failing to simple say "corner."

"Behind"

Remember earlier, when I spoke about all the hot and sharp things in the kitchen? Well, most accidents happen when people forget to tell others that they're walking behind them. Sense of urgency has professionals moving quickly, and with purpose, so they turn around without any warning. That can be catastrophic when holding a hot pan or a chef's knife.

There are, of course, many more unwritten rules. If you want your team to understand them completely, it's time we drag these unspoken expectations out into the open and talk about them with our teams. All business problems are people problems in disguise (I'm going to hammer this into your head until you say it in your sleep). Most of those people problems stem from poor communication and undeclared (or unspoken) expectations.

You have the power to fix this. Talk to your team.

The 4 Horsemen of the Restaurant Apocalypse – Knocking on Hell's Door

When you listen to people talk about their restaurant, there are subtle (and sometimes not so subtle) verbal statements that provoke a reaction—a negative reaction. As a consultant, when I hear these words spoken, I also hear a voice in the back of my head say, *"Wait for it…"*.

Usually, this voice isn't wrong. It could be a few months or a year, but eventually, those who knocked on Hell's door, end up eating their words.

What you say is a reflection of what's going on in that three-pound piece of brain matter nestled in your skull. The funny thing about the words we say to ourselves is we believe them after we've repeated them enough times.

The attitudes and associated phrases known as the 4 Horsemen of the Restaurant Apocalypse, uttered by short-sighted restaurant operators, **lead a restaurant straight to Hell's door**.

1. EGO: "WE'RE/I'M THE BEST"

When someone begins to rest on their laurels what they're doing is sending up the white flag of surrender—they don't realize it at the time. Claims that an operator is the best, even if they may be at the time, is a big fat waving white flag signaling that there's no room for improvement.

When you stop growing, you start dying. Declaring you've reached the top also sends a message to up-and-coming brands that they should set their sights on you to surpass you. Some people like to be targets for competition, but I believe it's better to let your actions do the talking and be the best in your market.

> *"Those who speak do not know. Those who know do not speak."* -
> *Lao Tzu*

False bravado tells others that perhaps someone is overcompensating for something. There's a fine line between cockiness and confidence: one is about talking a good game, and the other is producing results by executing the game plan.

2. PRIDE: "THAT WON'T WORK IN MY MARKET"

This one comes out before a person even *considered* an idea viable. They just shot it down before it had a chance to take form.

That's too bad because sometimes other people on your team will have some brilliant ideas. The owner or manager who feels like all originality must come from them is selling their potential short.

When you're stubborn (foolish pride) about considering new ideas, you shut down innovation and the opportunity to grow. Remember what happens when you stop growing?

When pride takes hold, it's hard to see the forest for the trees. You run your restaurant with blinders on and fail to notice little things that are hurting your brand. You develop what scientists call a scotoma or a blind spot. Those little things you don't want to see become bigger and more hurtful to your brand the longer they're ignored.

3. DENIAL: "I DON'T NEED TO CHANGE"

Change is a constant in the universe—you can't stop it or avoid it. Change is coming for your restaurant whether you welcome it or not.

Economies change. Markets change. Neighborhoods change. Guests want change. Look around, and it's a sure bet that something around you has changed in the last year. If you don't adapt and adjust to what's going on around you, you'll quickly find yourself outmaneuvered and weakened.

Not accepting change doesn't make it go away. Denial robs you of your power to invoke the changes needed to stay competitive in an ever-growing, ever-changing industry. Failing to take action is, in reality, an action, but it's not a *smart* action.

You can sit on the sidelines and think happy thoughts to yourself about how your business is fine, and you don't need to change or adjust to the market, or you can *get in the game*. Better to get up and face the reality of what's going on in your market. **Denial is for cowards**.

Ego, Pride, and Denial are the first 3 Horsemen of the Restaurant Apocalypse, and significant ones at that. *So, who, you might you ask, is the 4th Horseman?*

It's mediocrity.

4. MEDIOCRITY: "IT'LL DO/IT'S GOOD ENOUGH"

Mediocrity forms the foundation of failure. Once complacency takes hold, your dreams, along with your restaurant, will rot. Mediocrity comes in many forms, including being average, passable, common, and ordinary. You want your restaurant and your life to be **outstanding**—get off your dying restaurant horse and take charge; step up to the next level.

Watch your words because they truly shape the way you see your restaurant, truly reflect on who you are and how you feel about yourself. **Your unwarranted boastful or negative words are a call to the Four Horseman to visit your brand and, once they come into your restaurant, it's a battle to remove them.**

The best defense is never to allow the horsemen to set up shop in your brand or your head.

How to Tell If You're Ready to Expand Your Brand: The Expansion Trifecta

As you look at your restaurant, you might have thoughts of more locations. Maybe one or two more? Maybe a dozen? Perhaps you even have big dreams of multiple concepts spanning the country. Before you get too far ahead of yourself, this might be a good time for a little reality check.

Watch the movie, "*The Founder,*" starring Michael Keaton as the iconic Ray Kroc of McDonald's fame, and you'll likely get the idea that, with a great game plan, you can build a national - and even international - empire. Ray Kroc was a man with a vision, a very aggressive vision, and there was no way he was going to sit by and watch the two McDonald brothers stay in their comfort zones and just survive. Ray wanted to thrive and to do that he had to push the edge and make courageous decisions.

In your brand:

Who is willing to push the edge?

Who is willing to make sacrifices to get what they want?

Who is willing to make courageous decisions?

Many live in one world and dream of another. There is the restaurant they have now and the restaurant they dream it could be. To get from one world to the other, you need a means of transportation, and that's called a solid plan.

Strategic planning is what separates those who grow successfully from those who build a sort of "restaurant house of cards," where eventually it all comes crashing down. The success of any building involves one key component: the foundation.

Opening new locations is easy if you have the funding. Maintaining and growing multiple locations requires more planning than is realized. And, just because you have money doesn't mean your restaurant will be successful; it just prolongs the inevitable.

Realize these three things before you expand your brand:

1. A TALENT POOL

Many restaurants on an aggressive growth plan make this fatal mistake: they lack talented staff. You need to have a reserve of "A" list players you can pull from to staff the new location. Taking all your "A" players to the new opening is a short-term solution that can cause long-term brand damage. You took all your superstars to open and left the "C" players back at your home base? Guess what happens now: standards start to slide, and the frequency of guest complaints begin to rise. Brand integrity starts to erode, and before you know it, you're pulling people (mostly "A" players) from the opening team back for damage control. Now, the new team is fragmented with mixed players that have not had time to assimilate to your culture or be trained properly.

Just as soon as your team brings the original location back to your standards, the new location starts having problems. Now, your team is stuck in firefighting mode, just bouncing back and forth between locations and problems. Firefighting mode is not a long-term success strategy.

Please, don't overestimate how hard it is to staff for a new restaurant in today's market. Many restaurants are overconfident in their hiring approach to staff a new location and find themselves in "hiring handcuffs." When the opening day is set, the marketing kicks off, the pressure will begin to build up, and you'll start down a dark path by either:

Settling for "C" and "D" players; or,

Paying hirer wages than you estimated in your financial projections.

Both will dilute your brand and your integrity long-term. Short-term solutions don't fix the real ailment:

Bad planning.

2. SOLID TRAINING SYSTEMS

Not having a training system beyond "do as I say and watch what I do" is a sin you need to correct. Restaurants stuck in mediocrity think they can carry around all their training in their heads. Knowledge passed down by word-of-mouth has been in existence since man discovered language. Great for telling stories by the campfire, not so great for building a consistent brand. Today's workers want training on multiple platforms. They want printed materials, hands-on learning, and visual reinforcement (videos) of the proper way to do a task. Look at the popularity of "how-to" YouTube videos and the number of people that claim they "learned it on YouTube."

Having a solid system in place also results in training consistency, which contributes to brand consistency, and that's a key to long-term success. Many independent restaurants don't like having a "training system" because they feel it's too "corporate." Not to be the bearer of bad news, but a few independents could learn a trick or two about brand consistency from the corporate chains. There's nothing wrong with using them as a model and putting your brand-spin on what you learn from them. Corporate-speak can easily be changed to reflect the character of you and your brand. There are plenty of generic templates available on the internet, and they're great as a guide. Just don't use them without making changes that represent your culture and your brand voice. And, don't go reinventing any wheels! Use what has worked for others, and adapt it for your brand.

3. THE RIGHT REASONS

Why do you want to expand your brand? Is it a dream, a desire, a necessity, or a goal? If you answered the goal, then what type of goal?

There are two types of goals: push and pull. One sets you up for long-term success and the other for long-term failure.

- *Push Goals:* Here, you feel the push to make the new location happen. The real estate location is "too good" to pass up in your opinion. You feel the push to get another location open even though the other two requirements listed above—a talent pool to pull from and a solid training system—aren't in place. Push goals are a call from your ego that you should be doing this. Push goals are full of "rationalizations" that come from the little voice inside your head that tells you it's the right time and right thing to do. You can rationalize anything if your ego is invested enough. **Push goals come from your head, and they tend to be very financially risky because your ego is writing the checks.**
- *Pull Goals:* Here, you feel the goal deep within your heart. You feel an overwhelming compulsion that pulls you towards its attainment. It calls to you from somewhere outside. Authentic core values should pull you. Beware of "*surface* core values" that many people talk about because they *sound and look good*, are easy and convenient. **Pull goals are driven by your authentic core values; they are who you are.**
- Let's use the growth goal as an example:
- *Surface value growth:* I need to expand because that guy down the street just opened his third location, and I need to grow to keep up.
- *Authentic value growth:* I have such a diverse and talented team now that opening another location would allow many of them to expand their skills and assist in growing the brand.

See the difference?

You're truly ready to expand your brand when you can honestly say that you've achieved the Expansion Trifecta I've identified in this chapter. Or, you can place a bet if you have just one or two, get a short-term win, and potential long-term failure.

Or you can hold out for the big payoff and long-term success when you conquer all three.

The Number One Problem in Your Restaurant: Problems

All restaurants have them. You probably have a few, too.

It's okay.

Having problems is a good thing because they help you identify the gap between where you currently are and where you want your restaurant to be. The thing you don't want to do is ignore them. Problems can be a gift — ignoring them transforms them into a hungry monster anxious to consume your business. Always better to tackle the monster while it's small and doesn't require the National Guard (aka, a consultant) to be called in.

So, what problem do you face right now? What keeps you up at night?

Now, it doesn't matter where your restaurant is —the industry shares the same issues globally (I have seen this firsthand as an international restaurant coach). The struggle to find talent, the need to dominate your marketing, and the rising costs of doing business are all common problems that many restaurants face today. What is a restaurant to do?

The number one reason for the number one problem: people.

TO ERR IS TO BE HUMAN

I've established that all business problems are people problems, and the people part is usually due to communication issues. Human beings, for all the amazing things we can do, we have flaws that are supposed to help us on a survival level. Take all the information that is flooding into your brain right now: images hitting your eyes, sounds around you coming into your ears, smells wafting up your nose. The taste of food that dances across your tongue when you eat. If you had to process every little thing that came into your senses all at once, you would probably crash your human operating system, the brain.

Lucky for us, our brains absorb and process millions of information bits and does three things to help us:

Deletes information: We tend to think our memories are an accurate recording of the events in our lives. The reality is that those memories are more like an edited movie from which some key scenes have been cut out and left on the floor of the editing room. If you've ever remembered an event one way and someone else remembers it differently, then you have come across deleted information.

Distorts information: If you've ever heard someone say one thing and implied it to mean something completely different, welcome to distorted information. The same thing happens when you watch a scary movie, hear a noise by the door, and distort it to mean there must be a crazy killer trying to get in.

Generalizes information: You likely encountered some traffic the last time you drove to your restaurant. Did you notice every single make and model of the cars going in both directions on the road? Probably not. Generally, all you remembered were a lot of cars. If we weren't hardwired to store some information in the "general" category, we would constantly be stopping to figure out what everything is and who all those people are. Imagine if every time you walked up to a door with a handle you had to stop and say to yourself, "What is this thing? What does it do? What kind of material is it made from?" Generalizations help us navigate through the day with some ease.

How do you solve the people problem that plagues many restaurants? The best way is to make sure your communication skills are at the top of their game. To get there fast, you need to understand the one thing that all great communication has in common: clarity.

CLARITY IS THE KEY

There are *Four C's to Effective Communication* that need to be used in unison if you want to break down those pesky people problems. They have a synergy to them, and when applied together can have a dramatic and positive impact on your team (prepare to be amazed!)

Courteous: Make sure you're talking "to" people and not "down to" people. The basis of a team is unity. Embarrassing or degrading others only lifts *you* up, temporarily. Suppressing the team to make yourself look good is a losing position.

Complete: Remember back to distorted and generalized information? Your team has those natural biases too, so make sure you give complete information and don't assume they know what to do. Many people don't want to ask for clarification because they fear to look stupid. There are no stupid questions, only poor communication when complete information is not delivered.

Concise: Keep your communication on target. It's easy to get distracted and wander off topic. Keep your communication with your team focused, so information isn't deleted when it becomes too much. Jumping from topic to topic makes it difficult for your team to know what's important, so they delete, distort, and generalize to make sense of it. Then problems start.

Clarity: Your communication must be crystal clear and discussed. It's not only imperative to deliver the information from your end, but you must also make sure the people on the receiving end understand the information with clarity. Once again, assumptions in communication are the root cause of problems. Use active listening and ask the person what they heard. Stopping to ask what they heard is a game changer! You'll instantly see the Three Cardinal Sins of Poor Communication disappear (Deletion, Distortion, and Generalization).

With clarity also comes explaining your specific and detailed expectations for the task or project. Uncommunicated or unclear expectations do nothing but keep you from getting the restaurant you truly want. Here's a classic example:

You hand the new team member the standard job description (or worse, you assume they know the job requirements already). You have them read it over, and then they start. You don't verbally communicate all those "little things" that you expect and soon there's disappointment and frustration on both sides.

Contrary to your assumptions, people can't read your mind about what you expect from them. You need to communicate with clarity *exactly* what your expectations are or risk setting your team up for failure.

The number one problem in restaurants is communication.
The bad news is that means it starts with you.

The good news is that you can do something to improve it today.

The First Step to Developing a Better Restaurant

Do you want a better restaurant? *Of course, you do.*

You wouldn't be reading this book if you didn't. The great news is that you can have a better restaurant today.

Right now.

It starts with one simple decision defined by three powerful words: **Raise your standards**.

While it sounds simple on the surface, it's a little more complicated than that. *Saying* you want a better restaurant and *getting* a better restaurant is the difference between mediocrity and success. There are a few things to get out in the open before you can make the jump to the next level.

What lies between desire and results is action.

Many people think that the road to success is a straight line. In reality, success is more like a winding road with peaks, valleys, a few roadblocks, detours, and an occasional sinkhole tossed in for good measure. Even Ray Kroc, the "founder" of McDonald's, was quoted as saying, "I was an overnight success all right, but 30 years is a long, long night."

You need to understand what the word "decision" means.

If you look at the etymology of the word "decision," you'll find that it comes from the Latin dēcīsiō, which means "a cutting off." So, when you make a true decision, you cut off any other possibilities.

DECISION AND COMMITMENT GO HAND IN HAND.

When you make a clear decision that you're going to raise the standards for what you tolerate in your restaurant (and in your life), things will change dramatically.

Now, don't expect things to change overnight. The habits and standards you've held onto for so many years are not going to disappear quietly. Some things can be changed rather quickly; others might require more of an exorcism to displace the demonic shadow they've cast upon your business.

One thing you need to be aware of is that when you try to raise the bar and raise the standards in your restaurant, it's not like hitting the button from Staples that shouts out, "That was easy!" If change were easy, everyone would have the restaurant and life they desired. When you try to make changes, change will push back. The best thing to do is stay committed to your decision.

You'll want to give in and lower your standards back to where they were. *DON'T.* Raising your standards will start an internal fight with your comfort zone. That comfort zone you have is very much like the thermostat in your home: if you set it for 70 degrees, the air or heat automatically turns on and off to maintain that temperature. So, expect resistance because it will happen.

DROP THE EXCUSES

The first thing that will pop up on your quest to raise your standards will be some rather interesting excuses why it won't work. Excuses are nothing more than a bunch of bad B.S. You know how they define B.S. in coaching? *Belief Systems.*

When excuses pop up — and they will — you have to face them head on for what they are: *Fear.*

When you make a conscious decision to raise your standards, of course, fear is going to appear and try to rationalize with you. Here's a thing you need to understand about fear: It just needs to be recognized and respected. While danger is real, fear is a choice.

When you head into unchartered territory, there are no signs or references for where you need to go or what you should do. Fear will pop up and tell you this was a bad idea. If you've never raised your standards before, this will be a quest into the unknown. Face your fears, acknowledge the warning they're trying to give you and tell them to get back in line with all your other emotions. **Tell fear to go to the back of the line.**

TAKE ACTION

Now you have a clear understanding of some of the obstacles standing between you and the restaurant you desire. It's time to step up and turn those words into reality.

You're going to make three lists.

The first list contains all the things you're no longer willing to put up with in your restaurant.

Call this one, "A bad restaurant."

This could include sloppy appearance, using a cell phone during service, being late, gossiping, yelling, auctioning food off the table, name calling, not following recipes, not doing a menu, lack of teamwork, lack of leadership, negativity, low energy, poor communication (like asking a table "How is everything?"), lack of table management, failure to clean as you go... This list is virtually endless.

It's easier to start with a list of the things that you don't like. Once you have that list, writing down what you *do* want becomes a breeze.

The second list includes all the things that an outstanding restaurant will do. Not should do, will do.

*Call this one, "An **outstanding** restaurant."*

This list could include: opening the door for guests, refolding napkins when guests leave the table, never having to ask for a refill, writing personal thank you cards to staff and guests, taking a course to improve your leadership skills, invest in training your team, getting involved with a local charity, knowing your numbers, understanding the strengths of your team, marketing consistently, building value for your guests and your team, constantly recruiting for top talent, talking about your core values....

The third list is a personal one.

Call this one, "Who I want to be."

You need to write down who you need to be, as a leader, to make that second list happen. It's easy to sit there and say you want your restaurant to be legendary. However, you need to become the kind of person who can make that a reality.

You see, raising your standards for your restaurant is only 50 percent of the equation. The other 50 percent is raising your standards for yourself.

This list might include: scheduling time for self-care, investing in personal development, living your core values, leading by example, having integrity, self-discipline, controlling your emotions, appreciating your team, respecting yourself....

None of this advice works unless you expect more from yourself than you do from others. Throwing out blame and shame on other people is simply projecting your own unmet needs and insecurities onto others. Personal accountability should be a foundational element in your life. You need to take total accountability for everything that happens to you and your restaurant. This is usually the part that holds most people back from getting the restaurant they want.

It's so easy to point the finger and place blame on *this* person, *that* person, or the new restaurant down the street. Take a step back. Take a breath. Make this declaration: *My restaurant is exactly where it is because of me.*

All the good and all the bad are from the decisions you made.

The beautiful thing is that you can make new decisions, new choices, and create new standards.

Do Things Suck? Fall Back in Love with Your Restaurant, Now!

The relationship you have with your restaurant is like all the other relationships you've had in your life: *They all have their ups and downs.* When things are good, you're walking on sunshine. No clouds in the sky, the birds are singing, and there's a rainbow in every direction.

When things are bad, they can suck. People aggravate you for breathing too loudly. You sneer at others that cross your path. Everyone seems to be out to get you, and the universe is conspiring against your restaurant's survival. The dark clouds have moved in and constantly circle your life.

When the restaurant blues come to visit you (and if you own or run a restaurant, they will), you need a plan to get out of the rut and back on track.

Just remember that the only difference between a rut and a grave is the depth. Awareness is critical. When you see yourself in a proverbial hole...*stop digging!* Awareness precedes choice; choice precedes change.

Here are some of the warning signs you might be falling out of love with your restaurant:

- You don't look forward to going to work. You dread it.
- You keep putting off important projects because you say you're just not motivated.
- You are getting to work late and leaving early.
- You get easily irritated by seemingly trivial questions from the staff.
- You spend more time in the office "working on paperwork," even though you're not. You're also surfing the web more (Facebook and Instagram are your biggest distractions).
- You always have a headache at work.
- You find yourself either eating less or stashing a bag full of candy in your office that you chow down on throughout the shift.
- You start turning wine "tasting" into wine consumption.

- You bark at people for no real reason except that they're breathing.

Shall we go on?

Being in a slump is normal. You can't have sunshine every day; you need some rain in there if you want to grow. Successful restaurant owners and leaders appreciate the rainy days and harness their power into growth. How? I'm glad you asked.

BE GRATEFUL

It's easy to be angry and fucking bitter towards the world. Watch the news for 10 minutes, and it looks like a clusterfuck around us. Stop looking outward and refocus on the things you have going on that are good. Yes, having an attitude of gratitude is paramount to long-term success. When you're truly grateful for the things and people you have in your life, you'll find an inner peace that money can't buy.

Think of the people or things (like being alive) that you're grateful for right now. Oh, if you say there's nothing to be grateful for, reframe the statement to the things you *could* you be grateful for if you thought about it. Your mind is a magnet, and it attracts what you think about.

If you think **your restaurant and life are pretty much a shit show, that's what you'll get.**

THE 50

Here's a little exercise I like to do when I'm not feeling fully charged about my brand (yes, it happens to all of us from time to time). I grab a piece of paper and number it from 1 to 50. Then I start to fill in the reasons why I love my brand. Now, fair warning, getting to 20 and even 30 is pretty easy. After 30, you're going to have to dig deep into the well of emotions surrounding the time you first opened, like the excitement and thrill of turning an idea into reality.

That's right; you did something very few can: you took a concept and brought it to life. Keeping it alive depends on the love and energy you can maintain for it. Getting a little nostalgic and thinking back to the beginning is a great place to start.

VISUALIZE

Without a vision, people perish. Your restaurant and your life must also have a vision for the future. Without it, you have nothing pulling you towards a compelling horizon. You're stuck and spin your wheels every day just trying to maintain (protect) what you have. While you stand still, the competition starts to surround you and slowly cuts into your market, stealing your top talent and your guests.

If you're not growing both professionally and personally, you're dying a slow death of complacency. Better to go down fighting than to be forgotten due to lack of action.

TAKE BETTER CARE OF YOURSELF

Chances are you're not taking care of yourself as you should be. Now, you can blame it on the business we're in and serve up the bullshit excuse that you don't have time. Or, you can stop lying to yourself and admit that it's just not important to you.

Allow me to throw a little Stoic philosophy your way with a simple Latin phrase: *Memento mori.* It means "remember death." Yes, you and I are dying. We can't escape it. All we can do is live each day fully and become better humans, hopefully leaving an impact upon the world so others will remember us for the good that we left behind.

Legacy is what drives humans to have children and build monuments.

What will your legacy be?

What do you want people to remember about you?

I can tell you from firsthand experience that taking care of yourself needs to rise to the top of your list. Personal health is a taboo topic in the restaurant industry (along with mental health), and we need to address this as a community. Too many of us succumb to poor eating habits, lack of exercise, and abuse of alcohol (and drugs). We use those things to escape the world around us. Here's a thought, what about creating a world you don't want, or have, to escape from instead?

You've done it before.

You've taken ideas and transformed them into reality. You've bent time to be your bitch when you applied yourself, and yet now time is *your* master. You stopped creating the world you wanted when you got a little taste of success.

You took your foot off the accelerator of life and coasted. Now here you are, complaining about your restaurant and your life.

The time is now to get what you want from your restaurant and your life. How? It's simple in theory, yet it will become the biggest challenge you have faced in some time. You got soft when you got a taste of success, and you're going to need to get dirty to get that edge back. Think *Rocky III* when he had to fight Mr. T! You need to get your 'eye of the tiger' on! [Insert inspiring victory song here.]

*Step **One***: *Stop lying to yourself.* I wrote a lot of my first book on this topic. If your restaurant and life is not 100 percent the way you want it, you have to admit that it sucks a little.

*Step **Two***: *Take action.* Drive your ass to the gym and sign up today. Everyone talks a good game. Those who win the game take steps every day to ensure they win.

*Step **Three***: *Meditate at least 10 minutes a day.* With amazing apps available like Calm and Headspace, you don't have an excuse not to meditate. It will help you relax and clear your mind, and it's shown to increase happiness. If you say you don't have 10 minutes a day to meditate, then you must *make time* to meditate. In as little as a week, you'll start to see some changes in your behavior. Plus, those around you will notice, and it might shift their mind away choosing to jump ship from your restaurant.

*Step **Four***: *Eat better.* It fucking baffles me how crappy restaurant owners and managers eat. Hey, I did it too back in the day, standing over the garbage can, shoveling down a bowl of cold food before the next ticket came in on the kitchen printer. You don't have to be an animal and scarf down food in the corner. Sit down, chew your food, and enjoy it. Come on, you work in the restaurant business, and you don't even give yourself the same courtesy that you extend to your guests.

*Step **Five***: *Get some sleep.* I know that when you get home after a big dinner rush, there's a certain adrenaline rush you want to keep going. Many turn to alcohol or drugs to maintain that adrenaline high. The nights become longer and the days shorter because you slept through most of it. You wake up with just enough time to be at work on time. It's possible you don't even bother showering before work. Get control of your demons before they truly bring you down. If you can't do it alone, find help. *Professional help.* How can you tell if you have a problem? Here's a sign: if you find yourself at an ATM at 3:00 a.m., then you have a problem. Nothing good happens at 3:00 a.m. Yes, I've been there.

*Step **Six**: Work out.* I know you're on your feet all day. I know you don't feel you have time to exercise. You sound like a broken record of excuses filled with reasons you can't do it. Remember, step one? *Stop lying to yourself.* You do have time if you make it a priority.

You can excuse the shit out of anything! You can also find the internal drive to accomplish anything you desire. You need to turn those "shoulds" into "musts."

Remember that you never get what you *should* have, you get the things you *must* have. Make it happen.

Don't believe me? Try to hold your breath and not take another. Your body can hold off for a few minutes, but you'll gasp for air eventually. You must breathe to survive. That's the same way you get what you want in life — it has to be as important to you as taking that next breath.

We fall in love, and sometimes out of love, with our restaurant. If you're in the latter, you can save it, **if** (and it's a big if) you want to. That's a question you'll have to uncover for yourself. Do The 50 exercise and rediscover why you started your restaurant or got into the restaurant business.

There's was a fire inside you that you extinguished. Time to rekindle that love affair once again. Once it reignites, you must feed that fire every damn day.

"Death is not the greatest loss in life. The greatest loss is what dies inside us while we live." - *Norman Cousins*

Your restaurant needs your internal fire to burn brightly. Become a beacon for hospitality. Drop the bullshit, stop the excuses, and by all means, stop lying to yourself.

When you finally face the truth, you will become free.

4 Things Only Restaurateurs Know About Running a Restaurant

Many people dream of owning a restaurant: A place friends and family call home, and where you call the shots and have the freedom to run operations your way.

Be very careful what you wish for.

Owning a restaurant is not all sunshine and rainbows. It's hard to earn your stripes in the restaurant industry (which is probably why 26 percent of new restaurants fail in the first year).

So, you've got a few yummy drinks on your menu, guests love your food, and you've got long wait times each night. Big whoop—that's only a fraction of what it takes to run a successful bar or restaurant.

Looking for the inside scoop? Check out these four secrets to running a successful restaurant that only restaurateurs know:

1. YOU STILL REPORT TO SOMEONE

Even though you own the business and can come and go as you wish, you still have a boss: Your guests.

And let me tell you, your guests are fickle bosses. You need to make sure you're making your "boss" happy because you want them to spread the good word about your restaurant through all possible channels. Traditional word-of-mouth marketing has been replaced by marketing on social media and travel review sites like Yelp and TripAdvisor. Remember, anyone can find anything on the internet, including bad restaurant reviews or opinions of your restaurant; even embarrassing pictures!

A bad review and an accompanying defensive rant by the owner on the internet can make your restaurant's name go viral for all the wrong reasons.

Contrary to the popular cliché, not all publicity is good publicity.

Likewise, videos on social media of restaurant staff doing stupid things have a way of attracting eyeballs faster than you can imagine. Your restaurant's reputation will go down the drain just as quickly.

Dealing with disgruntled guests on the internet is tricky business. It's the world's stage, after all.

The best strategy? Pick your battles. Your guests provide the vital, life-sustaining cash flow needed to run your restaurant. The last thing you want to do is alienate your guests by mishandling interactions with them on the internet.

2. BEING A RESTAURATEUR IS A 24/7 JOB

Most restaurant staff get to go home at the end of one shift and don't have to think about work again until their next shift.

Being a successful restaurateur is a 24/7 gig. Even when you're not within the walls of your restaurant, you're thinking about your restaurant.

Ideas and inspiration for your restaurant will come in all shapes and sizes, at even the most unlikely of times.

Say you're out to dinner with friends and the conversation sparks an idea for new entertainment at your restaurant. Or imagine you're out to eat at another restaurant, and you have a lightbulb moment after taking note of how a specific dish is served.

Great ideas might even come to you in your dreams!

In today's competitive market, you need to be **obsessed** with improvement, innovation, and adaptation to stay above water. Being good is not good enough!

If you aren't constantly on the lookout for ways to delight your guests in new, fresh ways, you'll quickly be out-smarted, out-strategized, and out-maneuvered by your competition.

Being set in your ways is being lazy and a surefire way to kill your business.

As a small, independent restaurant, you can be agile and test out new things. Bigger, well-established brands don't have this luxury; their operations are often far too bureaucratic to institute change quickly. **When you see a trend hit the big brands, it's at the end of its 15 minutes of fame. Use this information to your advantage.**

3. SOMETIMES, KNOWLEDGE CAN BE LIMITING

While talking to Jeffrey Amoscato, V.P. of supply chain and menu innovation for Shake Shack®, at the *Hospitality Innovation Planet Conference* in Madrid, Spain, our conversation shifted to discussing how hard it is to "unlearn" things.

When you start a restaurant, you may be confident in all the operational aspects of running it; building an entire business is *completely* different. Likewise, as time goes on, the methods and strategies you use to run a successful restaurant will become outdated and stale as new techniques and technologies come on the scene.

Creating and growing a successful business is impossible without a solid foundation, also known as your vision. Though your strategy and operations will change as you gain perspective and insights, your business' vision will always remain the same.

To this day, Shake Shack still has the original napkin Danny Meyers wrote on to draft the ideas for the brand (it's framed in his office). It serves as a constant reminder of their original vision for the Shake Shack brand.

As you grow as a restaurateur and experiment with new entrepreneurial ventures, you'll realize that clinging to your old ways of thinking may be holding you back from exciting, profitable new ideas.

Therefore, it's essential to approach running a business with what's known in the Zen philosophy as "a beginner's mind." **Always be open to new ways of thinking, new strategies, new technologies**. This philosophy will help you run the restaurant of the future, not the restaurant of the past.

4. KEEP YOUR EYES OPEN

The restaurant industry is both extremely rewarding and extremely brutal.

If you go into running a restaurant thinking your concept is going to become an overnight success story, think again. Solid, successful, guest-adored brands that stand the test of time take time to develop, ask McDonald's® founder Ray Kroc.

As a restaurateur, be honest with yourself and always keep your eyes wide open for new ways to innovate.

Why do so many restaurants close? They didn't stand out. Being average (or even slightly above average) is a death sentence in an industry that's overwhelmingly oversaturated.

Keep your eyes open for fresh takes or insights, listen to the word on the street and in your restaurant, stay up on trends, and adapt quicker than your competition. *That advice is your recipe for survival in the restaurant industry.*

6 Signs it's Time to Rebrand Your Restaurant

All restaurants go through change. As I've said before, change is the one constant in the universe. Throw out the suggestion of "rebranding" to a restaurant owner, and you'll get a wide array of reactions, from contemplative to shock. It doesn't necessarily mean starting over all the time. Just like with a home, sometimes a restaurant needs a fresh coat of paint and a few minor adjustments to make it fresh again. Other times, it's better to tear it all down and start over.

The decision to rebrand is never an easy one to make because it's usually an emotional one. You have sacrificed and given a lot to build your brand—the last thing you want to do is think about change. Markets and technology are always advancing, developing, morphing, and changing. Those who fail to embrace change quickly find themselves playing catch-up in the market. You must avoid forcing your restaurant into a position where it's playing catch-up to the competition.

How does this happen? Failure to notice the warning signs. Failure to stay current on market trends and consumer behavior. Failure to put your ego aside. That said, let's look at the three most common red flags that it might be time to consider a rebranding project for your restaurant.

1. SALES ARE FALLING

When sales are falling or on a steady decline, there might be more to the cause then you realize. It's always a smart move to bring in a third-party company (a consultant or a mystery shopping service) to give you an unbiased view as to why sales are suffering. Falling sales are a symptom of deeper issues. *Side note: All businesses go through a normal sales cycle of ups and downs. You need only become concerned if you find your business down for a longer period than is normal. Don't let last week's slow sales cause you to hit the panic button. This is one of the many reasons why you must know your daily numbers!*

Look at your market: is there some new competition (or existing competition that you didn't think was a threat before) that snuck up behind you and started luring guests away? It happens to even the best brands — people like what's new. If you fail to give people what they want, they tend to go elsewhere, particularly if your food and service are average. Remember that average is a failing formula that keeps you stuck in the middle of the market (where most of the competition is).

So, what can **you** do? Take a hard look at your restaurant and ask yourself questions that require brutal honesty:

- Is my concept still relevant to current market trends?
- Has our guest profile changed?
- Does our brand tell the wrong (or outdated) story?
- Why do our guests come here?
- What do we stand for?
- Are we sharing the same congruent message across all our marketing platforms?
- What is our purpose, or why? *Side note: This can't be about making money. Making money is a result; it's not your driving purpose.*

You'll have to do some soul searching to get to the real answers. This is something you'll want to take seriously. If you want better results for your restaurant, it all comes down to **asking yourself better quality questions**. The truth is always in there.

2. YOU'RE ON A GROWTH PLAN

Maybe you're getting too big and expanding beyond your original brand identity. This can be a good thing if you take the time to set up your brand with a vision for the future. Let's say you're a small little Poké restaurant. You've opened your first location and business has just taken off. Soon, you've opened three more locations in your town. Then come the offers to expand your brand into a neighboring state. However, your website is pokecafearizona.com. That could be a problem, but it's an excellent opportunity to rebrand.

The above scenario is rather common. You started with something small, and it grew and grew. You went from local market hotspot to up-and-coming restaurant empire. Make sure you set yourself up for long-term rebranding success:

- Buy a domain name that will serve your brand now and in the future.
- www.joespastahouseboston.com is great if you never want to expand to another city.
- When you find a domain name that you like, you also need to make sure that you can use that same domain name for all your social media platforms. Nothing confuses people more than trying to remember all the different names you use for Twitter, Instagram, Facebook, and Snapchat. Look at Shake Shack and their consistent branding: on Instagram, their profile is @shakeshack, on Twitter it's @shakeshack, etc.

Have a marketing plan in place before you launch your new and improved website and social media platforms. Give your guests and your team plenty of time to adjust. The biggest thing to remember is to create excitement and hype it up. Launching a new website is the perfect opportunity to get your message back out to your guests about who you are and why you do what you do (review the seven questions from sign #1, above).

Being able to open more locations is a testimonial to your market that you deliver on your brand promise. Celebrate that. Share it. Brag about it.

3. YOU NEED TO UPDATE YOUR LOOK

Markets change, and the best brands adapt. Competition is entering your market right now to take guests away from you. You must become driven to stay at the top of guests' minds in your market. Several famous brands have done some "fresh look" rebranding to their logos to appeal to the demographic they service.

| 1952 | 1978 | 1991 | 1997 | CURRENT |

Kentucky Fried Chicken has seen a few revisions of their logo throughout the years.

1953 CURRENT

Probably one of the most iconic logos that is recognized around the world.

Even modern restaurants understand the need to refresh their look to attract the market on which they're focused.

~2006 CURRENT

Chipotle's logo has changed over time, with some criticism.

It used to be quite expensive to hire a graphic designer to give your brand a fresh, new look. Not anymore. With websites like Fiverr, 99 Design, and Upwork (which underwent a rebranding of their own, changing their name from Elance-oDesk), you can relatively economically hire graphic designers to help you pull together an updated look for your brand. Sorry, Microsoft® Publisher, you were good to us for a long time. However, we need to explore other graphic designers. No hard feelings, we still love Microsoft Word.

Whatever you choose to do in terms of design, make sure that it looks professional. ***In today's online competitive marketplace, your brand must make a memorable, favorable, and bold statement.*** Attention spans are shrinking—you need your brand to grab hold of the guest and keep them tuned in through consistency in everything you do: **branding, marketing, food, and service**.

4. YOU'RE STRUGGLING WITH PRICES

Your menu pricing is at its limit. There are times when your current brand won't be able to push the pricing envelope any further. If you're a moderately priced steakhouse, finding it hard to compete with rising food costs and shrinking profit margins, perhaps a rebrand is required.

The perception and impression your guests hold of your brand could be holding you back from raising prices. By rebranding, you can reshape the way your guests see your restaurant. There's a perception difference, for example, between Cowboy Café and Cowboy Prime Steakhouse.

5. YOU'RE NOT ATTRACTING TOP TALENT

Millennials want to work for cool and hot brands. If you don't see a steady stream of younger applicants coming in, you might need to adjust your (possibly diminished or outright lacking) hip and trendy vibe with a brand makeover. Older brands sometimes have a stigma that can be difficult to shake (think about Cadillac or Hyundai). While the Baby Boomers are all over Facebook these days sharing pictures of their grandkids, many Millennials stay away because that's where their parents hang out online!

Add a fresh look or some cool geo-tag filters to your Snapchat profile to update your brand for the younger generation since they prefer to communicate via social media. Above all, be open to new ideas. Don't be so stuck in your ways that you won't be able to see the new trends. *It's a brave new world on the internet, and you need to embrace it.*

Emergent cool and hot brands attracting new talent

6. YOU NEED TO DISASSOCIATE FROM BAD P.R.

Look at the headlines of the past several months involving major restaurant brands. The old saying that all P.R. (public relations) is good P.R. isn't accurate. Some P.R. that hits the news can cause a ripple effect of doubt and mistrust around a brand. If this happens, you need to act and *fast*!

Sometimes these issues are cultural. However, shifting focus away from the incident and showing that you're committed to improving as a brand is paramount to getting back on track with your guests. Be honest and transparent when rebranding from a negative image. Everyone will be watching, so move with purpose and conviction.

CHANGE FOR THE RIGHT REASONS

Now, be aware of what's known as "brand boredom." That's when an owner decides to constantly change and update their logo and image because they have become bored with it. Brand boredom is tied to "brand drift." When your brand starts changing too quickly, it starts to confuse your guests. People don't like to be confused. When you start doing that, they tend to drift away, because they don't know what to expect.

Just like human evolution, brands need to grow, learn, adapt, and change. If you've lost touch with your guests, if it seems like your message has become diluted, if you feel as if the spark has gone out of the relationship you have with your brand, ***maybe it's time to rebrand and fall back in love with your restaurant.***

3 Cold, Hard Truths Why Most Managers Suck

Here you are, running a restaurant as a manager—*How are things going?*

If you're like 87 percent of managers out there, you might feel a bit unprepared for the role you're in currently. Since you observed other managers before you became one yourself, you might have assumed that it was easy. Maybe you thought you could do a better job than that one manager who everyone hated or who did a shitty job of managing the restaurant. Then you were thrown into management and soon realized that it's anything *but* easy! To become a leader is a whole other step; and, well worth it to you and your employees.

Welcome to restaurant management. It's a lot like riding a bull: you need to keep your focus, or that wild animal will throw you and proceed to trample you very quickly. To be a champion bull rider takes courage and the ability to adjust quickly, staying centered on the back of that 1,600-pound beast. Restaurant management is quite similar to the rodeo arena wherein the forces around you are constantly trying to throw you off—do your best not to get stomped on in the process.

The journey you took to become a manager doesn't matter. The lack of management training doesn't matter either. What *does matter* is what you do from this day forward to take yourself from being just a manager to being a solid participant in the land of leadership. There are people who are leaders; and, there are managers who claim to be leaders. Claiming a title doesn't make it so. Truthfully, when someone claims to be something, that's the first sign they're not what they claim to be. How many times have you heard a manager claim to be the "leader," and yet there was NO leadership? True leadership isn't about titles—real leaders let their actions speak for them. A leader inspires and motivates, a manager controls.

"A leader is one who knows the way, goes the way, and shows the way." *-John C. Maxwell*

Before you can make the journey to the land of leadership (which can make the trip to Mordor in *The Lord of the Rings* look easy), you'll need to face a few hurdles (hard to hear truths) that could slow you down. All great quests have obstacles the hero must confront.

The following are *yours...*

1. YOU'RE NOT COMMUNICATING PROPERLY

On a scale from 1-10, with ten being **outstanding**, how would you rate your communication skills with your team? Most people are very kind to themselves and tend to rate their skills around an 8 (psychologists call this "Illusory Superiority"). Ask your team to be brutally honest, and they would probably give you a 4.

Communication skills are what separates leaders from managers. The leaders constantly work to improve communication with everyone they meet. *Everyone.* Don't think for a minute this applies to work and not your personal life. You might think that you can separate the two. You often hear that the key to success is to find "life-work balance." **Sorry to tell you this but there is no real life-work balance—it's all just life**. *One life. Your life.* Some days you're focused more on work, others on personal stuff.

How you talk to people is a habit. Habits become unconscious behavior that will creep into other areas of your life. If you talk down to people in your personal life, chances are you'll talk down to people on your team, too. Bad communication habits are the cornerstone of bad management. You can talk a good game and act one way in front of people you want to impress. It's what you say and how you act when those people are *not* around: that's the truth, that's YOUR truth.

Losing your temper in front of your team shows them you don't have self-control. Do you think people want to follow someone who has no control over themselves? You can argue that you're 'just passionate,' which is just an excuse for being weak-minded. If you don't get your emotions under control, they will control you.

2. YOU'RE A HYPOCRITE

The battle cry of the manager is, "Do as I say, not as I do!" When your words and actions don't match you create distrust within your team. Trust is an essential element of teamwork. Think of it like air. And, just like you need air, your employees need to trust if you have any chance of building them into a team. Become a leader, motivate your team by acting the way you expect them to act, drive your team to be **outstanding** by exemplifying this quality in yourself and discuss improvements and changes with the team to build trust.

You can post and share all the positive "pump you up" motivational stuff for your team—if they don't see you leading by example, then you're just like the boy who cried wolf. They see you coming a mile away and think, "Here we go, another piece of fluff and nothing will change."

If you want to be a leader, you must stop talking about it and start living it. The path to becoming a leader starts with being consistent and having integrity with your words and deeds.

> **You say you have integrity.**
> *What do you do when no one is watching?*
> **You say learning is a core value in your restaurant.** *How many books have you read in the last month? How many classes have you taken in the past year?*
> **You say health is important.**
> *Do you consistently exercise and eat healthy?*
> **You say you value community.**
> *Do you donate time or money to a local charity?*
> **You say people are your most valuable asset.**
> *Do you treat them as such?*
> **Do you feel a little uncomfortable now?**
> *Good—this is where the growth starts.*

3. YOU'RE FOCUSED ON TASKS, NOT PEOPLE

The restaurant business is fast-paced and loaded with a plethora of things that need to come together in harmony to create an **outstanding** restaurant. With so many variables that must be juggled simultaneously, many people new to management quickly become overwhelmed. Once again, not as easy as it looks. We don't want to drop the ball, so we add items to our go-to management tool, *the checklist*.

Checklists are a valuable tool when used *as a guide*, not the primary vehicle for task management. Checklists are inanimate objects. They have no emotions, no capacity for thought; they exist. Managers hand these out like it's the cure to all their problems. Then when their team doesn't do what's on the checklist, they become upset. "Hey, it was on the checklist, what happened?" You overlooked an important element, people.

Human beings are fallible. We make mistakes. We mess things up. It's our mistakes that propel us forward to grow and evolve. It's in our DNA. Mistakes and learning go hand in hand. (If people make the same mistakes over and over that's a different problem altogether). People also want to be recognized for doing things right.

The problem with checklists is that they're a double-edged sword. We create checklists to save time and use them to "manage" the team. But when people complete the tasks on a checklist, many managers glaze over and say, "Thanks, see you tomorrow." Epic fail. That person who just finished all the items on your checklist wants to be recognized. They want to be appreciated. They want you to inspect what you expected. One of our greatest human needs is the need to feel appreciated. If you fail to acknowledge your team, high turnover is right around the corner. You can say it's them, not you. **The turnover is likely due to you not being a leader.**

If you took the time to create a checklist, then you owe it to the team to verify that the quality and standards implied on that list are upheld. Not doing so robs you and your team of a valuable opportunity to be human. Connect. Communicate. Coach. Lead.

You made it into management based on your past skills, hard work, and character.

If you desire to transform into a true leader, you'll need to leave behind some bad habits. You'll need to open your mind to learning. You'll need to push past your comfort zone. You'll need to embrace change. You'll need to accept personal accountability for everything you do.

Will it be easy? Hell no.

Will it be worth it? Hell yes!

Why You Should Forget About Improving Your Restaurant

Wait! Am I telling you to stop trying to improve your restaurant? ***Hold on…let me explain.*** I just wanted a clever way to get you to read this section because what you are doing to improve your restaurant is <u>not</u> working.

Your restaurant is composed of thousands of details. All those details contribute to what your restaurant is today. The good and the bad. Here's the problem: with the new year comes the new plans to improve your restaurant — usually the same plan. You start strong, and around March, the best-designed plans start to fall to the wayside.

By June those plans are pretty much forgotten. In November you start to make plans for next year, and the cycle continues over and over, again and again, year after year. Perhaps it time to get off of this masochistic treadmill and get some real results?

The first thing to do is to stop trying to improve your restaurant. Wait? Did that last sentence say stop trying to improve my restaurant? Yes. It's not a typo. Improvement of a thing is like throwing new paint on a rusted-out car. It looks nice on the surface, but underneath, it's still a rusted-out piece of junk. Instead of trying to fix temporary issues, how about we dig deep down for **real, lasting change**? That starts with you being the leader.

Your restaurant is a direct reflection of who you are as a leader, owner, operator, or chef. When you're the one who is driving the brand, you have to know where you want to go! Too many people focus on temporary solutions that compound the real problem lurking underneath the surface … what is the real problem, you ask … well, <u>you might suck at running your restaurant</u>.

Here are a few things that contribute to your current state of mediocrity:

YOU FOCUS ON THE WRONG THINGS

There are probably days when you think that your restaurant would be awesome *if* it weren't for those other people screwing things up, day after day. You know, it's all *their* fault. Can't be *you*. Hey, let's invite a few more people to this pity party and turn it into a total bitch fest! Get a bunch of unhappy people together, and it ramps up pretty quick.

There was a restaurant owner who said to me the other day, *"My cashiers are a bunch of idiots!"*

My reply was rather calm, *"Who hired them?"*

"I did," he said.

"Well, maybe the real issue is the person who allowed them to work here in the first place?" I stated.

Yes, the truth will set you free. Yes, it's going to piss you off.

After a minute of silence, the owner replied, *"Yeah, I haven't done a very good job of screening people. I get desperate and hire anybody with a pulse!"*

I said, *"When you panic hire you solve a temporary issue and create a long-term problem that does not contribute to the growth of your culture."*

What are **you** doing to improve yourself and become a better leader?

What are **you** doing each week to recruit and search for better people to join your team?

The answer to these questions will prompt you to start focusing on the one thing you truly have control over YOU! Restaurants get better when the people in them become better people. You don't tolerate mediocrity in others, so why do you accept it for yourself?

YOU DON'T SCHEDULE TIME TO WORK ON YOUR PLAN

Let's talk about being busy. You're busy; I get that. The question is, what are you busy with? Are you blocking time during your day to move your brand forward? It's easy in the restaurant world to fill a day up with minutia tasks that have little long-term impact on growth.

Growth is not just about increasing sales. It's about becoming better. Better at marketing. Better at guest relations. Better at cultivating a team that lives your mission. Better at being a better person.

Time has the ultimate, "I don't care what you do" attitude. Seriously. Time does not care what you do with the 14,400 minutes you get gifted with each day. Waste it or invest it, it's always your choice. Remember that...you choose what is important by where you place your attention during the day. So, the "I'm too busy" excuse is a bunch of B.S. You should **be honest** and say that it's not important to you.

Finding small chunks of time and blocking them on your calendar is the one sure way to ensure your agenda (your life) moves forward. Take a tip for the most successful people on the planet...use your calendar to schedule

EVERYTHING! Don't take random meetings. Don't allow people to control your day by not having your calendar booked. White space on your calendar is the lazy person's life. Multimillionaire Grant Cardone is fond of saying, "If you want to meet the devil, have white space on your calendar." Your productivity will come to a halt when you have too much idle time on your hands.

What do you schedule? Everything! Gym time, breakfast, family time, meetings, phone calls, preshifts, computer time, reading time, meditation, and whatever else is important to you. I block some open time for things that might need my attention. I tell clients to contact me during these scheduled blocks of time. If you want to improve the quality of your restaurant and your life, then take control of your calendar and schedule everything!

YOU GET DISCOURAGED AND GIVE UP

Life loves to throw curve balls at you. Persistence and perseverance are required if you want massive success. Hey, things are not going to work *all the time*. It's ok. Even if your restaurant started with a Big Bang, as time goes by (and more restaurants move into your market), you'd start to become a little less appealing compared to the shiny new emerging restaurant brands.

You'll try something new to get your brand back on top. Maybe some video marketing on social media. You'll get a few likes, and then it seems to die off. Because of the lackluster response, you throw in the towel and throw out the excuse that your guests don't want this or that. You could be so wrong...

Marketing is not a one-time thing. It's a consistency thing. Throwing out that occasional video and then not promoting it is your downfall. You made a half-ass commitment, and the results show. If you want to play the social media marketing game, you need to put energy and effort in to get the results you want out. Is everything you put out there going to stick? Of course not! So, try something else! If that doesn't work, you try *something else*. If that doesn't work, you try *something else*. If that doesn't work, you try *something else*. If that doesn't work, you try *something else*. If that doesn't work, you try *something else*. If that doesn't work, you try *something else*. Get the hint?

You keep working and refining your message until you hit the nerve that gets a response from your guests. Then you market it **relentlessly**! Marketing is about keeping your brand in front (top of feed) of your market. If you don't want to spend the time and invest in promoting your brand, your competition will.

I think it's safe to say that almost everyone reading this knows what McDonald's is. Do you see McDonald's backing off on their marketing, ever?

Hell no. They keep their foot on the marketing accelerator all the time! When you see McDonald's slow down on marketing, you should follow suit. Until then, keep your brand at the top of social media feeds to keep your name at the top of mind.

Stop throwing caution to the wind.

Stop playing it safe.

Stop playing small in your market.

Stop trying to improve things that won't improve your restaurant.

Focus on becoming the best version of yourself. Control your calendar. Keep your marketing fresh and frequent.

Refuse to surrender to complacency and mediocrity!

Culture is Everything

"People don't buy what you do, they buy why you do it."

—Simon Sinek

It's Usually the Same Story

Joe (*real name changed to protect the not so innocent*) is a restaurateur who has four concepts in a small town. On the surface, he seems to have it all: the happy and supportive wife, the kids, the dog, the big house, and the Porsche.

Joe called me and asked me to help coach one of the senior leaders on his team. That's always an instantly waved red flag to me. I call it the "**Fix Fred Scenario**" because owners think that everything in their business will be perfect as soon I "fix" the one person they believe is holding back their team.

Here's the problem with that: it's always the owners who need to be coached. Besides, coaching is not about fixing people; <u>it's about fixing the thinking that causes the problems</u>. Once that's fixed, the problems tend to fix themselves. Owners don't like to hear that it's not someone else who's the problem; it's them. I make it a requirement that the owners participate in my team coaching program (The Summit Club). If they don't, it's doomed to fail—they'll never get the results that they want. I can predict the chance of restaurant coaching success by the amount of engagement the owner has with the program: the higher owner involvement, the higher chance of success. Period.

So, out I go on my standard site visit to spend a couple of days with Joe and his team. Well, let me tell you something about site visits and why they're critical to coaching: the things an owner tells me are the problems <u>are never the real problems</u>. The actual problems exist about five levels deeper, requiring me to see the owner and his team engaging with each other and their guests to uncover the truth. I always plan on at least three days. On the first day, everyone will be on their best behavior and show me what they want me to see. By day three, they get comfortable, and I see the real team dynamics.

I'm a big believer in behavioral surveys to help me get an inside look at what an owner's natural strengths are in a particular restaurant. Their kinetic energy, how they communicate with others, how they like to be communicated with, how they'll deal with stress, how they lead naturally, and how they accomplish tasks. It's all very powerful stuff!

Before my site visit to Joe's restaurant, I sent out invitations to take the ProScan® Survey and dug into the reports. I've seen more than 1,000 ProScan® reports from people in the restaurant industry, giving me insight into what creates a high-performing team. I can also identify possible challenge areas.

As I said, it seems that Joe has it all. When I arrived, things looked great…a little too great. I worked with Wolfgang Puck for five years. I've spent some time with catering at movie studios. It felt like I was on a movie set—everyone was playing for the camera. The trip was going well. I did a 360° interview with random staff, particularly the leadership team (I dislike the word "manager"). I have some off the wall questions that are designed to get people to drop their guard and tell me what's going on. One of them is the lifeboat question:

> *"Imagine you and your entire team are on a luxury cruise. Think of the Titanic. You're sailing along, and the ship hits an iceberg. The ship is sinking, and sinking fast. You find the last lifeboat and can only take five people who you work with onto it. There's no time to overthink this because the ship is going under. Give me five names. Go!"*

People usually give me one to three names without hesitation. Then, they pause for a second. You might miss the pause if you're not listening for it, but it's there. Here's what it means: The people they name with no hesitation are who they trust implicitly. The rest of the list consists of people with whom they have rapport (basically, they like them) or feel they "should" include. Now, if you were to ask a restaurant team this question, you'd be shocked by how many times the owner **isn't listed** in the first group. **If you don't have trust, you have problems.**

After I conducted my interviews with about 20 members of Joe's team, I saw a pattern. Only about 20 percent of the team trusted Joe. That's bad. The other issue was a common one: Joe thought he was an amazing leader! In psychology, they call this "illusory superiority." In a nutshell, you think you're way better than you are. You have a blind spot. This is one of the benefits of coaching—helping you realize you have a blind spot and helping you do something about it. It's so easy to see the faults in others and very humbling to see and admit you have faults too. *Side note: We all have blind spots and if you don't think you have one, that's your first blind spot!*

Joe proved to be a challenge. I love a challenge. So, he signed up for The Summit Club Team Coaching Program that includes The Restaurant Success Formula™, access to all of my online courses and resources at The

Restaurant Coach™ University, and a bi-weekly video coaching call with him and key members of the leadership team.

The first trip to Joe's restaurant occurred about two weeks into the coaching program. Calls were going great, and Joe was very engaged and seemed to be making positive growth. I conducted one of my signature workshops called **NeuroSelling**™ that shows the service team how to build rapport, use techniques from NLP (Neuro-Linguistic Programming), and understand the emotional dynamics of hospitality. The workshop routinely spawns an increase of **20 percent or more** in sales in just a few days. You see, a lot of restaurants teach the standard up-selling techniques, *few teach how to create and transfer emotions to the guest.*

During the workshop, Joe kept interrupting to add his own opinion. This is a common owner blind spot called "**the need to add value and be in control.**" When you study behavioral dynamics and have a ProScan® Survey in your back pocket, you see this with those who have the High Dominance trait. They like control. They have an inner urge to be in charge. *It's a pure alpha dog mindset.*

Now, whenever I experience this, I tread carefully. It would be easy just to shut them down and embarrass them in front of their staff, but I don't want to be the bigger jerk. So, I sidestep. I reframe their statement and put it on the back burner for discussion later (if they even remember it). "That's an interesting perspective. We should explore that later, let's continue." It would be easy to say, "No, that's not true," but then I would have an owner sitting there with his arms crossed like a chided child. The behavior of a child and an adult are not very different when they feel like they're disciplined— adults are just older and bigger. *Hit the right trigger, and you can watch an adult morph straight into an 8-year-old with a very bad attitude.*

The trip showed me a side of Joe, I had a sense was hiding. He came across like he was a people person and loved his team. Eventually, though, his actions started to fall out of congruency with his words. The other leaders on the team showed similar behavior to Joe: a lot of talk but little follow through. Joe was High Dominance and High Extrovert, a guy who could sell you pretty much anything. The issue with those two traits is they tend to have a blind spot for follow through. You can have great ideas, plans, and vision for your restaurant, but if you can't get those ideas organized and implemented, it's all just cheap talk.

Another problem with most owners or leaders in a restaurant is they tend to hire people who are like themselves! **Like does attract like.** We build rapport quickly with those who are like us. Do you see how having too many of the same personalities on the leadership team can be a problem? When you have too many High Dominance and High Extroversion individuals on your team, you get a lot of talk and no action, all show, and no go. If others on the leadership team are not like some owners, those owners tend to alienate them because they don't have a natural rapport. That's a major mistake because they need those other behavioral types to balance out the team.

Things were starting to become very clear in terms of why Joe was stuck. Here's where the tipping point was: *honesty*. People don't want to face their fears or be told that they're the problem in their business, and Joe was no different.

Another thing Joe was struggling with was his weight. The restaurant industry can induce a lifestyle that's not at all healthy if—and that's a big if—you allow it. You can throw out the excuses that you're too busy (*bullshit*) to work out or to eat better (*more bullshit*), but you're not fooling me. Excuses exist because you don't want it bad enough—it hasn't become a must.

Do this exercise: Take a deep breath and tell your body you're not going to take another breath again. How long did you it take before your body said you must take a breath? *Now, if you were successful not breathing again, then no need to keep reading because you're either dead or a zombie.*

Joe said he wanted to work out. He said he wanted to lose weight. Here's the thing, your words tell me what you want to do, your actions tell me what you will do to make it happen. When I travel, I commit always to find a gym so I can work out in the morning. I also invite clients to join me if they wish. Joe showed up the first day. His excuses for why he couldn't work out again showed up the next day.

Taking care of yourself as an owner or leader must become a priority. The energy you bring to your culture has a dramatic impact on your brand. All my clients know that self-care is at the top of my list for building a better restaurant. You must take time to recharge your internal battery and be at 100 percent when you hit your restaurant. This industry is all about **energy**. Your team and your guests will ask for your energy. If you arrive at 50 percent energy level, it won't be long before you're drained and exhausted. When you're out of energy, you go into survival mode, and that brings out the not-so-nice side of us.

It was on the last day of my trip that I saw this with Joe. It was around 8:00 p.m. His wife had just arrived at the restaurant and was a little shaken from driving in some inclement weather (okay, more like a blizzard). Joe unleashed a flurry of foul words on her. She started crying, and that made Joe look like even more of an ass. He noticed I didn't approve of this and added a rude comment for good measure, "Looks like The Restaurant Coach™ doesn't like me talking to my wife like this!"

I didn't.

I calmly said, *"How you do anything is how you do everything. How you talk to the people in your personal life is how you'll talk to the people in your professional life."*

Joe's reply? *"Whatever. I'm a millionaire."*

Nice attitude. His wife looked at me and silently mouthed the words, *"Thank you."*

I left the next morning. Two days later Joe sent me an email saying that he had to make some budget cuts (*even though he was a "millionaire"*) and was going to stop coaching.

Funny, I was about to send him an email dropping him as a client. He was trying to keep his pride intact. Good for him. I don't have tolerance for people who talk down to others. It won't be the first or last time that I've had to dissolve a coaching relationship. If you're not 100 percent engaged, don't listen to my advice (***plus take action***), or if you treat people like shit to make yourself look good to protect your fragile ego, we won't be working together very long.

When I come to your restaurant, I'm not going to lower my standards so you're comfortable.

I coach to make you and your business better; you can be mediocre all on your own.

The Trouble with Cultivating Culture

Look at any well-kept garden, and you'll see careful planning, care, and maintenance. You'll need to mirror those elements to create a restaurant culture that surpasses the average.

Culture is the secret sauce that separates the good from the **outstanding**. Restaurants can have the same ingredients and even the same menu items. What separates them is the one thing that's hard to copy: *culture*. Even famous rock bands that break up and go on to form other bands often find they can't recreate any semblance of the chemistry (or culture) they first created. *Culture is organic and alive.* Just like that immaculate garden, you need to understand the planning and work that go into creating such a masterpiece.

There are three key elements to cultivating culture.

SELECTION

You can't just pick plants and flowers for a garden without thinking about how they're going to thrive together. Some have different growth cycles, some require more attention than others, and some flourish in the heat while others prefer mild climates. The same can be said about the people on your team.

Think of your team members like plants and your restaurant as a garden. Some personalities grow well with others, and some prefer to grow alone. Some people need more attention than others. The thing is, you need a variety of people with a variety of skills and a variety of personalities to build a high-performance team.

It's natural to gravitate toward people who are like us. Because of this, owners and managers tend to make a common mistake during the hiring process: they choose people who are similar to them. This can cause a lot of the problems many restaurants experience. The things that annoy us about others can often be the same traits we dislike in ourselves. Be honest, have you ever looked in the mirror and not liked the person looking back at you?

You must look beyond just the position you're hiring to fill and consider how this person will impact the overall team dynamics. Look at your team's strengths and gaps. You can make smarter additions to your team by asking yourself better questions:

- *Does this person have strengths that will complement or complicate the team?*
- *Does this person have a personality that will integrate with our core values and culture?*

Answering these questions, truthfully will move you beyond hiring for skills and trigger you to focus more on personality. The ability of a new hire to adapt to your culture is imperative for the continued growth of your brand. Selection should always be a long-term consideration rather than a short-term solution, i.e., hiring to cover a shift or position. Temporary fixes only bring bigger problems down the road. Keep your eyes on your long-term goals.

NURTURING

It would be a waste of time, energy, and money to work so hard to build a great garden only to let it wither. Plants need nutrients and care. The same goes for the culture in your restaurant!

You might have the best intentions, but that's not enough. Without consistent attention and actions (your behavior) and the positive energy you feed your culture, you'll see it all fade away.

So, what do you need to feed your culture so it can grow and flourish?

Core Values: If you don't know what you stand for and why then you're going to find it very hard to get your team to buy into your culture. **Remember that all restaurants have a culture, either by design or by default.** Your core values are the seeds of culture—what you get largely depends on the values you plant.

Standards: These are your non-negotiables. Standards are the baseline for behavior. You must draw a line in the sand and stand there as a constant reminder of where that line is and what the consequences are for crossing it. This is where many owners and managers falter. They draw a line, but when it comes time to enforce the standards, they back down. If you back down from a standard you set, it wasn't a standard in the first place. Being a true leader means holding others (and yourself) to the standards at all times, not when it's convenient.

Energy: Everything in the universe is energy. The energy you bring every day to your culture is either negative, neutral, or positive. **Outstanding** leaders are aware of their energy and how it feeds the culture they've built. Self-awareness (part of Emotional Intelligence or E.Q.) is critical to cultural success. Your body language transfers energy to others. They sense when you're upset, when you're tired, when you're happy, your team and your culture are a reflection of your energy. If you can become mindful of your energy and create positive energy (known as *state management*), you'll be in the top 5 percent of leaders.

WATCH FOR WEEDS

A beautiful garden must be maintained and weeded, constantly. It's ironic that the things you want to grow take hard work, yet those nasty weeds grow without any help! Weeds pop up, and if you're not careful, they'll overrun your garden and ruin your efforts.

Without diligence and commitment to the selection of your "plants," and cultivation of your culture, the detrimental "weeds" will grow inside your restaurant.

What are some cultural weeds?

Gossip, lack of standards, negative team members with poor attitudes, stealing (scamming or taking tables from other servers), managers who have double standards, playing favorites within the team, an unhealthy front-of-house versus back-of-house mindset.

What do you do when you find a weed? You yank it out! You can't wait until "later"—before you know it that one weed is now two weeds, and then two become four. They grow faster and stronger than you thought possible, and you realize immediate action is the only cure.

When you find weeds in your garden, you pull them and spray weed killer to make sure more weeds don't grow in their place. When you find cultural weeds growing in your restaurant, you must remove them immediately. Then apply "weed killer" (training, communication, and crystal-clear expectations) to prevent weeds from growing in your restaurant's culture. This will also stop other problems from appearing.

People think culture isn't something they need to tend to like you would a garden. If you want to create an **outstanding** culture, you must take time to plant the desirable seeds that will take root deep inside your brand. If the roots are solid, you'll find long-term success through careful maintenance combined with meticulous selection, positive nurturing, and slaying the weeds before they take over.

The late actor Peter Sellers made a movie in 1979 called *Being There* in which he plays a simple man named Chance the Gardener who delivers tips for gardening that some high-level politicians and businesspeople took as words of wisdom. Chance the Gardener said, "As long as the roots are not severed, all is well. And all will be well in the garden."

If the roots of your culture are strong, all will be well in your restaurant.

Building a Restaurant Culture Free from Sexual Harassment

For many seasons on the popular HBO series *Game of Thrones,* we've been warned that "Winter is coming," foreshadowing a Great War to come. Well, winter is here for the restaurant industry!

The great restaurant storm is upon us, and many will need to form alliances (already happening), some will rebrand (already happening), and all will need to understand that people are what makes the difference (not there yet).

We, as an industry, perpetuate memes and jokes around the internet that display our world as overworked, devalued, and unappreciated. It's not so funny when we become the stereotypes we share.

> How do we change the sexual harassment culture that infests so much of our industry? How can we reverse the course we seem to be heading down to becoming the next Sodom and Gomorrah?

GET SOME VALUES

Restaurants become better when the people working in them become better human beings, and that starts with you. All great cultures start with a strong foundation: core values. You must know who you are and what you stand for. This old saying is quite true, "If you don't stand for something, you'll fall for anything."

Becoming crystal-clear about your core values is step number one. Your core values are something that you can't outsource. Your core values are a reflection of who you are. Write them down, make them real. Your restaurant is a reflection of you. Yes, you're going to need to get in touch with those things called emotions. Don't underestimate being authentic and being real. See the connection?

LIVE YOUR DAMN VALUES

Now that you have those pretty words - your core values - written down, what do you do with them? You put them into action by being the example. This is where many go astray. Core values are easy to verbalize but very challenging to live.

Integrity, respect, and punctuality are examples of core values that are easy to claim as yours, yet your actions may be telling a different story. Just remember that when words and actions aren't in sync, **your team and guests will always default to what you do over what you say**. Actions trump bullshit-words every time.

Creating a culture free of sexual harassment means living up to the golden words you flaunt for the public. You "respect and appreciate your team," yet you overlook "locker room" talk and gossip? That doesn't fly. *Respect is the new currency; it will draw people to your restaurant. True respect starts with respecting yourself and minding your behavior. Once again, it starts with you being a leader, not a coward.*

"THAT'S JUST THE WAY IT IS" IS BULLSHIT

Many people will claim the restaurant industry is "just this way" and "it will never change." **That's a real loser's mindset!** The most dangerous statements are those that are either complacent or encouraging of any behavior that demeans another human being. *What you put up with, you end up with.*

Stop accepting "the way it was" as the way it has to be. It's time to step up and be a leader in our industry; for our industry! Just because bad behavior has been a common practice in the past doesn't mean you shouldn't take a stand to stop it for the good of the future. Sarah Connor from the cult classic movie *The Terminator* said it best, *"There is no fate, except what we make."* Take a fucking stand, be the leader with integrity.

DON'T FOLLOW THE CROWD

Following the crowd is easy. The world is full of people who blindly follow the mainstream consciousness of thought and go along even when they know it's not right. Stop it. If you know it's not right, don't allow it. If you see someone being harassed, say something. If you see a post that spreads negativity, don't hit the "share" button.

We talk about being a better industry, **one** that attracts talent instead of repels it. There are plenty of people who want to work in restaurants, but we've foolishly driven them away by our inability to create a professional, inclusive, and safe environment and image. Reality TV chefs yell, scream, and degrade people. Yes, some act like that, but there are many more who don't! Professional people who honestly care about others are out there — we need your voice! Stand up and make some noise for the good of our industry. There's already plenty of negativity out there — we don't need anymore. Be positive, be the solid example we need!

Creating a non-sexual harassment culture starts with you knowing who you are, living your core values, and speaking up when you see people demeaning others.

Winter is here!

Are you ready for the great restaurant war coming?

Toxic Cultures Suck!

Your restaurant's culture is the life force of your brand. It creates energy that transcends and influences your staff. It trickles down, encompassing, and shaping the guest experience. To those on the outside looking in, it can be either a beacon that entices them in or a warning sign to steer clear.

A toxic culture is a symptom of a much deeper condition: the total absence of leadership. The good news is that toxic cultures can be recognized and treated. Determining how aggressive you need to be with the treatment will depend on how bad the toxicity has spread throughout your brand.

Like cancer, toxic cultures have one mission, and that's to destroy your brand one person at a time. Just like in the fight against cancer, early detection is your best chance of success and survival. How do you spot a toxic culture? How do you find out if you've developed one?

Check out these warning signs and see for yourself.

POOR MODELING

Most restaurant managers run on principles and techniques from the 1970s. Why? Because most are just passed along from mentor to student year after year. Nobody has stopped to say, "Are you sure this is a good idea?" It's the blind leading the blind. Just because it's always been done that way, doesn't mean it *should* continue to be done that way.

Think about it. Most managers are trained not to question authority and do what they're told. This is probably the number one issue that some people have with the Millennial generation because they're wired to question and not follow blindly.

If you've worked for and been mentored by **outstanding** leaders, then you're good. If not, then you're likely modeling the behavior of some bad managers. You might not even be aware of the behavior because it has become part of your unconscious mind and pure habit.

You may not want to read this, but here's the hard truth: **you're wired to be a conformist.** Human beings are herd animals. We thrive in highly coordinated groups. Individually, we're designed to pick up social cues, coordinate, and align our behavior with those around us.

So, if your model for management wasn't a good model, you unknowingly developed similarly bad behaviors. Now that you know the truth, you have options. Remember, awareness precedes choice, choice precedes change. Is your current management style serving you and those around you? If not, time to get off this road and head down a new one.

OUTDATED MANAGEMENT THEORIES

Have you heard of carrots and sticks? The old management theory based on the system of reward and punishment? This theory has been around since the 1950s. The problem with it is twofold:

- The reward becomes the only prize, and that has an addictive quality. The person soon needs a bigger reward, and for some restaurants, that's difficult to maintain when the reward is purely monetary.
- Usually, you base the carrot-and-stick system on what you think will motivate the employee. Assumptions are the last thing you want to use as a management technique. Have you ever asked what motivates a team member? It's better to sit down and talk with them to learn what they would like. The trick is avoiding leading their answers with questions like, "What amount of a bonus would make you happy?" Let them do the talking. Ask what drives them to do well and how they like to be appreciated; their answers will tell you what motivates them.

Carrots and sticks work only if you use them correctly. Here are some guidelines:

Don't make it all about money. This approach can offend some people because they'll think you're trying to buy them.

Sometimes small, unexpected rewards are better. Kind words, movie tickets, concert tickets, and other small gestures go a long way. Say "thank you," a little more often, and you won't need to break out the big rewards to keep employees engaged.

FEAR IS IN THE AIR

Here's another classic, outdated technique: break them down to build them up. The first thing to do is stop watching Chef Gordon Ramsay on *Hell's Kitchen*. **Drama is great for television, bad for restaurants.**

Yelling and screaming at people triggers one emotion: **fear**. Fear does **not** build a high-performance team. **Fear suffocates**. It takes the positive energy out of a room faster than fire does to air!

There was a restaurant owner who was overheard saying that his job was to make sure his employees feared him. He believed his mission was to put the emotion of fear into his staff. Do you think fear and hospitality can co-exist? No. One takes energy, and the other gives energy. If you haven't noticed, everything is energy.

Everything.

- Do you ever lose your temper in front of your team?
- Do you ever call people on your team degrading names, either in front of them or behind their backs?
- Do you ever think of your team as lazy and incompetent?

If you said yes to any of these questions, you have a toxic culture. If that serves you and you enjoy high turnover, then, by all means, continue. Otherwise, it's time to get that raging toxic monster under control. Oh, and stop watching reality TV shows!

POWER IS APPARENT

It's been said repeatedly that power corrupts and absolute power corrupts absolutely. If your restaurant is big on titles and hierarchy, you are modeling a destructive power paradigm (the use of power or force in your organization). It's a battle as old as time. The tighter you wrap your hands around things trying to control them, the more things slip through your fingers.

Power and its cousin fear come as a package deal. One feeds the other. The more power you get, the more fear appears, whispering in your ear about all those things that could happen if you lose control.

Managers motivated by power are easy to identify. Their moral compasses are obviously out of whack, AND these behaviors may seem too common:

- They seem to have a lot of "private" conversations with only some people on the team.
- The message their sending is: if you're not in the inner circle, you can't be trusted.
- They have the belief that without them, the restaurant would fall apart. They make this known to everyone whenever they arrive for a shift or break, "I leave for just two hours, and everything goes wrong!"

Yeah, it's doubtful that *everything* went wrong. People who use power to control also use what's known as "all or nothing" vocabulary. "Everyone," "always," "never." Some of their favorite phrases are, "*Everyone* is lazy," "You *always* mess up," and "You're *never* on time." Any of those sound familiar?

- They keep teams separated. The last thing someone in power wants is for the team to figure out that together they're stronger than the manager. They'll use words to keep people apart and build imaginary walls. Front-of-house versus back-of-house, this location versus the other, day staff versus night staff ... All designed to keep the staff from forming into a team.

Now, before you say, "Well, I'm *not* replaceable," let me say this: every position in your restaurant is replaceable. People are not replaceable, that's for sure. You're unique, one of a kind. There will never be another you. Your job, though? That's another story. Maybe your replacement won't do it just like you—maybe they'll do it better. Either way, *tell that voice in your head named Fear to sit the fuck down and shut up, it's ruining your culture.*

Many restaurants have lost key leaders or been sold to new owners, resulting in great success. Colonel Sanders and Ray Kroc have been gone a long time, and both their brands **still** bring in billions of dollars in revenue. Yes, that's billions with a "B."

If you're sitting there thinking that you might have a toxic culture in your restaurant, the first thing to do is stop it. Realize that you can't make things better until you first stop making them worse. Will it be easy? Of course not. Anything worthwhile requires effort, energy, and consistent action.

If you're willing, to be honest and take a hard look at yourself and your restaurant, if your culture is showing signs of being toxic, you have a chance to save it.

That is a choice only you can make.

Choose wisely.

Act now.

Transform Your Team into Brand Fanatics

Today's market is a lot like flying coach on a major airline — there's not much room. Standing out is imperative if you want to make an impact on your guest's experience. The easiest way to make an impact is to turn your team into brand ambassadors for your restaurant. Your team is a natural amplifier of your brand message, good or bad. Your team is talking about the restaurant, and you, when they aren't at work, so take time to make sure they're sharing the same love you have for your restaurant. All restaurants have two types of customers: internal and external. We focus so much on the external customer — or guest — to turn them into raving fans that we lose sight of a vital customer base right in front of us: our teams.

Why invest your time in turning your team into brand advocates? Because just like with any investment, you're looking for a return and the stats don't lie. Getting your team more engaged and transforming them into brand advocates is just smart business. Gallup's meta-analysis of employee engagement shows that business units with high employee engagement have 28 percent less internal theft or shrinkage, and 21 percent higher productivity (Dvorak and Kruse, 2016).

You might have a solid marketing message and brand already, so why not amplify that? Companies with strong employee advocacy programs increase their visibility. **Messages shared by employees went 561 percent further than the same messages shared on a brand-owned channel.** Brand messages are re-shared an average of 24 times when distributed by an employee rather than just the brand (PostBeyond™, 2018).

YOU saying you're good is one thing — when your TEAM says your brand is good, you make it into the bonus round.

So how do you go about transforming your staff into solid brand advocates? You commit to exercising the tactics below...

ONBOARD LIKE YOUR LIFE DEPENDS ON IT

During the interview, a new team member is most likely very fired up about starting. They look forward to a new opportunity and chapter in their life. But when they show up for the first day and are told to read the 45-page employee handbook, their enthusiasm disappears. No warm greeting from the management team, sit in the corner, read the manual, and fill out paperwork. **Epic fail**.

Instead, hold a new employee-welcoming party. You want to make their first day is memorable (in a good way). Make sure to clear your calendar, so you have time to focus on really getting them excited about joining your team. Once again, remember that your new team members (*internal customers*) must be treated just as well (and maybe even better) than your guests (*external customers*). Onboarding sets the tone for how the new employee connects with your brand. Take it seriously. Put some energy into it. Craft your onboarding process into an **outstanding** experience.

MAKE THEM THE HERO

Everyone wants to be the hero in the movie. Everyone wants to be heard. Everyone wants to know that they matter. Too many owners and managers treat this desire as a liability and not the asset it is. <u>The funny thing about people: they tend to rise to your level of expectation.</u>

If you think someone is lazy and entitled, you tend to find yourself surrounded by lazy and entitled people. Look, and you will find. People are a complex puzzle of both good and bad traits. When you focus on the bad, you tend to get more of it.

Instead, focus on your team's natural strengths. Find ways to help your team flourish by accentuating what makes them strong. This requires you to talk to your team more and find out what makes them tick. Allow them to voice concerns and make suggestions. Talk to your team regularly (and not always about work) and make them the hero. Talk to them about their dreams, goals, and desires. Find a way to help them achieve those, and they will go into battle for your brand.

NEVER MISS AN OPPORTUNITY TO APPRECIATE

The two most powerful words you can say to another person are "thank" & "you." Think of how great it feels when a guest walks up to you after a meal in your restaurant and says thanks to you. It feels pretty good, doesn't it? Your team wants to experience that as well; give it to them often.

Saying thank you is probably the greatest thing you can do when transforming your team into brand advocates. The best thing about it is that it costs you nothing. Sincerity and appreciation are paramount to any experience. Thank your team openly. There's a good rule of thumb when feedback is concerned, "**critique in private, and praise in public**." Wise words. Follow them.

Take to social media and showcase your brand ambassadors. Celebrate their birthdays, life events, and accomplishments. Your restaurant is more than just the food and drinks you serve. The restaurant business is really the people business. **Make time to appreciate and share the stories the people on your team.**

SHIFT FROM GX TO TX

Look around the internet, and you'll see the hot topic is the GX, or guest experience. If you truly want to improve your guest experience, then focus on the *TX* or team experience. **Remember, your team is a powerful amplifier for your brand message.** When they become brand advocates, they become a megaphone for your message and mission. *Don't neglect that.*

To help you focus on the TX, ask yourself these questions:
- Does the team have access to an employee-only area?
- Does your team have access to employee meals or discounts on food?
- Does your team have health benefits?
- Do you offer paid time off?
- Do you offer advanced training, coaching, or mentorship?
- Do you offer education scholarships?
- Do you offer anything different or unique as a benefit for your team?

Little things make a difference when it comes to creating brand advocates.

SWAG, BABY

When your team buys into your brand and are transformed into advocates, you'll want them to spread the message even when they're not at work. Cool swag like water bottles, clothing, baseball caps, backpacks, cool stickers, or whatever's hot at the moment, goes a long way toward promoting your team's brand advocacy. Don't give them the same T-shirt you expect them to wear at work. Make it special. Make it unique. *Better yet, ask them what they would like. (wow, what a concept!)*

When your team members start incorporating your restaurant's brand into their personal lives, you'll know you've finally transformed them into brand advocates. If you can get them to tattoo your brand on themselves, you've turned them into brand fanatics.

Brand tattoos are a topic for another day ... and tequila shots!

Is Your Restaurant Culture a Monster Out of Control?

Culture is one of those business elements that's created either by design or default. It can be like a subtle song playing in the background, or it can be a booming cinematic soundtrack that blasts throughout your brand. It's there — *have you noticed it?*

Culture and your brand are in a symbiotic relationship. Together, they cooperate and succeed or fail. Your culture is your brand, and your brand is your culture. When you started your restaurant, you brought an idea to life. Along with that idea came the dynamic every business and society needs to successfully survive: culture.

Think of it like that memorable song mentioned earlier. If your brand message is the lyrics, then your culture is the beat. You can put incredible, soulful words into a song; but, if the music or beat doesn't provide the right background, your tune won't find an audience. Can you see how they need each other to be a hit? Can you see why so many miss the mark?

IS YOUR CULTURE A MONSTER?

Maybe your focus was on building sales, and you didn't pay a lot of attention to how your culture was growing. That's the same as planting a tree and being more concerned about the fruit it bears than it taking root and long-term-growth.

When you're in your restaurant, watching your team and guests, does something feel wrong? Is there something not quite right about the culture in your restaurant? Does it feel like your culture has grown into a little monster that's difficult to control? It's much better to deal with it while it's small than when it grows into Godzilla and consumes your brand.

> **Fair Warning**: When you try to change something, anything, even the seemingly small shit, change will push back on you. Sometimes it pushes back rather harshly. Like the line from the famous Dylan Thomas poem, change will "rage, rage against the dying of the light." Change goes against the human drive for comfort, which is most people's natural set point. We seek it, we want it, we crave it.

The first you need to do is avoid beating yourself up about it, too much. This happens to even the best brands. When your brand and culture suffer from a disconnect, you need to get back to the fundamentals of what creates a winning culture.

Being comfortable is the last thing you want for your brand! So, rage and rally against it.

GETTING BACK TO BASICS

So, you've strayed off the beaten path? If you have, don't worry too much. Even a plane flying from Los Angeles to New York makes course corrections.

It's time to make your culture course correction.

You should always be aware of what's happening in your restaurants and adjust as needed but adjust ONLY if it is needed. *Don't change for the sake of change* or you'll end up driving your team crazy with your pursuit of the next new, shiny thing.

Pick your battles carefully. When you encounter a battle, you truly believe will move your brand and culture forward, act with precision and *ruthless execution.* Oh, and give it time to succeed. Not much kills culture faster than giving up too soon when things don't happen as fast as you'd like.

Get your culture back under control using these five culture fundamentals:

1. CONNECT TO WHO YOU ARE

At the epicenter of all cultures is core values. You can't escape them if you want to build a culture that attracts talent and guests to your restaurant brand.

If your culture has grown into something with which you're unhappy, you need to return to square one and identify your core values. **An understanding of what you stand for, who you are, and why you do what you do are essential to the roots of your "culture tree."** Put some deep thought into understanding the values that drive you and your brand. Remember that core values are a reflection of you. Connect with words and phrases that resonate deep within you.

An easy way to start is to write down words that spark an emotion inside you. Happiness, family, sustainability, innovation, leadership … Do any of these words trigger emotion? The important thing is to find words that you truly believe in and are part of who you are. Don't go for words that sound good on the surface or that you think make you look good. **Core values need to have a true connection to who you are.**

2. GET UP AND PREACH!

Once you have your list of core values and corresponding reasons why get up on your soapbox and preach those things to your team every single day, you want to become **obsessed** with talking to your team about your core values and what drives you.

You want to approach talking about core values the same way that Joel Osteen does a sermon: with a **disciplined conviction**.

Your duty as an owner or leader is to talk every day to your team about what drives you, what inspires you, and what makes your heart sing. That's the stuff that great cultures are made of. This must be done every day without fail. Enthusiasm is contagious! You don't build an incredible culture by speaking about your core values occasionally or just during a new hire's orientation. Talking about your core values must become a daily habit. When your team sees what drives you, what you are passionate about, what you believe it, they will either get on the bus or get off the bus. Those who stay will be beside you for the entire ride.

3. BE THE EXAMPLE, NOT THE WARNING

Once you've made a habit of talking about your core values every single day to your team, you need to back your words up with actions. Hypocrisy is a culture killer. Words are mere words; it's through our actions, exhibited every day, that we build credibility.

Credibility leads to trust, and trust builds culture.

A lot of restaurant owners and managers talk a great game. However, watch them in action, and you'll see there's a big disconnect between what they say and what they do. If you selected the core value of integrity, you better live up to what that word means. People love to see a hypocrite fail. That's why your deeds and words must be in total harmony.

What separates a manager from a leader? A leader leads the team through consistent actions and takes personal accountability for those actions. A person is *assigned* the role of a manager; anyone can be a manager. Leaders step up to lead.

Leadership is respected.

Leadership is trusted.

Leadership is earned.

4. CHOOSE WORDS THAT BUILD CULTURE

Do the words you use regularly have an impact on your culture? Hell yes, more than you think. Words are powerful, particularly the right words. Do you use the word "customer" or "guest"? Are you still placing subconscious divisions between guest-facing roles and the kitchen by referring to them as "front-of-house" and "back-of-house," or do you use the word "team"? Do you have a "management team" or a "leadership team"?

Great restaurant cultures are very clear on the nomenclature they use. They choose words that resonate with their brand and reinforce the culture. Think about words and phrases from your own life. Do you have a "problem" or do you have a "*challenge*"? Do you want to be great, or do you want to be **outstanding**? The words you use amplify your messages and experiences (good or bad). You need to be very careful about the words you use with yourself and your team.

Everything that happens in your outer world starts in your inner world. Be mindful of the way you talk to yourself. If culture truly flows down rather than up, that starts with you. Therefore, how you see yourself is very important. Traits common among successful leaders include demanding more from themselves than their teams, being harder on themselves than others, and expecting more from themselves. Successful leaders do NOT beat themselves up mentally and emotionally to the point it affects their confidence and self-esteem.

Spend the next week being very conscious of the words you say to yourself and others. Remember, awareness precedes choice, choice precedes change. You must be aware an issue exists before you can fix it. After a week of taking mental or written notes on some of the keywords you say, find some empowering replacement words to start using in their place. A great one to start with is the word "should." You know you *should* do this and you *should* do that. Whenever you find yourself using the word *should* change it immediately to the word "*must*." If you change the things you *should* do into the things you *must* do; you'll see a radical improvement in the quality of your life, culture, and restaurant.

5. NURTURE YOUR CULTURE <u>EVERY - SINGLE - DAY</u>

Culture is a living thing, and just like any living thing, it needs to be cared for and cultivated. If your culture grew into a monster and got out of control, it's because you didn't nurture it correctly. Once you start getting your culture back under control and on the right path, you'll want to dedicate more energy and effort to feeding it the proper way.

That means spending time with your team observing, guiding, coaching, and leading by example. This also means that you may have to get rid of the bad apples that have spoiled your culture with negativity. Remember, your culture is like a garden. If you want a meticulous, beautiful, and thriving garden, you must tend to it daily. Weeds will grow without help, so you must be vigilant and keep them from overgrowing your garden. The same goes for your culture — you must be relentless in your pursuit to weed out negativity as soon as it appears in your culture.

Negativity, once it has taken root, is very difficult to eradicate. You don't want it to burrow deep into your culture. Get a hold of it while it's small and rip it out before its roots take hold in your culture. Nurture the elements you want to grow: **trust, confidence, hospitality, growth, teamwork, creativity, learning, respect, gratitude, energy, and community**. These elements of culture need to be tended to and encouraged every day, without fail. You must become diligent in feeding your culture the positive traits that you wish to see blossom.

Culture is a lot like the ocean — you don't want to turn your back on it for too long. It can become quite nasty in a very short time if you don't watch it. If your culture has grown out of control or gone in a direction that you don't like, it's not too late. Will it be easy to change? No. It will be a hard-fought battle to change the culture that has grown out of control. However difficult, it's a battle that you must take on and commit to seeing through to the end.

It's worth it and necessary. If your culture has grown out of control, the only one you have to blame is yourself. Like most things in life, you are your problem *and* your solution. Time to dig in, make a solid plan, and get to work.

Think of culture as the soul of your restaurant.

What would you do save your soul?
Whatever it takes.

Let's Talk About Why Your Teamwork STILL Sucks

"You can get everything in life you want, if you will just help enough other people get what they want."

—Zig Ziglar

Hit the Ground

One of the schools we attended during the Pararescue Pipeline was the U.S. Army Airborne School in Ft. Benning, Georgia. I was particularly pleased to be going to this special training because my father was a member of the 82nd Airborne in World War II. Getting my jump wings would be a great accomplishment for me. Something to show off to my father (yes, I was the proverbial young man seeking the approval of his father).

Airborne School was a three-week course that consists of ground week, tower week, and jump week.

GROUND WEEK

Even though you get to Airborne School super gung-ho about wanting to jump, they prefer to teach you a few things before you get thrown out of an airplane. Ground week focused on one main thing: learning how to hit the ground and rolling properly. The Parachute Landing Fall (or PLF) is very critical if you don't want to twist or break your leg upon landing in a drop zone (DZ). Getting to the battle is one thing; being ready to fight when you get there is another. Back in the '80s when I attended Airborne, you spent that first week in the pit, a row of short cables with handles that you grabbed on to. You stepped up on a block about three feet off the ground, slid down the wire (kind of like a zip line), and then let go to practice your PLF in somewhat soft dirt (really a mix of sand and small pebbles).

Since I had just received my second-degree black belt before leaving for Airborne School, I was maybe a little overconfident that I could learn to roll properly. I quickly realized that the way they wanted me to roll, and the way I rolled in martial arts were quite different. I had some bad rolling habits and only a week to correct them. Game on.

I kept wanting to roll over my shoulder as soon as my feet hit the ground, dispersing the energy along a line that went from my right hand to my left hip. The Airborne Instructors (known as "Black Hats") were not fond of my "Hollywood Stuntman Roll." *Yeah, I did a lot of pushups that week.*

In the PLF, when your feet hit the ground, you redistribute the energy on one side of your body (with your feet and knees together). If you're coming in on your right (due to wind) you make contact with your feet, collapse to your right calf, right thigh, and right hip, using the hip as your pivot point. You finish by rolling onto your right side (your lats). My biggest challenge was learning to be great at executing a PLF from *both* sides! My right side cooperated very well. My left side was a little slower... okay, it sucked. The instructors made me endlessly repeat the PLF on my left side. After the second day, I had a bruise up my left leg that looked like a truck had run into me. I remember getting back to the barracks that evening and thinking, "Fuck. This is only day two!"

Day three was not fun. I'd hit the right side and roll perfectly. But then came the left side.

Motherfucker—that hurt! I recalled my mindfulness training and centering from my martial arts training. "Center yourself," I would say to myself. "Pain is just weakness leaving the body." You would be shocked by how powerful the mind can be. My martial arts instructor, Sifu Byron, had horrible back and knee pain from a couple of tours in Vietnam. He used meditation and self-hypnosis to control the pain. When I was 17, I took a pretty good fall during a sparring match and tore some muscles in my back. He taught me his technique for pain control and, fast forward to Ground Week at Airborne school. I was so grateful he did.

By day four, my left side was finally getting the hang of it, and I was no longer a target of the tough Airborne Instructors. Day five was the test, and then I was off to the tower.

TOWER WEEK

When you first arrive at Ft. Benning, you can't miss the sight of two luminous structures rising above all else: the 34-foot tower and the 250-foot tower. The first part of tower week is the 34-foot tower to get you used to the sense of falling and how to exit an aircraft properly. Getting out of a plane the right way is more important than you might think. During this part of tower week, we had to run up the stairs of the 34-foot tower with our mock reserve parachute in front of us, always keeping our right hand over the ripcord to protect your reserve chute. You do *not* want a Black Hat to see you not protecting your shit. At the top of the 34-foot tower, we placed our hands on the outside of the mock airplane door. When the instructor screamed "GO!", We went! We needed to exit the plane strong and then start counting to see if our main chute had deployed. "One one-thousand, two one-thousand, three one-thousand, four one-thousand, check main canopy!" If all went well, you had a beautiful T-10C parachute to look up at. If not, well, we were so happy for the second part of tower week.

The second part of tower week involved training for all the shit that could go wrong, aka malfunctions. How to deal with risers, steering the chute (it isn't very cooperative at times), what to do when faced with a variety of malfunctions (like twisted risers, the Mae West, partial deployment), and dealing with a total deployment failure were covered. We were taken up the 250-foot tower to take a few drops. Learning to steer our elephant of a parachute that, depending on wind conditions, can be more of a wild, uncontrolled ride. You need to go with it, doing your best to properly prepare for hitting the ground (safely).

After week two everyone was psyched because during jump week we got to jump out of a real plane!

On the last day of tower week, everyone gathered for a final pep talk by one of the Lead Airborne Instructors. He was built like a rhino (or maybe being up on a stage looking down on us made it appear that way). The seasoned vet had a thick southern accent, and I remember his words to this day:

> *"Airborne, we've spent the last two weeks getting your sorry asses ready for next week. Jump week. If you pass next week, you get to wear with pride your Airborne Wings. You won't be considered a leg* [a person not Airborne qualified] *anymore, and you can join the elite few. Now, Airborne, I cannot promise that when you hit the drop zone next week that you will remember to do a proper PLF Airborne, I cannot guarantee that you will do a proper exit from the plane. And Airborne, I cannot guarantee that if you have a parachute malfunction that you'll remember the procedure we drilled on this week that could save your life or the life of another soldier. But, Airborne, I will guarantee this, Monday morning when you jump out of that plane at 1,200 feet, you will hit the ground!"*

Nice pep talk, Sargent.

JUMP WEEK

This was it! Two weeks of training, and it was GO TIME. Just like a lot of things in the military, we got to the airfield early, put our chutes on, and then sat on the tarmac at Larson Army Airfield waiting for plane preparations to be completed. I could tell a few of the guys in class were having second thoughts. You can sense it. Now don't get me wrong, you always want to have a little fear when parachuting. Fear keeps you sharp, and alive if you can control it and not let it control you. When you don't have a little fear back there keeping you focused, it's time to stop jumping. Overconfidence can get people killed, and it's usually someone else that pays the price for arrogance.

Finally, the plane was ready, and we filed in. I was the eighth person in the "stick." I counted because you don't want to be number 13. Not that I'm superstitious, but why take a chance (LOL)?

I saw the Jump Master kneeling, looking out the door which was opened and ready for us. We had our static line attached to the cable that would deploy our chutes as our bodies fell from the plane. There were two lights by the door, one red and one green. The light was red. The Jump Master stood up and yelled at the first man, "STAND IN THE DOOR!" The light turned green. "GO!" I was so excited! I would finally get my chance to stand in the door and perform my exit just like in tower week.

It was like a fast shuffle and the next thing I knew I was out of the plane, falling! I immediately started counting, "one one-thousand, two one-thousand, three one-thousand, four one-thousand, check main canopy!" I looked up. A beautiful and perfect T-10 chute was above me. I gained control of the risers and got myself oriented. I was coming into the DZ, right on target. Then those conversations occurred in my head, "Wait, is that a big mud puddle? Oh fuck. I don't want to hit that. Pull on a riser and try to steer clear. Come on, turn! Shit, the ground is coming up fast!" Boom.

I think I did a PLF—I can't remember. I didn't break or twist anything, so I went with the standard Airborne truism, "**Any jump you can walk away from is a good jump!**" I gathered my chute and headed over to catch the bus back to Larson Army Airfield to get another jump in. You need five jumps total, including one nighttime jump. You jump in a variety of configurations, including no load (known as Hollywood) and with full combat gear (where you waddle to get to the door with 80 pounds strapped to your back).

After the final jump, we fell into line to receive our jump wings, right there on the DZ. Now, they will ask you if you want "blood wings." A few of the guys ahead of me in line declined, but when the Black Hat asked me, I figured sure, I'll take blood wings. Normally, when they pin your wings on you, they reach through your uniform, place the wings, and give you the little backings to secure them. When you get blood wings, they use the bottom of their fist to imbed them right into your chest! That's going to leave a mark.

Going back to the barracks that evening was a night filled with stories of valor and facing the open door at 1200 feet above the earth with determination and courage. Someone asked me what I thought just before I jumped the first time. I said, "I didn't have time to think at all." He said, "You're lucky. I was thinking about all the different malfunctions and what could go wrong."

> *"We don't rise to the level of our expectations, we fall to the level of our training."- Archilochus*

Reflecting on my time in Pararescue and the martial arts, I can say with absolute certainty that it was the training that made the difference. **Peak performers always train more than the average person.** Even after tower week, I spent most of the weekend going over the malfunctions in my head, working out multiple scenarios, and going through the motions. I became the best I could be through determination, practice, and execution.

In Special Operations (Spec Ops) you train and rehearse constantly. You throw a variety of "what ifs" at yourself and your team, so you don't have to think too long about what to do. Sifu Bryan used to say, "He who hesitates meditates in a vertical position." You want to be ready for anything in the restaurant industry. I've seen some wild shit in my four decades in the industry. Thumbs cut off on slicers, a cook putting his entire arm into a fryer to get his tongs, I broke up a knife fight once between two cooks and some things that will remain a secret to protect those who aren't so innocent.

How you train your team is how your team will perform. You don't train for the ideal situation; you train for contingencies. There's a saying in Spec Ops: *"If it walks like a duck and talks like a duck, better have a plan in case it's a chicken."*

What's the plan for a steak that's overcooked? What do you do when you need to cut a V.I.P. off because they appear to be intoxicated? What about the manger you just caught making out with a server on a busy Friday night? What's your plan when tickets hit an hour in the kitchen? What's your plan for everything you can think that could go wrong? What about those things that you haven't thought of? Come up with a few gold-standard remediation rules that might save your ass in an unexpected situation. I'm not telling you to become gloom and doom, focused on the worst-case situation. What I'm saying is that you need to think about your plan if shit happens.

Being prepared makes you confident and reduces stress.

Be ready for whatever Murphy's Law throws at you.

Got Crabs? How to Spot the People Killing Your Culture

Have you ever seen a bucket full of crabs?

The strangest thing: people don't put a lid on top of a bucket of crabs to prevent them from escaping. Why? *The crabs keep each other from getting out.* As soon as one climbs above the rest, another crab will grab it and pull it back down.

Sadly, I see the same thing in restaurants way too often. People who are supposed to be a team constantly bring each other down, so no one gets ahead. This widespread mentality screams, "If I can't have it, neither can you!" Ugh. Really?! Grow up.

Spotting the signs of a Crab Culture is easy.....

- There is no accountability. No responsibility. The crabs blame everyone except themselves.
- It's all about entitlement (You deserve it, right? You paid your dues?).
- Too many people think they're the only positive workers, or do all the work. The song from Stealers Wheel comes to mind: "Clowns to the left of me / Jokers to my right..."
- Passive-aggressive remarks, like "I don't do it like that, but if that works for you..." are aplenty.
- Rampant use of playing favorites (schedule and sections based on likability, not performance).
- Cliques (sometimes not consciously formed, like "the chefs").
- Inconsistent standards. Sometimes no standards, usually because nothing is written down as the standard. This is also known as "tribal culture."
- Average performance. People tend to adjust to the average output of the group and then perform at that level. This is also known as "team performance set point."
- Leaders with a superiority complex. They think no one is better than them, so they keep people suppressed instead of helping them grow.

This type of "leader" tends to use the phrase, "No one can replace me" often.

- No one volunteers. The staff has to be recruited or commanded.
- People who excel or make positive efforts are quickly shamed and ridiculed by the group. This is a form of bullying and creates a hostile work environment. It is also strong negative feedback that is NOT helpful.
- Extensive gossip that is out of control. Entrepreneur and author Dave Ramsey had a great company policy in place: If you're caught gossiping, you're given a warning one time. The next time it happens, you're gone. Ramsey doesn't tolerate people who gossip because it's the foundation of other poor behavioral habits.
- Backstabbing.
- Two-faced managers.
- Double standards on rules. This is particularly prevalent among owners and managers. Commonly illustrated through the phrase, "DO as I say, not as I do."

I think you get the hint...

If you have a Crab Culture, you need to isolate the crabs who are pulling down the team. It's time to step up and be the damn leader! You need to remove crab personalities from your organization, right now! It doesn't matter if they're an incredible sauté cook or are the server with the highest sales—destructive personalities only damage your culture and brand long term!

If you can't spot the "crab" on your team, then there are two possibilities:

1. You have created an **outstanding** culture free of crab personalities.
2. *It's you.*

If it's you, you'll need to do some deep thinking into why. No, I'm not going to say you should quit your job, give up your life, and become a Buddhist monk seeking the path to enlightenment...*well, not yet.*

So, why am I telling you to get rid of others who have a crab personality and not yourself? Because you can only change yourself, you can't change others. Take that message to heart: *You can only change you.*

You can set the example, provide coaching, offer tools, and be a positive role model for others but they'll only change when they're ready, not when you *think* they're ready.

If it turns out the problem is you, you're engaging in self-sabotaging behavior, likely due to poor self-esteem.

Now, you might say, "But I'm very sure of my skills and abilities!"

Okay, that's **self-*confidence***. Self-*esteem* is your sense of self-worth. Do you feel you deserve success? Do you feel you're trying to prove something to others? I must admit that during a good portion of my professional career, I was trying to prove something to others. Now, the only person I need to prove anything to is myself. That's the upside of getting older — you give fewer fucks about what others think.

When you feel you don't deserve success, you're more likely to act out so that the mental scorecard in your subconscious is even. This is referred to as "protest behavior.**" You can only rise to the level of what you feel worthy of receiving**. Up in that beautiful brain of yours is your crab mentality. When you rise above what you think you should be or have, you do stupid shit to bring yourself back down. That's your comfort zone. That's where you feel is where you *should* be. Bullshit...get up and stay there; make your new awesome self the new comfort zone!

Right now, you may be protesting, shouting, "I want to be successful! I want more!"

If that's true, why aren't you where you want to be?

Why haven't you taken your foot off the brake pedal and hit the accelerator?
What excuses do you have now?

Those excuses and the reasons why you can't stop sabotaging yourself are crabs pulling you down. It's time to have a "mental crab boil" and kill those suckers!

Remember, your words tell me what you say you want — your actions that tell me what you're willing to do to get it.

How to Interview Millennials, a Step-by-Step Guide

If you are like many restaurant owners or managers in today's market, you might have noticed that the number of applicants for your restaurant seems smaller than in the past. It might even invoke a little panic. Perhaps you've become a little jaded by the younger generation that appears, to you, to be different and lack motivation.

Here's the good news and the bad news. The good news is, yes, they're different. The bad news is that you probably aren't embracing their beneficial differences, and you ask the wrong interview questions.

STEP ONE: CREATE A CULTURE THAT ATTRACTS TALENT

If you see fewer applications for your job openings, it's time to ask yourself a very hard question: Why? We all want to hire A-level talent. The issue is that A-level talent (which includes many Millennials) aren't attracted to a restaurant with a C-level or average culture. Maybe, just maybe, it's not them, it's **your culture**?

Case in point: Did you know it's harder to get a job at Zappos (the online shoe retailer) than it is to get into Harvard? It's true.

Culture is the secret sauce that separates **outstanding** restaurants from the rest of the crowd. You have access to the same ingredients as other restaurants. You have access to the same equipment. You also have access to the same labor pool in your market. So why do some seem to get the A-team and others are just trying to find a warm body to work a shift? **It's culture.**

Like it or not, your culture either attracts or repels people from working at your restaurant. What kind of culture does your restaurant have? What can you do to improve it?

STEP TWO: CREATE A COMPREHENSIVE TRAINING PROGRAM

Millennials look for opportunities to learn and grow. Don't confuse growth with money and promotions.

For many Millennials, learning and contributing are more attractive than the dollars on a paycheck. You're employing or working with a generation that can access information immediately — they like to know the why behind an activity.

You can tell a person to stand behind the host stand, smile at everyone who comes in, say hello, and seat guests promptly for the next six hours. However, you'll be looking for a new host in less than two months. If you want to avoid hiring for the same position over and over, teach and train your employees the soft skills that will make them a better person. Communication techniques. Reading non-verbal body language. Stress management skills. The list goes on.

If you only train them to *do the job*, you'll get a temporary employee. **If you invest in them to make them a better person, you'll develop a loyal team member —** time to take a deep look at your training programs and see where you can make improvements.

STEP THREE: ASK BETTER INTERVIEW QUESTIONS

During your interviews, you're probably asking the same questions you have been for years. And you're probably getting the same boring, predictable answers.

> The goal of an interview is to find the best team fit, not the best job fit.

Too many times we interview just looking for someone with availability to fill a slot on the schedule. Major mistake. **You need to dig deeper and see if this person has the behavioral match to improve your team machine, not just be a generic clog in the wheel.**

Demand thoughtful responses with these interview questions:

1. Do you prefer working alone or with a small group? Why?
2. How many people from your last job are your friends today? Why?
3. What's your favorite social media platform? Why?
4. Is there a charity that you volunteer for or support? Why?
5. Have you ever eaten at our restaurant before? If so, how many times? If not, Why?
6. What did you like best about your friends in high school? Why?
7. What do you like about living in this town/city? How would you improve this town/city?
8. What's your favorite thing to eat? Why?
9. Tell me in your own words what this job position is?

10. Why is working here important to you?
11. Do you have any "rules" among your friends?
12. What kind of relationship do you want to have with your coworkers? Your manager?

What you're looking for is a good behavioral fit for the team. Hiring Millennials isn't difficult if your restaurant and culture are attractive to them. Get feedback from current Millennial members of your team about what they like and don't care for in your culture and training. Improve those areas, and you'll start to see more of the younger generation starting to come to you and **asking to join the team**.

When you have a solid culture that fosters learning, appreciation, and professionalism, it will become a signal to the world that you're the employer of choice for restaurants in your market. As we all know, a referral from someone on your team is more valuable than a cold lead from a help wanted ad on the internet.

Aim for more referrals by improving the culture of your restaurant.

What Will It Take to Win Over Generation Z?

For the past few years, we've been wondering how to get Millennials into our restaurants. Well, I have some good news and some bad news. Millennials aren't the problem you think they are. That's good news. The bad news is you're going to need to shift gears for the generation quickly coming up right behind them: Generation Z.

Born between 1997 and the present, this young demographic demands transparency about what they eat. While they only make up 25 percent of the market, they're an influential 25 percent that wields a big digital impact. This generation takes to the internet to start revolutions, and one's coming to your restaurant soon.

How can you win over this "fresh-centric" generation? Here are a few ways to get them to embrace your restaurant brand.

1. YOU NEED VALUES

While it's easy to pull words out of the air and say they're your culture, Gen Z wants to see if your words are backed up by your actions. Say you're into locally sourced produce yet you don't have any suppliers they recognize on your menu? Strike one.

Gen Z has heard all the talk from Millennials and Gen Xers, and they won't support unauthentic brands. They have no issue with the size of your brand, unlike the older Millennials who favor smaller brands. **Gen Z wants you to be honest**. That means having strong values with which they can identify and align themselves. Know who you are and be authentic about it.

2. PICK A BATTLE

Gen Z loves a good cause to get behind. There are so many causes out there with which you can align: non-GMO food products, equality, immigration.

Pick a cause that you *actually* care about and your brand will feel good getting behind, and then commit to it. Oh, and please don't pick a cause just because you think it's the issue of the month. Remember, authenticity is the key, and you must pick a cause about which you are passionate about. Don't be too concerned with the possibility that it will "rock the boat" in your community. That's a part of standing behind a particular cause. Rocking the boat, shows you stand behind your beliefs, and that goes a long way to getting people of all generations behind you. *Integrity is a powerful thing.*

3. BREAK FROM TRADITION

Gen Z wants to eat when it fits into their schedule. So, break away from traditional dayparts and have shifts available to serve the "snacking generation." They love breakfast all day (thanks, McDonald's), they love the convenience (either online ordering or delivery), and they love having a space to hang out with friends (community tables are hot if you have Wi-Fi).

Offer late night or reverse happy hour menus (Gen Z's are hitting drinking age). However, be smart and plan to have designated drivers or rideshare services available for guests. Be known for looking out for your guests, and it will come back as good karma. Billy Dec from Rockit Ranch in Chicago offers free transportation between his many different concepts so guests can have fun and still check out his other venues. That's smart business.

4. TELL ME A STORY

Gen Z grew up with foodie parents and Food Network. They know food, and they like to know where it came from. Smart brands like Sweetgreen go the extra mile to tell their story (complete with video — Gen Z loves video), share their values, state their mission, and even discuss their food ethos which includes profiles of their ingredients and sources. Now *that's* transparency in food operations!

You're going to need to dig deep to uncover your why, as Simon Sinek suggests in his bestselling book *Start with Why*. To paraphrase Sinek, remember that people don't buy what you do, they buy why you do it!

You might have amazing food and service, but if you can't translate that into a story that Gen Z can relate to, you're missing the opportunity to turn them on to your brand.

WHAT WILL IT TAKE TO WIN GEN Z OVER?

Honesty.
Solid core values.
Transparency.
Story-telling.
Having the courage to declare your beliefs.

The Staff Bill of Rights

The restaurant industry is a hot mess!

Don't take that the wrong way — it's a good thing. Perhaps it's a little dramatic to say it's a hot mess. It's more like there's a storm brewing and some people better get it together before it hits them like a Cat 5 hurricane. However, preparing ahead of time is, unfortunately, not how most restaurants operate. If you're reading this book, congratulations — you have a better chance to survive the storm.

The Founding Fathers of the United States created the Bill of Rights to guarantee certain rights for the people. Our industry needs a similar Staff Bill of Rights. You need one, so your brand can survive the looming restaurant storm on the horizon.

The time has come to work collectively as an industry and raise the standards for how people in every restaurant are treated. Food trucks, mon 'n' pop, fast casual, fast food, fine dining, and elite Michelin Starred restaurants all need to support this.

The Staff Bill of Rights

YOU HAVE THE RIGHT TO BE PAID ACCORDING TO WHAT YOU CONTRIBUTE TO THE BRAND.

Don't be naive and think that all positions in every restaurant offer the same compensation. Staff members have the right to get what they contribute or bring to the brand in terms of value. If they're not happy with what they're currently being paid, they have the right to ask an empowering question: *What can I do to become more valuable to the restaurant?*

There's plenty of culinary talent out there that can cook but, not a lot of culinary talent that can run a profitable P&L and lead a team. Asking for a raise without bringing more value to the brand is a sign of entitlement.

Entitlement language can be spotted by the following tone of: "I deserve because I am me."

YOU HAVE THE RIGHT TO BE TREATED FAIRLY AND WITH RESPECT.

We need to talk about expectations. Many people don't ever have a real job description beyond "whatever it takes." Some owners are very clear about what they expect from their employees. Correspondingly, staff members should make their expectations of ownership clear.

Healthy expectations are needed for long-term success. Things can get crazy, and there will be times an employee is asked to perform a task that might fall outside their job title or description. There's nothing wrong with asking a staff member to jump in on dishes on a busy night. However, paying someone a server's wage but expecting them to wash dishes, too, isn't okay.

YOU HAVE THE RIGHT TO VOICE YOUR CONCERNS.

There are some things that a staff member may see in this business that will make them question the behavior of others and maybe even themselves. Employees have the right to step up and voice their concerns. They should do so in a professional way without placing blame or shame on others.

If someone's a line cook, and they hear another cook make a crude sexual comment about a server, they have a duty as a human being to say something. They need to draw a line and say they don't appreciate language that degrades others. The restaurant industry has negative energy that we must change if we want to become a viable employment option for future generations. How do we change an industry? *One person at a time.* And it starts with us.

YOU HAVE THE RIGHT NOT TO LIKE YOUR COWORKERS.

A common misconception about teamwork is that people must like their coworkers. Not true. Nobody has to like the people with whom they work, but they must **respect** them. Some coworkers may become friends. That's a benefit, not a requirement. In any case, make sure to be a professional and do the job.

Staff members should avoid using this right as a barrier to not to talk to people or get along. In a restaurant, the staff tends to come from a variety of backgrounds, and not everyone will want to hang out and talk about the game last night. To each their own. Coworkers should identify the skills and strengths of their coworkers, celebrate the healthy diversity, and work together to reach a common goal: to wow the guests.

YOU HAVE A RIGHT TO WORK WITHOUT FEAR.

Nobody should have to work in a state of fear and intimidation. Old school managers who lead through fear are a dying breed, but they're still out there, clinging to outdated management techniques like "break them down and build them up." When people are broken down, they're rarely, if ever, built back up (in a positive, stronger way). Besides, do you want broken people working in your restaurant and interacting with your hard-earned guests?

Fearful staff members and harmful managers are a recipe for failure. Operators who fail to understand this may as well install a revolving door for employees since they'll come and go so quickly.

Fear breeds negativity. Nobody can build a successful restaurant brand on fear and negativity. Those two elements are the catalyst for a toxic culture. Sure, there may be a few brands out there known for their culture of fear that appears to be doing well. The reality is that they're just limping along and are always stuck. They will never break through the negative force field, keeping them in a perpetual *Groundhog Day* scenario.

YOU HAVE A RIGHT TO CALL IN IF YOU ARE TRULY SICK.

There will be days when an employee is as sick as a dog. They may have a fever, be throwing up, or worse. A sick staff member shouldn't be encouraged to come to work. Part of being in the restaurant industry is food safety. Being sick sucks. Bringing that to work and risking getting others sick is irresponsible and unsafe.

Of course, employees shouldn't use this as an excuse to get out of work.

YOU HAVE A RIGHT TO BECOME BETTER.

It's a safe guess that anyone reading this book is interested in self-development. That means they need to occasionally ask for feedback about ways to improve their skills and increase the value they bring to the brand (see the first *Right*).

Many managers say they don't have time to train. They have the time; they lack the coaching or training skills and use lack of time as an excuse. For the record, time is never the real reason: the real culprit is a lack of planning and priorities.

So, that leaves it up to individual staff members! They should seek out online education, follow industry experts, read about communication skills, and listen to some podcasts. Smartphones are for more than posting to social media and texting.

YOU HAVE A RIGHT TO WALK AWAY.

If a staff member's current work situation violates most of these Staff Bill of Rights, they have the right to look for another restaurant that would be a better fit.

If we want to turn the restaurant industry around for the better, all of us need to up our level of professionalism.

Owners and managers need to treat their staff members with respect and have a plan for individual growth. They need to pay what's fair and become leaders in their markets when it comes to benefits.

Staff members, for their part, need to be respectful and consistently give their best performance. Many show up and give their best for only a few days (or hours) each week. That doesn't make them an asset to the brand; it makes them a liability.

The bottom line is this: We all need to make sure we're creating and working in environments that allow everyone to improve and be their best every day.

We must use this Staff Bill of Rights as a platform to live our best lives.

Got Entitlement? Here Are 3 Warning Signs

About a year ago, I worked with a challenging chef. He wasn't open to new systems or following through on some projects he had started. He just wanted to order high-end ingredients and play with food. He didn't care about food or labor costs because that would stifle his "creative genius."

We had a coaching session one afternoon during which I mentioned the challenges associated with our changing industry and the fact that he had to adjust his skillset to focus more on business. His only comments were that he felt he worked his ass off, deserved a promotion (a better title), and wanted more money.

As he walked away, I felt frustrated. And a little pissed off.

How could he be so blind to his true potential?

How could he not see that he was focused only on what benefited *him*?

I knew that unless something changed, we would be having a different conversation shortly, one about him leaving the company. (*Side note: That conversation happened about two months later.*)

Write this down: There is no room for an entitlement mindset on your team. None. It creates a passive team, and there's no place in today's market for anyone on your team who's passive or uninterested about their work and their development. The restaurant industry is changing, and those who fail to adapt will become extinct.

Keep an ear out for the three phrases of entitlement and their variants...

"I EARNED IT."

This is the boastful attitude of a person who believes a restaurant's owners should be overcome with joy even to have them on the team. These people think the business would fail if they left. This person loves to tell stories of past successes but appears unmotivated or even lazy when it comes to doing the work needed for the restaurant to succeed in the future. They live in the past and revel in what they supposedly accomplished.

You can't win today's game with the points you scored last week. A boastful person never thanks you for the opportunity to work on your team or expresses gratitude for the compensation they receive. They respond to carrot-and-stick motivation, but they don't like the stick, and they're never happy with the carrot you give them; they always feel they've earned a bigger carrot than the rest of the team.

"IT ISN'T FAIR."

What is fair? What one person thinks is fair might not be the same for another person on the team. Fairness is defined by the individual's perspective of fair, not an independent measure. In other words, it's subjective. A person who complains that things are "unfair" are comparing their current work environment to one from the past and are resisting change. A common phrase uttered by this person is, "When I worked at [insert restaurant name] we did [insert task] this way [insert how a given task *isn't* done at your restaurant]."

They also spend a great deal of time comparing their job, their position, and their work to others both inside and outside the company. Their own bias clouds their view — they have no interest in little things like facts. Watch for the person who uses "fairness" as the measure for their performance.

The Fair Crusader also tends to think that restaurant owners make "tons" of money and are being too greedy. They forget that most owners have worked hard for years to earn money, sacrificed personal relationships and possibly their health, and opened their restaurant (maybe with heavy debt) to get where they are today. Entitlement mindsets want shortcuts to avoid spending the time or making the sacrifices required for long-term success and rewards.

"THE COMPANY OWES ME."

This individual easily loses sight of the full contribution of the team. They focus on themselves rather the organization, and they often feel superior to others. No reward or amount of recognition is ever enough. There's not a restaurant out there that thrives based on one person's performance, but this person believes otherwise.

Often, their view that the company owes them is based on some past event or contribution. They feel that because they did something great yesterday, they deserve the rewards for that specific bit of work forever. This individual may hold personal grudges and try to undermine leadership.

An entitlement culture is often lazy with undercurrents of defiance and protest behavior, i.e., leaving early, not following through on tasks. This is a culture where the focus is on the individual rather than the guests you serve or the restaurant as a team. There are lots of "I" statements in an entitlement culture, and few "we" statements. Watch out for this as it's the catalyst of a toxic culture. Address it with urgency before this mindset spreads like weeds.

Do you know how to deal with weeds? *Aggressively.*

It also usually requires removing them.

How to Create a Training System that Gets Results: 3 Easy Steps

What separates good restaurants from **outstanding** restaurants is the quality of their training. This is rooted in whether you have a training culture or a learning culture. Not sure which you have?

Answer this question:

Do you train only when people join the team (the onboarding phase) and maybe throw in a few training "sessions" throughout the year (training culture), or do you have training scheduled consistently all year long (learning culture)?

An **outstanding** restaurant owner understands that school is never out for the true professional. If you want your restaurant to stand out in your market, you need to become **obsessed** with training. Many people look at the word "**obsessed**" as a bad thing. If you want to reach the pinnacle of your game, being **obsessed** with training is required.

Most restaurant training systems are just generic manuals or templates that were downloaded from some website. It's the standard "yadda yadda yadda" that gives most training systems their well-earned bad reputation for being boring. Think about how much time and money you spend recruiting people to come to work for your restaurant. You make it seem like your restaurant is an incredible place to work. The new team member is excited and can't wait to start. On their first day, they're handed a training manual that looks like every other training manual they've seen. Look in their eyes, and you'll see their excitement fade away.

How do you fix that? By taking three easy steps toward ensuring your training system stands out and matches the energy of your brand. You want your training system to be like the Fourth of July in a big city, not a package of sparklers that you light up in your driveway.

1. MAKE IT INTEGRATED

Most training systems focus purely on hard skills. While technical training for a job position is an integral part of any training program, it shouldn't be the primary focus. The standards, policies, procedures, and expectations need to be explained, but, other information needs to be included in your training materials as well.

Don't miss out on often overlooked soft skills like communication, time management, conflict resolution, influence skills, how to set goals, how to break bad habits, personal accountability, and state/energy management. These people skills are needed to elevate the team past the point where only hard skills alone can take them. Hard skills are important; however, when used in conjunction with soft skills that help people maximize their potential.

As the leader, you need to set the example for soft skills. Leadership only works when the leader lives up to their standards and expectations. The old cliché of "do as I say, not as I do" is a surefire recipe for failure in any training system. Human beings have mirror neurons in their brains, the primary function of which is to help us learn faster and create social connections. If you're walking down the street and smile at someone who makes eye contact with you, chances are they'd smile back. That's mirror neurons at work.

When you're sending out mixed messages, like saying one thing and doing another, your team has a hard time getting their mirror neurons to fire. **Having an integrated training system is not about training people to do their job; it's about developing people so they can become better human beings, which in turn benefits them AND the restaurant.**

2. USE DIFFERENT LEARNING STYLES

Most restaurant's training consists of handing out a manual and having new hires follow someone on the team for a few days to learn the position. This is effective on some level but misses the boat for many people due to the limitations of *how* it trains people: it doesn't take into consideration *different learning styles.*

There are four basic learning styles: visual, auditory, read-write, and kinesthetic. People learn by using a variety of all four. However, everyone has one primary style.

Visual learners: These people tend to be fast talkers, exhibit impatience, use words that build visual images, and learn by seeing. In this case, a picture truly is worth 1,000 words.

Auditory learners: Tend to speak slowly, are great listeners, process information in a linear manner, prefer to have things explained verbally instead of written down, and learn by listening and verbalizing. For these people, try to incorporate lots of conversation and feedback.

Read-write learners: This type of learner prefers information in a written format and likes taking notes. These people want to make sure you have detailed lists and a notebook available. They like to write out their interpretations of what's being taught.

Kinesthetic learners: The slowest talkers. They take longer to process information and make decisions, learn by doing and solving problems on their own, and approach things with a hands-on mindset. They learn best by rolling up their sleeves and participating in training activities.

As you can see, if you're training system doesn't incorporate each learning style, you'll quickly lose people's interest and attention, and you won't be training adequately. Having a variety of different training activities is the best way to keep all of your trainees engaged. Use traditional printed materials, training videos, hands-on sessions, and demonstrations by people on your team who have honed their skills to high levels. The last thing you want to do is have someone who has only been working for you for a week training the new staff.

3. MAKE IT EASY TO ACCESS

If you're still relying on Xerox copies of your training materials, maybe it's time up your onboarding and training game. Granted, printed materials are usually needed for training systems. Just don't rely on them as the only vehicle for learning. Training videos can be easily created with your smartphone or tablet. Interactive quizzes and tests can be created using online resources like Survey Monkey.

As restaurants embrace more Millennials and Gen Zs entering the workplace, they'll need to do a better job of delivering training content in multiple formats that are mobile-compatible. As discussed earlier, people have different learning styles. They also have different rates for how they process information and different preferred ways to access information. Some people need more time, and if you only have your training materials available during a limited window, they won't be able to learn. Make it easy for your team to learn. Stimulate their different learning styles by providing multiple formats. Create a private YouTube channel with your training videos! Make learning fun, and make it easy for them to review the materials.

If you truly want to develop a learning culture, then you need to make learning a priority. Give your team access to e-books, reports, and links to blog posts. Share videos from YouTube. Restaurants truly get better when the people in them become better people. That starts with you wanting to become your best.

Set the example.

The Formula for Better Hires

Hiring can suck. In an uber-competitive and growing industry like ours, you can feel like your back is against the wall. Desperation creeps in as you attempt to find a warm body to fill those empty spots on your schedule. It's easy for that desperation to become panic, leading you to do the one thing that signals the decline of your culture: you compromise your hiring standards. This is commonly and aptly known as the *Panic Hire*, and it's safe to say that every restaurant manager or owner has done it before. I know I have.

I know the cost you will pay for allowing this to happen. You don't see it right away. When you Panic Hire you feel relieved at first. You think, "Finally, someone showed up for an interview." And they were breathing!

You try to convince yourself. 'It will all work out.' The Panic Hire 'just needs some training.' 'The nose ring that hangs down to their chin? It will be okay.' Denial *is* your friend in times like these.

Here's the first rule to better hiring: *Stop lying to yourself.*

Reality check time. Are there restaurants in your market that have amazing staff? Do you have at least one A-list player on your team? If you answered in the affirmative, there's some real talent in your market. In that case, it's **your** formula for hiring that needs to be changed.

Your hiring formula (or recipe) has probably served you well over the last few years or possibly decades. Look around, and you'll see that times are changing. Those who fail to update their hiring formula, and follow it, will soon be left with the less desirable employees. Cream rises to the top, as I'm sure you've read and heard before, and those with the best talent gravitate toward the restaurant brands with a solid reputation and huge success.

Update your hiring process with this 5-step formula.

1. RECRUIT BETTER

It all starts here. Recruiting is the only way to secure top talent. Placing help wanted ads on the internet or social media and waiting for people to contact you is passive and returns little in the way of rewards. Besides, it's probably a blow to the ego when you don't get as many applicants as you thought you would. *Time to take the game to them.*

The first step is to make sure you have a culture that screams, "You want to work **here**!" Replace some of those food photos you post every day with a few of your team having a great time. You must communicate that your brand is *the* place in town where the A-list players are appreciated and want to work! If you don't go out of your way to show potential employees that you're different than the thousand other restaurants in your market looking for staff, you'll look the same. **Same is equal to being average. Average attracts average. Average fucking sucks**.

The next step is to become a recruiting ninja! There are talented and personable people in your market right now who could be working for you — you just haven't met them yet. The sad thing is you'll never meet them if you fail to activate your recruiting radar and keep it on all the time. That smiling, kind, and friendly young lady at the front desk who checks you in at the gym, and always tells you to have a great day when you leave, is she happy there? Abso-fucking-lutely! You want your staff to emulate her. Make that happen.

That young man at the car dealership who gladly opens the door for you and goes over in great detail what they did to make vehicle purr, and is so proud of it, and just so happens to mention he loves to cook and thought of being a chef, could he fulfill those aspirations working with you? Abso-fucking-lutely!

You don't know unless you ask. You should always—*always, always, always*—have some business cards with you. Hand them out with a sincere compliment. Something like this:

"Look, you're amazing with people, and I think you would shine at my restaurant. I'm not sure if you're looking for a new opportunity, but if you are [hand them your business card], I would love to discuss it with you. If nothing else, have you been to [insert your restaurant name here]? You should at least come by and see what we do. I would love to be your host."

Does this work every time? Of course not. Probably only 2 out of 10 will contact you. You only need one A-level player to start. Soon, you'll get another. Then another, and another. Be patient and alert, and you'll eventually recruit and build an all-star lineup. It's the A-level staff snowball effect: bring one, show appreciation, and many will follow! Pretty soon you won't be able to stop it.

You might say there aren't any good people out there. The truth is you've been closed-minded when looking around. Open your eyes.

2. INTERVIEW BETTER

Now that you've improved your recruiting superpowers, it's time to check out your interview game. Those standard, boring questions that everyone asks at every interview have got to go:

- Tell me what you liked about your last job?
- What would your last supervisor say about you?
- What are your 1-, 3-, and 5-year goals?

Zzzz...zzzzz...zzzzzzzz...zzz...

You're setting yourself up for failure when you throw easy questions at a candidate. Most candidates for a job have rehearsed for the expected interview questions. How are they able to figure out what they're going to be asked during basically every interview? Everyone asks the same lame questions! You need to challenge their thinking and bring down the wall between the person you think you're interviewing and the real person behind the façade. Ask unexpected questions, see how they respond, do they smile, show passion??

- If you had a superpower, what would it be and why?
- So, why *did* the chicken cross the road?
- Without overthinking, quickly — tell me one person, any person, you would want to have dinner with tonight.
- What's your favorite junk food? Why?
- Name one of your guilty pleasures.
- If you had a time machine, what year would you visit first?

Now we have a hot and interesting interview game! **Develop a series of questions that challenge applicants and require them to show some** *personality — that's what you're hiring for anyway.* You can train almost anyone if they have the right personality. We tend to have our focus backward when interviewing. We look for the skill first and personality second. *Flip that around, immediately.*

You must look at interviewing as a game of chess and not checkers. You must be strategic in your questions, using each one to reveal another layer of an applicant's true self.

3. ONBOARD BETTER

Okay, you're a recruiting badass, and your interview game is back on point. Now what? Welcome them to your team like it's a homecoming for a long-lost family member!

Sadly, onboarding is where many drop the ball. Picture this:

You're working at a retail store, and the owner of a restaurant complimented you on your natural people skills. They hand you their business card and say to call them. You think about how you've wanted to go back to school part-time and that the restaurant might be a better opportunity. You call.

You land an interview during which the owner introduces you to the general manager, and you're asked thought-provoking questions. They ask some odd questions that make you laugh and think. You like the energy here. They say you'd be a great addition to their team and want you to think about it tonight and call them at 10:00 a.m. sharp if you want the position.

You're excited and tell your friends about your new opportunity. You call the next day, right on time, and they're as excited as you that you want to be on the team. They tell you to come in on Monday at 9:00 a.m. for orientation.

On Monday, you walk in the door a few minutes earlier than expected, excited to start your new journey. A manager you've never met before asks if he can help you. You tell him this is your first day and he says nobody told him anyone was starting today. He tells you to have a seat in the booth in the corner. You wait 15 minutes, and he finally comes back out to hand you a stack of paperwork and a pen. You're told rather unenthusiastically to fill everything out and wait for the lead server to arrive so you can shadow her. You sit there filling out paperwork, questioning whether this was a good idea. Your excitement? Gone.

That scene is probably very familiar because it's played out in many restaurants every day, and owners and managers wonder why they have a hard time getting A-list people to work for them. They've developed a bad reputation for a lot of hype during the recruitment and the interview, and a big letdown of an onboarding process.

Here's the new rule: If you hired them, you should be there on their first day! Is this always possible? No. However, you can communicate with the new hire and the team what the game plan is for their arrival. Introduce them with a conference call or include them in an email explaining what the steps are going to be when they start:

9:00 a.m., Meet the manager

9:15 a.m., Orientation, and tour, meet the team

9:30 a.m., Paperwork

10:00 a.m., Introduction to the brand/culture

10:30 a.m., Training schedule, and outline

11:00 a.m., Day one training

Not taking the time to properly onboard new hires is *lazy*. Lazy doesn't instill confidence and trust in your team or your leadership. ***Do better by being better***.

4. TRAIN BETTER

Another classic failure is lack of training due to hiring someone to fill a shift or role when you're in panic mode. In 2 days, you rush them through training that should take at least 7. They jump into the fire of a busy dinner rush and struggle. The young manager is barking at them all night. Feeling anything but positive about the restaurant and lack of leadership, they go home and get online to find a new job.

Selection is critical to long-term restaurant success. **Who you allow on your team is crucial to the development of an outstanding culture. Training is the fuel that feeds that culture.**

If you purchased a world champion Thoroughbred horse with the dream of winning the Kentucky Derby and didn't train the horse properly, your chances of winning are nonexistent. The same can be said for hiring great people and failing to give them the tools and resources to become their best. You spent all that time and energy recruiting, interviewing, and onboarding to watch them leave sooner than you expected. That's just stupid!

The sad thing is that you can stop slow turnover bleeding by committing to training your people better than any other restaurant in your market! **It should become a burning desire, training like your brand depends on it; because it does.**

Train your team consistently and constantly. High performers want to grow. If you've done your job in the first three steps, you'll have the makings of a team that can help you dominate your market. Take it to the next level by creating a learning culture in which personal growth plans are formulated and required.

"We don't rise to the level of our expectations; we fall to the level of our training."

— Archilochus

5. RETAIN BETTER

This is the final step. You've spent considerable time and resources getting here, and the last element is probably the most important: **do everything you can to keep your new hires.**

Here's where it's easy to take people for granted. There's a common psychological term, The Law of Familiarity. In a nutshell, the law states that when you're around things or people, you tend to take them for granted. It's like falling in love. When you first date someone, you're head over heels for, the world is just so amazing! Then after a year (or two or three), you stop making the same effort. You stop doing the little things you used to do to show appreciation. It's not that you stopped caring; you just committed the number one life sin: **you became complacent.**

How do you change that? **Decide today to treat your team with respect and appreciation every day**. Treat them with the same energy and enthusiasm today as you did when they first started working for you. Fall back in love with your brand and your restaurant. Look for the good things your team is doing instead of nagging them about all the crap they're doing wrong. (By the way, if you're constantly training your staff, this should fix most of those issues.) Say "please" and "thank you." It doesn't make you weak to be polite and respectful; *it makes you a leader.*

Hiring is a formula you must get right if you want your restaurant to thrive, not *just* survive, in the years ahead. The storm of restaurant saturation is coming. Be proactive, be prepared.

Those who see the warning signs and make adjustments today have the best chances of making it.

Working with Family Can Suck

There are a lot of restaurants that reference *family* to describe their culture and approach to teamwork. While on the surface, this can sound great; *being* in the family business is different. Working with family members can be a real challenge for restaurants.

I had the opportunity to work with my father; twice. The first time I vowed I wouldn't do it again. After the second time, **I meant it.** Working with family members is anything except easy. Depending on the family dynamics, it will have an impact on how your restaurant functions.

Speaking from personal experience, some can make a family business work to their advantage. Let's explore the upsides and downsides of working with family.

THE DOWNSIDES

Rivalry
This isn't something that rises to the surface openly when talking about family dynamics in restaurant operations. Rivalries run deep and can sometimes really hurt restaurants. When decisions are made out of spite or to show-up one another, the focus shifts from what's best for the brand to what's best to win the internal (and very damaging) competition that lurks beneath the surface.

Who's the boss
The power struggle among family members can present a very real challenge. It's always best to clearly define the roles and responsibilities for *everyone* from the start, or at least before things get too out of hand. When it comes down to it, one person must be able to make the decisions that are best for the brand. There must be *only* one primary decision maker, THE boss.

This isn't home
Reality TV is fun to watch. However, it is NOT much fun to live through a dramatic reality show in your restaurant. Drama is great for television ratings,

but it fucking sucks for restaurant brands. Leave the demeaning yelling and exaggerated screaming to TV celebrities like the overly dramatic Jon Taffer. When you air your dirty laundry and past grievances in front of your team (or worse, your guests), you damage your reputation. That's hard to recover from —*ask Chipotle.*

THE UPSIDES

Trust
Truthfully, family members are trusted more than anyone else, most of the time. Trust is something that you want to cultivate among your team, and sometimes working with a family member you trust sets a great example.

Dependable
One thing about family is that they'll be there when we need them, always loyal and dependable. Once again, this can set a very good example for the team.

Time together
For some people, working together in a restaurant is also a way to spend time together. Spouses often work together to find time which would otherwise be spent apart due to the demands of the restaurant industry.

A confidant
We all need someone we trust to talk to and vent about stress. Family members can be great for that as long as they know that some conversations need to remain confidential.

Common goals
Many family-owned brands are built from a sense of legacy and contribution to the community. Your family-run restaurant can become the inspiration that changes people's lives. Strong core values, vision, and a passion for serving others can build million-dollar brands. Just look at Chick-fil-A.

Now, if you have a family member who you don't trust, who isn't dependable, or can't keep things confidential, or share your vision (or core values), they shouldn't be working with you. You must look at family members just like you would any team member you would interview for a spot on your team. Just because they're family doesn't mean they need to, or should, work in your restaurant with you.

The key to managing a family-owned business is to be fair and consistent with your standards and policies. The first time I worked for my father (back in the early '80s), I thought I had different rules when it came to being on time for work. After the third time, I was late; my father fired me. Now, for a 16-year-old, that was shocking. He told me, "You will always be my son. However, when you disregard the rules, you disrespect the restaurant, and as the chef, I cannot allow that."

About two months later, two line cooks quit, and my father asked me if I wanted to return.

I did.

Oh, and I was never late again.

5 Misconceptions Your Staff has About Owners

Look at you, a restaurant owner. So many people dream of owning a restaurant that might be considered *the* American dream. It's true that while it's easy to open a restaurant, it can be a challenge to keep it open. There are so many variables that come into play when trying to carve out a brand in today's very crowded market. Competition can, at times, be a dichotomy.

For some, it pushes them to create a brand that stands out in the market. For others, the pressure causes many to become complacent. In an aggressive market, that's the last thing, you want to be, complacent.

The troubles for many come from both sides of their world. They feel the push from other restaurants in their market, and they feel the pull of discontent from their staff. What is an owner to do?

"If there is no enemy within, the enemy outside can do us no harm." – *African proverb*

It's difficult to fight two battles at the same time. And like the saying goes, "If you chase two rabbits, you will not catch either." In the medical field, they use a system called triage to set priorities and get to work saving lives. The most critical patients with life-threatening injuries receive attention first. If you have dissension among your staff, you had better treat it like a life-threatening injury or slowly risk bleeding to death.

Unhappy staff is an epidemic among restaurants, and it's because of the way we treat the staff. The good thing is that we can change — we need to be aware of the misconceptions our staff may have about restaurant ownership. Educating your team is a primary mission all restaurant owners and leaders must commit to if they want to rise past the internal struggles that hold their businesses back year after year.

2. THEY THINK YOU'RE RICH SINCE YOU OWN A RESTAURANT.

Yes, some restaurant owners do very well. However, most independent restaurant owners are far from what would be defined as rich. Most have gone to great lengths and borrowed against their homes, asked family for loans, and groveled to bankers for lines of credit. There's an old joke about this business that if you want to make a million dollars, start with *two* million. Sad but true, for some.

Solution

Be open about your P&Ls (please tell me that you consistently run financial reports). Being open with your team about what things cost and the very slim margins that restaurants operate on is eye-opening. This must be done if you want to tear down walls between ownership and staff. Remember, trust builds teams, and that trust must be across the board. You can't trust your team on certain things and hold back on others. Share your losses and your victories.

Show them and educate them on the real business of running a restaurant. Do they understand how much each plate or glass they break costs? Do they understand how much refrigerator repair costs when they don't maintain and clean the reach-in? Do they understand what the reservation system costs you each time a guest makes a reservation? Do they know about your expense for music or utilities? These things can help them understand that running a restaurant is a business, and the purpose of a business is to make a profit.

2. THEY THINK YOU DON'T WORK HARD.

Now, don't get all defensive just yet. Perception is projection, and if your team only sees you walk through the restaurant and sit in the office with the door shut, they'll think you're not working. Owners and managers know that there are a lot of admin duties that an owner must perform to keep a business going. You need to spend some quality time behind a computer to review Point-of-Sale (P.O.S.) reports (you *are* using a report-rich P.O.S. system like **Toast**, *right?*), balancing bank statements, marketing, doing payroll, recruiting, negotiating with vendors, and the other duties that the team doesn't know happen behind the scenes. *You* know all that owner stuff — *your staff* may not.

Once again, education is powerful. The problem with being great at what you do is that you make it *look* easy. Since it looks easy, your staff assumes it *is* easy and thinks all you do is hang out in the office and play golf. Most people learn by observing. Observing **your** model, **outstanding** behavior is how your team will learn best. They will begin to mimic or repeat your behaviors, so those behaviors better be what you want. We are, at our core, tribal: leaders set the tone and communicate what behaviors are acceptable within the group. Now, you might need to take a good, hard look at yourself in the mirror. Do your behaviors set an example of good or bad habits?

Solution

You might have a great routine and like to spend time in the office doing owner stuff, and that's fine. However, your staff will never understand you if you don't take the time to understand them. Tell them some of the things you're working on and maybe even ask for feedback. Perhaps you're thinking that being on Snapchat would be good for your brand. Ask a few people on your team who use that platform what they think and get feedback from them. **Being open and receptive to input from your team doesn't make you a weak person; it makes you a true leader!**

3. THEY THINK YOU'RE A HYPOCRITE.

Actions speak louder than words. Your team knows this. You know this because you've probably preached to them about it, yet you probably don't act on your own words. When your words and actions are incongruent with each other, the glue that holds a team together—truth— breaks down.

The words of Shakespeare in *Hamlet* ring as true today as they did 400 years ago, "This above all: to thine own self be true." Do the right thing; that's great advice. Here's another: do *what* you say you're going to do *when* you say you're going to do it. Hypocritical owners and leaders cripple teams. **If you're a hypocrite, you're not a leader — you're more of a manager.**

If you're a hypocrite, it's not the end of the world because you can do something about it: change your behavior. Is change easy? No. However, if you want to start breaking down the barriers between you and your staff so you can start building a team, it's a requirement. If you don't want to change or don't feel a need to change, that is, of course, your prerogative. Just be ready for high-turnover, low-morale, theft, and pretty much remaining stuck wherever your restaurant is today. Sucks, doesn't it?

4. THEY THINK YOU DON'T CARE.

So, you have fancy checklists and tools like Slack, Jolt, or Basecamp available for the team to communicate with each other (all are awesome, by the way), yet when your team posts something or completes a checklist you don't reach out and give kudos to reinforce the positive behavior.

Positive reinforcement is sadly lacking in a lot of restaurants today. Is it because we've become so familiar with our teams that we assume they know we appreciate and are grateful for the work they do? Maybe. How would you feel if you never received positive feedback about your food or service? Would you start to have doubts? Would you start to second-guess your brand? Would you be worried about the stability of restaurant sales? How do you think your team feels when you don't give them any feedback? Hmmm … kind of makes you think, doesn't it?

You must give credit where it's due. A little appreciation and gratitude go a very long way in helping reinforce team dynamics. And you know the best part? **It's free**. A few kind words are more powerful than you can ever realize. The deepest human need is the need to be appreciated.

5. THEY THINK YOU'RE A TERRIBLE LEADER.

There are incredibly talented chefs out there who can't lead a team. Some owners are financial geniuses who would have a panic attack if they had to talk to people. Some managers can work magic on the floor but can't balance their checkbooks. See, everyone has strengths and weaknesses.

Great restaurant owners and leaders play to their strengths and minimize their weaknesses. They do this by building a team around them that mitigates their flaws and creates a synergistic, complementary, powerful team dynamic. Each person on the team, of course, brings a talent to the table. However, it's the combined strengths of the team that make it unstoppable. Think of it like the *Avengers*.

Sometimes, it takes self-actualization and a little bit of honesty to see if you're the best person for the job. Maybe you're very good — is someone on the team *better*? True leadership is about doing what's best for the team and, therefore, the brand. Sometimes that means putting ego away, taking a step to the side, and letting someone else step up.

Now, if you're not the world's greatest leader, here's the bright side: you can learn and improve your leadership game. While there are natural leadership traits, the skills required to become a great leader are teachable and coachable. Seek out a mentor or coach that can help you raise the bar and elevate your game. If you don't act to become better and push your limits, you're the living embodiment of the colloquial definition of insanity:

> *"Insanity is doing the same thing you are doing now and expecting different results." —Attribution unknown*

Bridging the gap between owners and their teams is easy to accomplish if all are willing to be open to communication, honesty, integrity, trust, and vulnerability. Don't expect your team to take the first step in closing the distance between you — that falls on you.

YOU need to take that first step and become the owner or leader they've been waiting for.

7 Things Your Service Team is Screwing Up Big-Time!

There are some things you never forget: your first kiss, your first car, an amazing movie, and horrible service. Great service can sometimes be an elusive creature, much like Sasquatch. Incredible service is not only comprised of mechanical aspects like serving food from the left and clearing from the right; it also contains the human element — hospitality. When you combine the mechanical and human elements, it creates a synergy that today's guests have come to expect.

Here's the real secret to amazing service: it must be constantly managed and monitored. I'm a big believer that incredible service teams are orchestrated and guided like a well-choreographed ballet.

I eat out at restaurants around 260 times a year. I've seen the good, the bad, and the downright ugly. When you dine out that much, you tend to see patterns in behavior. At this point, I can read the team dynamics, much like Neo can read the matrix.

Here's my short list of the seven things your service team might be screwing up.

1. THE GREETING. WOULD IT KILL YOU TO SMILE?

Nothing sets the tone, good or bad, like the greeting. I'm still shocked and surprised by the staffing choices some restaurant operators choose to make when placing people in positions where perhaps an outgoing and friendly disposition would have a big impact.

Consider the following scenario. I've driven across town to dine at your restaurant. I'm hungry, and I've decided to spend my money in your establishment. Then I'm greeted by a hostess or server who can't even muster up a smile that conveys the message, "I'm glad you're here." *Strike one.*

2. STUFF ON THE FLOOR.

They say that the devil is in the details, and that's very accurate. You must understand that **guest perception is paramount to the overall guest experience**. If the guest thinks your restaurant is dirty (particularly the bathrooms), their perception is that your kitchen is probably dirty, too. Unfortunately, whether this is true or not, it doesn't matter because your guest will have already formed a negative opinion of your business.

I ate at one restaurant and found food under the table that must have been two weeks old judging by the fur that was growing on it. *I've never been back.*

3. TAKING THINGS FROM THE TABLE.

Now this one falls into the category of absolute service no-nos. Service teams should be trained to *replace* and never *take away* from tables. Here's an example:

A server just dropped off my entrée and noticed that my iced tea was almost empty. They ask me if I'd like a refill. Since I just got my entrée, yes, I'd love more iced tea. The server reaches over and takes my glass away. Now I'm sitting there with food and no beverage. If the server had brought me a new iced tea, placed it on the table, and taken away my empty glass, it wouldn't have felt like I was in an episode of *Seinfeld*: "No soup (iced tea) for you!"

4. NOT BRINGING ME THE "EXTRAS" BEFORE MY FOOD ARRIVES.

Here's another one that should go under the list of absolute service no-nos. Please, and I'm seriously begging *please* here, bring me everything I need to enjoy my meal before my food arrives. Don't drive your guest's crazy by making them flag down someone for something as simple as ketchup to enjoy their entrée.

5. NOT READING THE TABLE.

It's amazing how much human beings communicate nonverbally. Some studies claim this to be as much as 55 percent of how we communicate with each other (Mehrabian, 1972). Your service team should always be aware of the tables in their section AND the entire dining room.

Yes, restaurants divide the dining room into sections for better service and flow. There aren't any dotted lines on the floor or walls separating one section from another, yet some servers seem to strike a territorial posture ("That's MY table.") or see a barrier when they're asked for something ("That's not my table."). Damn. *Strike two.*

6. ASKING THE STANDARD DESSERT QUESTIONS.

Of all the cliché questions asked in a restaurant, the desert question has to be the most common. Eight out of 10 times when I dine out, this is how the dessert dance goes down: A server comes up to me, and while they're clearing my entrée plate they ask one of the following questions:

"Would you like to see the dessert menu?"
"Did you save room for dessert?"
In most cases, my answer is usually "No."

If you want better results, you need to ask better questions at optimal times. I'm a big believer in planting the seed for desserts when *taking the entrée order.* Yes, when taking the entrée order! If a server tempts me with the idea of dessert *before* my entrée comes out, I'm much more inclined to save room and order one.

7. FORGETTING ABOUT ME AFTER I'VE PAID.

Too many bad servers are guilty of this crime. Once I cash-out, I don't see them again. This can be particularly frustrating if I'm entertaining clients at your restaurant. We're having a great conversation and decide to linger and talk a little longer. Water glasses are empty, dirty plates are still on the table, and our server has moved on to new guests.

I paid for dinner, I left you a tip, and now you've forgotten about me. You've now taken away the human element and transformed my dining experience into nothing more than a business transaction. For the prices, you charge, I could've stayed home and had food and beverages much cheaper. *Strike three.*

In today's market, guests expect good food and service. To go beyond that, your restaurant must connect with its guests at the human level. Mediocre restaurants are a dime a dozen and fine with just being "good." Most don't last.

Great restaurants embrace a culture of excellence and attention to detail, thriving on creating an atmosphere of hospitality.

5 Myths About Restaurant Teamwork - Busted

What is it about teamwork that gets us so excited and frustrated at the same time?

At times, it seems like we have a love-hate relationship with the concept of being a team. Maybe it's hard-wired into our genetic code for survival. Human beings have worked together since the first formation of societies, helping each other, and pulling together for the common good of humanity.

Our motivation has changed somewhat over the centuries. We went from surviving wild animal attacks and nomadic bandits to fending off power-hungry coworkers and the hordes of cookie-cutter restaurant concepts opening up all around us.

Wait — maybe things haven't changed that much...

We still feel the need to come together for the common good of the brand. Most restaurants benefit from working together as a collective. The biggest obstacle, however, is that we have so many misconceptions about teamwork that they cause teams to fail.

Let's explore some common myths and the truths that lie beneath.

MYTH #1: TEAMS ARE HARMONIOUS.
TRUTH: TEAMS ARE A COLLECTION OF PERSONALITIES.

I'm sure you've heard this before: There is no "I" in team. A lot of people hold onto the fantasy that working on a team is a magical experience, and everyone gets along. While there's some truth behind stating there's no "I" in team, there *is* a "me" (it's just scrambled). Understand that teams are a collection of individuals who all have different personalities.

Think of team member personalities like spices in a recipe. Some flavors work well with others, harmonizing and elevating one another to levels that could not otherwise be achieved. But some spices *don't* go together, particularly if they're bold and aggressive on the palate.

Building a team is very much like creating a recipe; you must be very careful about the personalities that you put together. You and too many strong or dominant members have a team loaded with people fighting over who's going to be in charge. The opposite can be just as debilitating; too many submissive members means no one will step up to take the lead. It's a balancing act.

MYTH #2: CONFLICT IS UNHEALTHY.
TRUTH: CONFLICT IS ENERGY AND CAN BE USED AS A RESOURCE.

Conflict has gotten a bad rap. Perhaps this is due to our perception of conflict as a negative. Many people imagine conflict as a hostile, possibly even violent, encounter. Most tend to think that in a conflict, there's always a winner and a loser. That's not necessarily so.

Conflict, in reality, isn't so bad…if handled properly. Conflict can promote growth, change, and, on some level, brainstorming of solutions. If — and only if — you maintain a level of respect. It's okay to have divergent ideas from the rest of the team. It's okay to speak up and voice your opinion if you think there might be a better way.

What isn't okay is being disrespectful to the other people on your team. You see, respect must exist if a team is going to survive and succeed. Respect is one of the main ingredients of real teamwork. **Remember this: You don't have to like everyone on your team, but you must respect them.**

A telltale sign of disrespect is passive-aggressive behavior. Passive-aggressive people act like they're part of the team but work to subvert it at every turn. The tools they use to undermine the team agenda are procrastination and gossip. When you find these people within your team, the best thing you can do is remove them. They're not worth giving a second (or third or fourth) chance because all they do is violate the second core ingredient to teamwork: trust.

Trust is the social glue that holds a team together. Without trust, you don't have a team, you have a collection of free agents all out for themselves. The Beatles told us that "all you need is love." For a team, what you need is respect and trust.

MYTH #3: BUILDING A TEAM IS THE HARD PART.
TRUTH: KEEPING A TEAM'S MOMENTUM IS THE REAL CHALLENGE.

Putting a team together is easy. Just grab some people, call a meeting, and declare them a team. See? Easy. The real work comes when you try to get the team to work together toward a common goal and mission.

Getting a team to pull together has, at times, been described as herding cats. *You need to be very selective about who you allow on your team.* One of the most important roles of an owner, operator, or chef is selecting who they allow to be on their team. Therefore, the team selection process must be clearly defined and methodical.

> The last thing you want to do is pull a team together based on emotional reaction or desperation. The Panic Hire is a classic example. You lose a team member or two and become desperate to fill the position(s). You place an ad for the job and very few people apply. Your anxiety grows and grows. Finally, someone comes in to apply for the job and you hire them right there on the spot. Big mistake.

If you're going to allow anyone onto your team based solely on the requirement that they're breathing, you should also hand over the keys to your car, the deed your house, and let them do whatever they want with your personal property. It's the same thing. Indiscriminate hiring will cause more disruption to your brand and your profits than you realize. Always screen the team with a highly selective filter. Always.

MYTH #4: IT'S THE LEADER THAT MAKES OR BREAKS A TEAM. TRUTH: THE TEAM, AS A COLLECTIVE, MAKES OR BREAKS ITSELF.

Leadership is important to the formation and direction of any team. However, it's the strengths of the individuals on a team that produce the results. Sure, a leader can take credit for bringing the team together. However, it's the team members themselves that figure out how best to do the work. Look back at the famous Michael Jordan-era Chicago Bulls. Phil Jackson certainly played a major role in the winning of 6 championships, but it was Michael Jordan and his teammates who put points on the scoreboard, working together and leveraging each player's unique skill set.

Two vital elements contribute to an **outstanding** team member's success, skills & character (also known as core values). *Skills get you into the game, and character keeps you there.* There are a lot of incredibly talented people who work in the restaurant industry, yet they don't last because they don't have the character to sustain "playing the game" at the highest levels. Too many times, owners and operators are impressed by skill alone. You need to make sure the person has character and heart to be able to maintain a spot on your team.

MYTH #5: ALL WORK IS BEST WITH TEAMWORK.
TRUTH: SOMETIMES, TEAMWORK CAN SLOW DOWN THE PROCESS.

While working together as a collective or team is advantageous much of the time, there will be times when you need to allow someone on your team to go it alone. A byproduct sometimes created by teams is bureaucracy. Waiting for consensus and everyone to get on board with a plan can put a damper on results.

Sometimes you need to allow highly skilled employees to function outside the framework of the team. Now, they still need to function within the standards of respect and trust, or the entire team dynamic will suffer. You're just sending them out on more of a reconnaissance mission.

Keep communication lines open and report results back to the team constantly. Lack of communication flow is a death sentence for teamwork. It can honestly be said that poor communication prevents teams from reaching their peak — it keeps them in a perpetual orbit of mediocrity.

Communication must flow unhindered from leadership to the team, among teammates, and from the team back to leadership. Too many restaurants communicate one way. When you communicate in only one direction, you're telling the team two things: you don't respect them, and you don't trust them.

Forget what you think you know about teamwork. It's like that old Zen story of a teacher who invites his senior student over for tea one day. As they sit down in the garden, the teacher starts to fill the teacup of his guest. When it reaches the top, he keeps pouring. The student reacts harshly, exclaiming, "What are you doing? My cup is full!" The teacher calmly replies, "Yes, I know. You've come here to learn, but your mind is full of your preconceived notions, opinions, and beliefs. You won't be able to learn until you first empty your cup."

There are a lot of myths about teamwork, and most are preconceived notions, opinions, and beliefs we've been handed throughout our careers in the restaurant industry. You can't move to the next level if you're keeping one foot on the level below.

It's time we empty our cups.

How to Build a Badass Team in Just 90 Days!

Here you are. Running your restaurant full speed and things are in either one of two states:

A. *You are rocking it beyond your wildest expectations!*
B. *You are already looking forward to next year; you just need to survive until then.*

If you are in state A, congratulations — you may stop reading here because the rest doesn't apply to you. Now, if you are in state B, sit down because we need to talk.

Your successes and failures are caused by your ability to gather and build a high-performance team around you. Sorry to break the bad news to you, but it's hard to build a successful brand alone. You might think you can, yet here you are, just spinning your wheels and hoping that next week (month, quarter, etc.) will be better. You have to catch a break. Well, hope is not a strategy for running a successful restaurant or bar. Hope is for suckers who play the lottery as a retirement plan.

So, what can you do? Allow me to bring out my soapbox and give you a sermon on how to get your shit together and build an A team that can save you from evil and deliver you to the promised land of profits! Can I get an Amen?

STEP 1: ADMIT YOU SUCK A LITTLE AS A LEADER.

Hey, it's okay—this is between you and me. I'm not going to point fingers at you on social media or make you feel bad. If you can cowboy up and admit the truth, then I can say with certainty that you are savable.

You have to know you have a problem before you can solve the problem.

STEP 2: STOP MAKING EXCUSES FOR YOUR LACK OF LEADERSHIP.

And quit placing blame and shame on others! Stop your bad leadership habits. Under your bad leadership, your team has run amok and does whatever they want to do. That stops now.

It stops when you say to yourself, "I am done bullshitting myself. I accept where I am, and now it's time to take action."

STEP 3: SEPARATE YOU'RE A PLAYERS FROM THE C PLAYERS.

If you have a shocked look on your face right now, here are the answers to the questions floating in your head at this moment:

Yes, you have some C players on your team who are dragging your brand into the ground.

No, you don't have an obligation to keep C players.

Yes, that might mean running short staffed.

No, you are not going to fail because you let the deadwood go to another restaurant.

Yes, your A players are going to love you for getting rid of the slackers.

Get a piece of paper and draw a line down the middle. Don't overthink this exercise because you'll try to rationalize things and it won't be effective. Believe me when I say that human beings can talk themselves into pretty much anything. Be aware of this glitch in your cognitive processing and avoid it.

So, on one side are your A and B players. On the other side are the C and D players. In all honesty, you should never have any D players. However, I give you a pass since you just woke up to the fact that you're now the leader.

Once again, without overthinking this, start putting people in one column or the other. Your first instinct is usually right, so don't second guess yourself. Now you should have a clear list of the C & D people you must replace. Time to move to the next step.

STEP 4: GET BUSY RECRUITING.

Recruiting isn't placing help wanted ads on the Internet or social media — that's job advertising. No, you'll need to get out there and recruit. That means taking the first step and reaching out to people you might not know. Yes, that's scary for some — suck it up and do it. If we're going to get you an A team in 90 days, you need to get going … like, **today**.

Use your social media accounts like LinkedIn to search for people in your market who have a similar job title or job description for what you're looking for. Say you need to upgrade from a C player-manager. Search for "restaurant (or bar) manager" and look at the profiles. If you have a premium account, send them a short and simple message like, "I was looking at your experience, and I think you could be a great fit for our team. I'm not sure if you're looking to make a change. However, if you are, message me, and we can set up a time to talk." Consider the example I used above, about the young man at the car dealership that impressed you, ask him if he's interested in working with you. Don't be shy, ask. Be a leader.

Now consider that this is a numbers game. It's a lot like digging for gold: You will have to sift through a lot of dirt to find a gold nugget. No one said recruiting was easy. Recruiting is required if you want to build a real high-performing A team. Commit each week (that means schedule it) to spend time recruiting.

Top talent (A players) do not last long on the market, because they're a hot commodity, so you need to keep your eyes open for them before your competition snaps them up. Always have your business cards on you for when the opportunity (an A player) presents itself. It could be anywhere, so stay sharp and keep your eyes open. Great candidates are people who have the important soft skills that make them shine, like:

- a sincere smile
- being helpful
- taking initiative
- liking people
- being concerned with their appearance (not **obsessed** by it)
- being comfortable talking to others
- demonstrating attention to detail
- moving with purpose and urgency

There are thousands of people in your market right now who have those traits and others.

Interestingly, many don't work in the restaurant or bar industry. Why not recruit people with soft skills and train for hard skills? Many restaurateurs have that equation ass-backward: they look for job experience and hard skill sets. We tend to hire for skill, and then we fire them for their behavior. Flip that around, and you're on the way to building an A team.

Can you do this in 90 days? Yes, because I've done it many times.

Get rid of the poor performers and make a commitment to schedule recruiting time each week. keep your eye out for A players everywhere, and step up to be the damn leader your team is looking for (drop all the B.S.), then you'll find the A team promised land.

Why Thinking Like an Owner is Bad

If you're a restaurant owner or manager (ugh, I do *not* like the word "manager," but bear with me), you've probably either spoken these words or heard them said to you: "You need to think like an owner!"

I have issues with that statement and approach to management. Let me tell you why...

MANY MANAGERS DON'T WANT TO BE OWNERS!

Like a lot of things in life, we assume others want what we want. Sorry to burst your bubble, but most people don't want to be an owner (or even a manager). If you're highly driven, you'll likely have a hard time understanding why others aren't driven to want what you want.

Here's a "revelation" for you: Everyone has different wants and desires. I know that's not groundbreaking news, yet we tend to generalize and group people via the way **we** see the world.

Have you ever promoted someone thinking that they wanted the new position and responsibilities, only to find out later that they never really wanted it? They most likely took the promotion because they didn't want to disappoint you. As a leader (not a manager), people will follow your suggestions. That's why being a true leader is so powerful. You must leverage that responsibility ecologically.

What does "ecological leadership" mean? It means leading with concern for the relationship of your team and the environment in which they work. To obtain this symbiotic balance using ecological leadership, the decisions you make must fit all three of these criteria:

- *It must be good for you.*
- *It must be good for the other person.*
- *It must be good for the guest (or community).*

Many owners and others in a position of authority and power are only concerned with number one: themselves. Many *managers* "manage" a shift, and never get past what's in it for them. A true *leader* looks at what's best for the guest, the team, and finally, themselves. That's one of the main reasons true leadership is so rare to find in our industry. We're hardwired for self-preservation, but flipping that model on its head is what facilitates the manager-to-leader transformation.

MOST HAVE NEVER BEEN AN OWNER, SO THEY CAN'T COMPREHEND THE APPEAL, AND FRANKLY, DON'T CARE ABOUT IT.

Being an owner is not the big party you might think it is. As a restaurant owner in my past, I can tell you that if you want to be at the top of your market, it must become a 24/7 obsession. Even if you're not at your restaurant, you're obsessing over it. When you go to other restaurants, your mind is working, comparing it to your own.

Now, obsession is required if you truly want to thrive and not just survive. Most restaurants operate in the realm of average, also known as mediocrity, mainly because they aren't 100 percent **obsessed** with improving.

> **That brings me to another topic: "110 percent." You can't give more than 100 percent, so please, for the love of all that is sacred, stop using this tired cliché! If most would (or could) give 80 percent, they'd be fucking astonished by their results. You only have 100 percent — aim for that, and you're on the right track.*

Okay, let's get back on topic...

Saying, "Think like an owner," particularly if the individual has never been one, is like me saying to you, "Think like a fish!" *Have you ever been a fish?*

What do fish think about?
How does a fish act?

If you have a puzzled look on your face, you now understand the same look your staff gives you when you tell them to think like an owner.

Owners have had experiences that few can truly understand:
- Working more than you ever imagined (or cared) because you see and need to reach your goal.

- Worrying if you're going to be able to cover payroll or a check to a vendor.
- Wondering what those three new restaurants, opening a few miles down the road, are going to do to your business.
- Working months — maybe even years — without a steady or normal paycheck.

The list goes on and on. Here's the thing: you're the owner. You signed up for all of this, good and bad, whether you knew it or not at the time. You signed the loan papers and the lease agreement. If things go bad, the creditors are coming for *you*, not your team. Hard for them to think like an owner when they don't have the same level of personal investment, responsibility, or context you have.

How about this instead? Let's focus on taking *personal accountability*.

Everyone can take personal accountability for three things:

1. What they focus on.
2. What they say.
3. What they do.

FOCUS

At any given moment, you have a couple of million bits of information flooding your five standard senses. Once that information filters through your brain, everything that happens next is on you.

Some take that information and infer that the world is a cruel, evil place and that people suck. This is called being a victim. The world is working against you, and everyone seems to have it out for you. This is a bunch of B.S. (aka Belief Systems) at work (okay, maybe a little bullshit, too). **What you expect or focus on, you tend to get, much like a self-fulfilling prophecy.** Focus on the perception that your staff is working against you, and you'll probably be "proven" right. *It's funny how people rarely tend to exceed our expectations.*

I asked an owner once during our first phone call, "How many people do you have working *with* you?"

His reply? "About 25 percent."

Yikes. All I wanted to know was how many people he had working in his restaurant. I learned a lesson about framing questions that day, and that people harbor their self-fulfilling perceptions.

WORDS

Words are so powerful, and I spend much of my time on coaching clients to help them understand the power of the words that they say, not only to themselves but to others as well.

Words inspire. Words heal. Words can cause damage, too. A massive leap toward becoming a true leader is acutely aware of your word choices. So, before you speak, run your words through the three gates developed by the 13th-century poet and theologian Rumi:

1. Is it true?
2. Is it necessary?
3. Is it kind?

Did your words pass all three gates? You must answer all three positively before you respond with your chosen words.

ACTION

You are responsible for what you do. What actions you take. Personal account-ability, at its core, is about taking action and doing exactly what you said you would do when you said you would do it. Hypocrisy runs rampant in the world, right alongside its cousin mediocrity. Those two travel together, running amok, laying siege to all the best intentions and plans.

> You must back up your words with solid action. *Your words tell me what you say you want — your actions show me what you're willing to do to get it!*

What are you doing right now? Okay, I know you're reading this chapter; I *mean* right after this. Are you going to share what you've learned and get motivated? *Why don't you get up and take some action that will change you and your restaurant?* Sign up for a webinar to learn something new. Register for a food show that has educational sessions (not just free food samples). Do something today that your future self will be grateful for.

Restaurants truly change when you stop talking, stop overthinking, and start doing.

Building a Service Team That Dominates

You have a problem that we need to address. It's your service team. Okay—that's not exactly accurate. The problem is you; *you* did not train your service team **to dominate**.

Sure, you trained them…maybe once, maybe twice. But half-ass efforts yield half-ass results. Oh, and please, for the love of all that is fucking sacred, don't throw out the excuse that you don't have time. *You never had time, to begin with.*

Things get done when you make a decision and develop the self-discipline to get what you want. If your service is so-so, the effort you placed into training them was at that same energy level. Water truly does seek its own level; **mediocrity is attracted to mediocrity**.

Don't think so?

How many powerful or successful people do you know who seem to be friends? Do they run in the same circles? Successful people like to associate with other successful people.

How do you get there? How can you create a service team that dominates your market? I have a 5-step plan for you!

1. UNDERSTAND YOUR ROLE

When you're the leader in your bar, nightclub, or restaurant, you become a source of energy that feeds the culture, much like our sun radiates heat and energy into the solar system. People tend to give the most energy to those who are close, and who they like the most.

Those close to the energy source have it good. But if you're like Pluto or Uranus, your days are relatively cold and isolated. No one wants to be Uranus!

You're the energy that creates the culture, good or bad.

bad culture —— bad energy —— bad leaders

It's not a complicated equation. If you can take ownership of the idea that your service team gets their energy from you, then you've managed to take a big step forward toward a better restaurant.

2. BECOME OBSESSED WITH BECOMING BETTER

If you're the energy source for your restaurant (as discussed in step 1), you'll need to become freaking **obsessed** with becoming a better person. Now, you might quip that becoming a better person has nothing to do with being a leader, generating profits, creating culture, or building a service team that dominates the market.

Au contraire — it has everything to do with those!

Defining 'better' is quite personal, quite subjective. It is up to *YOU* to define *YOUR* better. It could be that you become more focused, dedicated, or committed.

Restaurants get better when the workers in them become better people. You can't raise your restaurant without raising yourself. Most people learn and do based on what's known as modeling: we imitate the actions or behaviors of others because we're chock-full of mirror neurons. The mirror neuron system helps us learn at a fast pace, and we need the entire system for survival.

You've been modeling the behavior of others your entire life. From your parents to your siblings and friends to those you admire, like teachers, mentors, and coaches. You might not have realized it before now, but your behavior is a collective of other people's behaviors to which you've been exposed — the good, bad, and ugly.

Once you become **obsessed** with becoming a better person, you can build a service team that dominates your market. But you must become **obsessed**. I mean, really fucking **obsessed**. The word "**obsessed**" gets a bad rap because many associate it with being out of control. And yes, that can be true if an obsession can't be kept in check. In other words, you either control your obsessions or **let them** control you!

Read, listen to podcasts, watch YouTube videos, substitute audiobooks for music while driving, go to seminars, find a mentor, get a coach … Becoming a better person does not require you to sit at the top of a mountain, shave your head, and meditate for hours on end; it just requires you to become **obsessed** with learning one new thing each day and implementing it in your personal and/or professional life!

We build better restaurants by building ourselves. Leaders are forged through chaos, pressure, and discipline. Anyone who says that leadership is easy is full of shit.

3. PRACTICE UNTIL THEY WHINE, THEN PRACTICE MORE

Now that your energy is amplified and you're becoming a better person, it's time to train. Here's where the path you're traveling on comes to a fork: you can either confidently step toward dominating your market or meekly shuffle toward settling into mediocrity.

Mediocrity is the easy path. *Easy doesn't get you shit.*

Elite athletes who want to win an Olympic gold medal know that they must commit to training every day. They're aware that they may need to train multiple times on some days. To dominate and become elite, you must make a new commitment to training your team every – single – day.

There are no days off from training if you're aiming for the top!

You must be as dedicated to training as you are to becoming a better person. You must be **obsessed**. Following the most straightforward path to greatness is crucial for success. Here's one of the easiest ways to find **your** greatness:

1. Get a blank index card. Pick your favorite color if that makes you happier.
2. Draw a line down the middle.
3. On one side write "My 3" and on the other write "Team 3."
4. Choose 3 things you're dedicated to improving for yourself for the day on the "My 3" side.
5. Pick 3 things you're committed to training your team on for the day on the "Team 3" side.

Fair warning: Your team will not like to be pushed out of their comfort zone. That zone was established and burned into their souls after working in the past for mediocre restaurants that only gave training when they first started; and shitty training at that. So, be aware that they're going to complain. They're going to whine. They're going to push back. They won't like it. They'll try to get you to stop this new obsession you've discovered. They'll try to lure you back to the comfort zone.

Stay the course with this new mantra: You're either <u>on my side</u>, <u>by my side</u>, or <u>in my fucking way</u>. *Choose wisely.*

4. ASSET ALLOCATION IS KEY

Look at the people on your team right now. Would you honestly say that they're all at the same skill level? Of course not. You have your A players, B players, and C players. (You shouldn't have any D players working in your restaurant. If you do, fire them and give yourself a time-out for bad team selection.) Now, look at your team again. Do you have everyone playing to their strengths? Most likely you're just filling positions and shifts. You're not looking at your team as assets; you're treating them the same or worse than they are.

Checkers vs. Chess

When you treat all your employees the same and try to be "fair," you're playing a big game of checkers. Now, when you look at each individual on your team for their unique strengths and position them to leverage their useful abilities, you're playing chess.

Managers play checkers — **leaders play chess**.

You'll never develop a service team that dominates by standing in their way. You need to let them do their job so that they can learn and grow. You can't do their job for them; you have your job to do. Do you want to lead, teach, coach, and train? Hell yes! Do you want to take learning, growing, and developing away from someone else? Hell no!

Let me provide a few examples of taking growing opportunities away from the team:

- The general manager who is working the expo when he should be on the floor orchestrating the guest experience.
- The chef who pushes people out of the way on the line grabs the plate and finishes the dish.
- The floor manager who seats everyone and has three hourly hosts standing behind the host stand doing nothing.

If you're in a salaried position and you're doing the job that's usually fulfilled by an hourly position, you're not managing your assets properly. When you take growth opportunities away from people, they leave to work at a restaurant that will help them grow.

5. KEEP THE CYCLE GOING

Now it's time to follow the same directions on your shampoo: rinse and repeat. Excellence, greatness, and market dominance require one critical element, and that's consistency.

It's not about taking one step toward being a better person, a better leader, training your team, and suddenly achieving greatness. You'll never be "all set" that way. It's about developing the discipline to take many steps and following through, even when you don't want to do it!

> *"Don't expect to be motivated every day to get out there and make things happen. You won't be. Don't count on motivation. Count on discipline." — Jocko Willink, Retired Navy SEAL Commander*

How you develop yourself determines how your team will improve. How consistently you train your team determines how consistently they'll perform. How much you allow others to grow will determine how much your bar, nightclub, or restaurant will grow.

It's time to step up and into your potential. Once you start down that path, a true leader inspires others to step up into their greatness.

It's all synergy. Each element on its own is great — combined effectively, they become unstoppable.

Stop Lying to Yourself About Time Management

"You get to decide where your time goes. You can either spend it moving forward, or you can spend it putting out fires. You decide. And if you don't decide, others will decide for you."

—Tony Morgan

The Real Reason Your Time Management Sucks

If you're not driving a car or holding a chef's knife in your hand at this very moment, do this: look at either your watch or a clock near you. Notice the time. Now, stop time. You can't. See, that's the thing about time—it never stops.

The key to understanding time management is that you don't manage time, you manage attention. You probably hear this quote often, "Time is money."

Sorry to be the bearer of bad news: time isn't money, *money* is *money*. You can always make more money—you can't create more time. Your attention is the real currency in time management. What you focus on is where your energy goes. Energy and attention are how the most successful people in the world get stuff done. We all have the same number of hours in each day. The difference between those who get want they want in life and business, and those who don't is how they use their 24 hours.

THE SECRET OF AN ITALIAN ECONOMIST

Vilfredo Pareto was a man who recognized a very unusual pattern in his garden. Eighty percent of the peas were produced by just 20 percent of the pea pods. It made him wonder if that strange imbalance was just in his garden, and his research showed it was not contained to just peas. He uncovered that 80 percent of the land in Italy was owned by just 20 percent of the population. Thus, the Pareto Principle was born. Known also as the 80/20 Rule, it states that roughly 80 percent of your results come from only 20 percent of your activities. That's easy to understand—the hard part is identifying your 20 percent.

What activities can you delegate to others who may be better at executing them than you? Don't let foolish pride get in the way: If a task is not something that you're amazing at doing, you might be better off having someone else on your team tackle it. Always play to your strengths. Yes, you can struggle through that Excel spreadsheet to prove something, but why? Better to focus on your 20 percent and maximize your results. **Remember, time is ticking—invest your time in activities and priorities that get you and your brand the best return.**

TIME TRICKS

The human mind is a fascinating creation. For only weighing roughly three pounds it uses around 330 calories a day. It also consumes about 20 percent of the oxygen you breathe in. The human brain also has some unique wiring or shortcuts called heuristics. These are mental shortcuts we've developed to help us make decisions faster. They were formed to make sure we survived millions of years of human evolution.

They also can hurt us when it comes to time. Cognitive biases are the ways our brains make sense of all the information that bombards our senses. Think about all the information that you take in at any moment: all the visual stimuli, every little sound, the physical space around you... It's a lot.

Here are a couple of tricks to getting a better grip on time:

PARKINSON'S LAW

Work expands or contracts to meet obligations. If given a week to work on a project, most people won't feel the pressure to do anything until a few days before it's due. If you've ever crammed for an exam, you've experienced this firsthand. It's better to set a tighter deadline for yourself and commit to reaching that target. Be tough on yourself and exercise your willpower muscles.

That might mean saying no to that hour or two of T.V. you like to zone out to at night. Stop chatting with people at work for long periods discussing what you think might happen on your favorite binge worthy television show. Discipline is the key to getting the distraction monkey off your back. Saying no is sometimes more powerful than saying yes.

This can also work wonders for getting your team to control time better. If it's Monday and you want a project done on Friday, ask for it by Wednesday. In the kitchen, when you give a cook a prep list, make sure to provide a deadline along with it for its completion. There are some cooks who, if given 12 items to prep in 8 hours, will use all eight. Give them 12 items, make it clear that they have only 6 hours to prepare them, and you'll see that many will pick up the pace under the time pressure.

SCHEDULE IT!

If you looked at your calendar right now, chances are it's 90-percent-filled with appointments, meetings, or phone calls that are from other people. The demands of others are killing your ability to gain control of your life.

You either control time, or it controls you, *period.*

Gaining control over your calendar is paramount to learning to control your attention. The key is making sure you schedule time for things that are important to you, things that move you closer to your goals.

DO YOU EVEN WORK OUT?

Most people in this industry love to throw out the excuse that they don't have time, and it's true—no one *owns* time. You make time and schedule it for things that are important to you. If working out and keeping healthy isn't important to you, it will only happen when you find the "opportunity." You'd have a better chance of hitting the Powerball numbers four times in a row than working out if you're waiting until the opportunity presents itself. Taking control of time and your life requires you to step up and own the things you have total control over, your calendar, and your attention (which means taking conscious action).

Want to get to the gym? *Schedule it.* Want to get the schedules done on time? *Schedule time to work on it.* Want to read more? *Put that on your calendar!*

YOUR CALENDAR IS A REFLECTION OF THE QUALITY OF YOUR LIFE.

If you have a lot of white space on your calendar, chances are you live a life driven by the demands of others, or you're doing things that only give the appearance that you're busy. Yeah, you worked a 12-hour shift, but what did you get done? You might say something like this: "Well, there was this thing that popped up, and then I had to go to the store because someone forgot to order limes."

Stop lying to yourself.

Stop coming up with excuses for why you're not getting the things done that can have an impact on not only your restaurant but your life!

You're not rewarded in business or life for being busy; you're rewarded for the results you get. If you want to make more, do more, and become more, stop fighting against time—that's a battle you'll never win. The only thing you control is your focus at this moment.

What are you going to do with this information? Are you going to keep fooling yourself and stay in denial, or are you going to take control of the one thing you truly can control?

That's what you do at this moment: take control!

The Most Effective Tool for a Productive Week

Tick tock, tick tock... People always wish they had more time. They're always trying to manage it, to bend it to their will.

We all wish time machines were real so we'd be able to control the uncontrollable. When you run a restaurant, time can either become your ally or a malicious nemesis. Most people choose the latter, seeming to fight with time constantly.

So how can you stop this love/hate relationship with time? Here are some simple ways to work *with* time rather than against it.

RESPECT TIME

Just like a lot of things in life, you need to give before you can receive. Respect is a common theme in all relationships. It's the same with time. You need to have a deep respect for your time and that of others.

One of the greatest gifts a person can give is their time. Remember, it can't be saved or traded. When you give your time and attention, you've given away a valuable and precious commodity. That's important to realize and respect.

It all starts with self-respect. You need to respect time for the gift it is. You need to respect yourself. You are powerful beyond measure—if you develop real self-respect and make a sacred pact to honor that you'll realize your full potential. Everything in your outer world started first in your inner world.

> When people don't respect themselves, it becomes rather apparent in their behavior. Your words say one thing, but your actions say everything. This behavior will manifest in many ways. One of the most common is overcompensating behavior. The person who is loud, obnoxious, and demeaning to others is quite often suffering from a lack of confidence and self-respect for themselves. If people don't have respect for themselves, it's hard to get them to respect other things.

This is a fantastic interview question! Ask them, point-blank, "Do you respect yourself?" Then ask them to give you at least three examples of how they respect themselves. You might be shocked when you see how many people's faces go blank when asked this question.

CONTROL YOUR FOCUS

You might see clever T-shirts that says, "Time is Money." That's not entirely true. Money can be saved; time cannot. So, time is not money—money is money. *Focus* is the real currency for being productive. How someone spends their focus is a window into what they value.

Watching T.V. for four hours a night is a typical escape for many people. Let's say that they do this for five nights a week. That's 20 hours. In a year, that becomes 1,040 hours. Now, let's take it further and throw in the variable of a person's hourly worth. If someone endeavors for their time to be worth more than others' time, they first need to be worth more to themselves. This goes right back to respect. So, let's say they want to make a $100K a year in salary. In a normal 40-hour work week they'd need to be worth $45.79 per hour to make that kind of money. If they spent that time watching T.V. and put a dollar value to it, they'd need to pay out $47,621.00 at the end of the year! Ouch! I don't know too many people who would write a check out for $47K for watching T.V.

How do you take back control of focus? Start being more selective about where your attention *and* focus go. The restaurant industry moves fast, and it's easy to get dragged into the demands it throws at us. If you want better results, you need to ask better quality questions. Here are some examples of questions you should be asking yourself:

1. *Am I the best person to do this?* No. Seriously, you don't need to do everything yourself. The people who are always doing everything are also the same people who love to play the martyr. They don't respect or trust their team, and if someone treats their team that way, well, they don't have a team. Instead, they have a one-man or one-woman show with support. That rarely works out. People like this either have very high turnover or they bounce from restaurant to restaurant, never finding deep, fulfilling success.

2. *Who on my team could benefit?* Yes, think beyond your own needs. When you hold your team back from growing, you hold back the business. One of our human needs (not want, *need*) is to contribute. When you take control of everything and don't give others a chance to

contribute, you'll soon see they stop asking for more responsibility. Next, you'll see their drive and motivation dwindle. After that, you have zombies working for you. Or no one at all.

If you want to see where your time goes, conduct a time audit. Get a notebook and write down everything you do and how long you spend on each task for an entire week. This exercise can be a real eye-opener for most, as long as they're brutally honest.

We tend to think we get a lot done, but when we look back on the real data, it can be a little disheartening. You can't change without first becoming aware of the habits you've allowed to take hold of your life. **Awareness precedes choice; choice precedes change...*if* you make a conscious effort to want to change and act on that desire**. Remember, the road to Hell is paved with good intentions.

RESULTS MATTER MORE THAN EFFORT

"Busy, busy, busy," the battle cry of anyone working in the restaurant industry. We're all busy. We're called 'human beings' when in fact we should be called 'humans doing.' Life moves quickly, and the human race is always pushing to be faster, better, stronger. We're driven by a need for more.

It's not a bad thing to want to be better and want more. The self-help industry is a multi-billion-dollar conglomerate that serves that drive with books, audio, video, and workshops.

If you're not moving fast enough, you can quickly be labeled a "slacker" by others. The issue is that we've concluded that being busy is the end goal. We think someone busy is successful. Not so fast! It doesn't matter how busy you are. Being busy for many people is just a form of distraction. They use it like a magician does: "Look over here and see how busy I am so you don't see what I'm doing!" **What matters are the results you get**.

Write this down: Never mistake being busy for being effective. You're rewarded for the results you get, not the effort.

A line cook works a 10-hour shift and is moving quickly. He appears to have a lot of prep going. On the surface you might think that he's a workhorse. But at the end of the day, that cook knocked out just four items on the prep list. Epic fail.

It's not being busy that matters. Sure, someone can stay busy all day. However, when all is said and done, their productivity can be just average (or below average). Mediocrity loves to disguise itself as being busy.

PLAN THE DAY BEFORE

Here's one you may have heard: "Proper planning prevents piss poor performance." Hands down, the most effective tool for a productive week is this: **plan your work, and then work your plan.**

We know that this business is fast-paced and demanding. It's easy to accept the status quo and say that you don't have time. What have we learned about owning time? Remember, you only own your attention and what you focus on. Your brain is wired to get you from want *to* want. Your brain is a problem-solving machine, and as such, you tend to achieve the results tied to the questions you ask yourself. Ask poor questions, get poor results.

If you ask, "Why does this always happen to me?" your brain will give you the following answer: "Because you're an idiot." Ask a better question, like, "What is the lesson here, and how can I use that to be better?" Seek, and ye shall find.

Ideally, you want to tap into that problem-solving part of your brain to help you become more effective. That starts with having a game plan the day before. When you write down what you want and decide what you're going to do to get it, something amazing happens—you start to see results.

So, could you eat an entire cow? Yes, one steak at a time. The best thing to do is cut your day down into three tasks. Here is a low-cost system to get you started: index cards. Pick up plain white or multicolored index cards at the store and start today. Take out an index card and draw a line down the middle. On one side at the top write "Task" and on the other side, write "Action." Write down the three tasks you must accomplish for the day, the most important tasks that can move you forward. These need to be big and bold.

Remember:

> *"Dream no small dreams, for they have no power to move the hearts of men." —Johann Wolfgang von Goethe*

After you've written down your three tasks, in the next column, write down the actions that will help you accomplish your tasks. Most big dreams and goals can't be achieved through one or two actions. If they can, you need bigger goals!

If you do this the day before and review it before you go to bed, your problem-solving brain will go to work. It will help you the next day when it comes time to get busy making things happen. Stacking the deck in your favor is always a smart move.

Smart restaurant owners, operators, and chefs always have a plan.

How to Achieve Work/ Life Balance in the Restaurant World

Balance. You've heard that word thrown around often in our industry. It seems like the Holy Grail— many seek but never find it. Is it that hard to achieve work/life balance? No, not really. It just requires a shift in mindset and habits.

The first shift is to understand that you'll never find real balance. The idea of balance carries with it the false implication that things are equal. Life isn't fair, and it's not equal. Does that mean you shouldn't try to find balance? Of course not.

But many who work in restaurants are out of balance to the point of burnout. They put so much into work that they have no life! Let's stop that all the "all work and no play makes you tough" bullshit right now. Life is meant to be lived. There are times to focus on the work side of life and times when you must stop to smell to the roses. *You want to seek life-work integration.*

GET CLEAR ON WHAT YOU MUST DO TODAY!

There are a lot of things in this business that we feel we *should* do. "Shoulds" are nice to have, but they're not "must-haves." When you hit work, you want to have a clear plan for the day on what you must do to move your restaurant and your life forward. **Here's where many fail: they lack a plan**. They go to the restaurant with the thought that they'll "roll with the punches." This is no time to wing it. Rolling with the punches indicates you're ready for a fight. That's not a healthy way to look at your restaurant.

Without a clear plan, you'll end up reactionary and living in the time dimension called Demand. Here, other people's agendas take control, and you're a buoy floating in a sea of chaos. *That's no way to live.* You must have your plan and schedule small blocks of time to work it. If you want to become a better leader, you're going to need to block off time to learn and grow your skills.

FOCUS ON BEING EFFECTIVE, NOT BUSY!

Many people fill their day with tasks that are just not productive. Some managers build their careers around looking busy. We tend to think busy people are successful but, as I've made clear, I find that assumption to be false.

You need to know that throwing more hours at work isn't always the right action. If one manager takes a 12-hour shift to do the same thing that another manager can do in 8 hours, which is more valuable? It's a sure bet that if you tracked the 12-hour manager's day, you'd find they're unproductive a significant amount of the time. **Stop putting in time and start focusing on results!**

When you stop thinking in hours and commit to becoming more productive, you break free from the shackles of busywork and wasted effort.

YOU NEED TO TRUST OTHERS.

Getting away from work and enjoying time off comes down to another critical element of success: you gotta trust people. So many don't want to leave work and experience self-imposed anxiety attacks when they take a day off. Your team needs to know you trust them.

When you take away trust, you don't allow people on your team to grow and develop. That's the selfish behavior of a self-centered ass. Taking away the opportunity for others to learn violates inalienable rights! Everyone has a right to learn, grow, and develop themselves.

Will your team make mistakes? Yes. Humans are fallible—no one is without flaws. Mistakes hold within them the opportunity to learn. You've learned more from the mistakes you've made than you ever have from so-called beginner's luck. Don't deny your team and others around you the chance for personal growth.

Finding work/life balance is attainable if you're willing to stop looking at work as the end-all, be-all of life. Your life is meant to be big, bold, and multidimensional! Live it that way!

You're not defined by the work you do or your title, you're defined by the person you become.

Go to a bookstore. Learn a new skill. Join a cause. Become a local at the corner coffee shop. Get to the gym. Go for a damn walk. Spend time with people outside the restaurant business.

Stop being held captive by a quest to find work/life balance and just live. Seek integration, not balance.

Why Your 80-Hour Workweek is Stupid

Hustle.

Rise and grid.

Get some.

Just do it.

These sayings flood the internet and social media daily with a call to get up and get after the day. They're the battle cries of the new order.

"You gotta hustle to make it."

"Outwork everyone."

"Be on 24/7."

"Only losers quit."

Yeah, how about, "Only fools get stuck on the time treadmill, racking up workweeks that top 70, 80, and sometimes 90 hours,"? Let's sit down and have a little chat about why long workweeks aren't a badge of honor, they're just stupid.

ALL TIME IS NOT EQUAL

You're going to have productive parts of the day. But you're going to find that you're not as productive as you think you are throughout the rest of it. However, if you change your mindset, you'll come to realize that the hours you put in have little to do with the results you achieve.

We've become addicted to **busyness**. Looking busy and declaring how busy we are is the new status symbol. When you say, you're "so busy" what you're saying is that you're too lazy to prioritize your day or life. You're stuck on the hamster wheel of life, running as fast as you can, getting nowhere.

When you can finally muster the courage to be brutally honest with yourself about where and how you spend your time, conduct the time audit I mentioned previously for one week. Write down everything you do and include the time you allocate for each task. If you have an iPhone running iOS 12, check out the *Screen Time* feature that shows you how much time you spend on your device and where that time goes. Both tools will give you a rude awakening as to how much time you spend doing things that aren't important.

LEARN A NEW WORD: "NO"

Yes, this is the hospitality business and you've had it ingrained in you to want to say "Yes." But problems arise when we say yes all the damn time, to the point we become overcommitted and are pulled in too many directions at once. Let's clear the air right now: you're a human, not a machine. You have a breaking point—everyone does. The "phenomenon" known as burnout is a direct result of pushing past your breaking point. **Burnout isn't something that happens to you, it's something you do to yourself.** Remember that, because it gives you power and puts you in control.

That control starts with not saying yes to everything that comes your way. The word psychologists use is "boundaries." You need them to keep your sanity in an industry that is anything but sane. Having solid boundaries protects you. They allow you to say, "This is who I am and what I stand for." Without healthy boundaries, you'll overcommit to too many things. Sadly, that's when your results will start to suffer because you're doing too many things half-assed.

Here are some common boundary issues:
- Fear of saying no.
- Overcommitting.
- People pleasing.
- Inability to make decisions.
- Feeling responsible for other people's emotions.
- Taking care of others' needs but not your own.
- Taking on the moods or emotions of others around you.
- Being overly sensitive to criticism.

Setting boundaries does not mean going from one extreme to the other. Don't go from being a yes-person to a no-person overnight. Instead, be a little more flexible and don't say yes right away. I use this easy way to decide what tasks and projects to tackle: it's either a "Hell yes!" or a "Hell no!" There's no in between for me. If I'm not passionate and committed to a project, it's hell no. **You must seriously consider passing on things that don't kindle a fire inside you.** I get it; sometimes, there are things you must do as an owner or leader. Just start being more aware of what you allow on your plate.

The chances are that if there's something you don't feel is a good fit for your natural strengths; there's someone on your team for who it would fit perfectly. You need to know your team better, and how to use each person's strengths to build the business, this is otherwise known as resource allocation.

When you don't allow your team to learn and grow, you increase the odds that they'll leave for another restaurant. Why? Because people need to grow. They need to contribute. They crave it. Give those who want to develop their skills the opportunity to do so, and you'll build a solid team.

YOUR RESULTS SUCK!

Okay, I said it—it's out there now, so let's deal with it. Your energy level throughout the day is like a battery. Here's the inside secret: everyone's internal battery level is different. The issue is that most don't properly recharge their internal battery enough to take on the demands of the day.

Imagine, if you will, that you went to work one morning with your cell phone only charged at 25 percent. Now, if you couldn't recharge your phone all day, how long would you make it before it died? 3 hours? 5 hours? It would depend on how much you used it, right? Well, most managers are just like that partially charged cell phone when they go to work. They haven't taken steps to recharge their internal batteries so, they run out of energy before the day is out.

What happens when your internal battery runs low? Here are some warning signs:

- Short temper
- Easily agitated
- Stressed
- Unfocused
- Impatient
- Overeating (need sugar for energy)
- Caffeine dependency
- Snapping at people
- Overly emotional
- Depressed

Not much good comes from running your internal energy below 50 percent. Bad things happen when you get below 25 percent. Managing your energy must become a priority if you desire to break free from the mega-hour syndrome. *Energy is everything to outstanding leaders.*

A BETTER WAY

So, if energy is everything, how do you ensure you have plenty to make it through the day and still have some left over? Easy—take care of yourself first. I'm not talking about becoming a self-centered asshole who only thinks about themselves. I'm talking about becoming responsible for your energy and taking better care of yourself. You can't give to others without first giving to yourself. Self-care is not selfish; it's smart.

How to recharge your internal battery:
- Working out at the gym
- Walking
- Hiking
- Meditating
- Swimming
- Reading
- Writing
- Playing an instrument
- Taking a class
- Joining a club
- Spending quality time with family or friends

Anything that activates other areas of your brain and body is good for recharging. You truly are limited by your imagination. Just make sure to schedule it and follow through. "The road to Hell is paved with good intentions," the quote goes. Stop talking about taking better care of yourself and fucking do it!

The best way to accomplish this is to develop a routine and set a time each day for your self-care habit. Without setting a firm time, you'll find it difficult to anchor the habit into your neuro pathways. *Outstanding habits create outstanding leaders.*

It starts with the simple habit of getting a good night's sleep. Too many run their lives with the mindset that sleep is for the weak. *Sleep is for the high achiever!* Your body needs quality sleep—without it, you risk going a little loco in the head. Lack of sleep has some of these common side effects:
- Brain fog
- Irrational behavior
- Irritable
- Overly emotional

Have you personally experienced any of these side effects? I'm willing to bet you have. Pushing harder and further is not always the answer. Your body is a lot smarter than you think and there are times you need to listen to it. Aim for getting 6 to 8 hours of quality sleep each night. Your body and brain need it to repair and reboot. Lack of sleep is a major contributor to many health issues. Take measures to fix that by setting steady bed and wake times, and following through.

GET BETTER RESULTS

Here's the trick to getting more done: you have to set yourself up to accomplish more! The key to this is to reduce the distractions that bombard you all fucking day long. The restaurant business is full of distractions that pull at you. You also have a lot of personal distractions that compete for your attention. Emails, text messages, Facebook, and other social media notifications, and pop-up conversations are distractions that kill your productivity.

Set up some time to unplug and dial in your focus. The most effective way to do this is to schedule short "focus blocks" throughout the day. These blocks are 20 to 30 minutes you use to go dark from the world and get shit done. Now, you may think that 20 or 30 minutes isn't much time to get anything done. I'm going to tell you that the amount of pure focus is life changing! You'll be amazed how much you can accomplish when the only thing you focus on is getting shit done!

Ideally, you need to schedule these focus blocks like you would any other important meeting. I recommend a minimum of two focus blocks each day. If you can get more in, that's great. The key is to start blocking off time to get 100 percent focused.

This is how you implement a focus block:
- Set a timer for your allotted time (20 to 30 minutes).
- Turn off all notifications.
- Turn your phone to "Do Not Disturb."
- Have what you need to get to work ready. A focus block is designed to get results, not run around getting materials ready to get work done.
- Stay on track.
- Track your results.

You want to measure your productivity during each focus block. An easy way to do this is by giving each session a score from 1 to 10, 1 being least productive and 10 being ultra-productive. Whenever you have a score under

8, take notes of what could have been done better. Do this for a month, and you'll see a dramatic improvement to your results!

GET OFF THE HAMSTER WHEEL

Okay, we now see that the 80-hour work week is for people who seek to play the victim and want to keep the drama high in their life.

Working long hours in a restaurant is not a badge of honor, it's a mark of stupidity, piss poor planning, lack of priorities, failure to develop your team and schedule focus blocks, depletion of your internal energy levels, and fear of saying no.

The answer isn't more hours, it's less bullshit.

It's facing the truth.

Create a Menu That Sells, Not What Your Ego Wants

"The ego is the single biggest obstruction to the achievement of anything."

—Richard Rose

How to Create a Menu that Makes Money!

You look at your menu over and over until you feel like your stare could burn a hole in it. Hey, it looks good. Maybe even great. You decide it's ready to be rolled out and you decide to launch. Sales jump, and you get excited. Then.... they seem to level off. What happened?

A fresh menu design is like buying a new car. At first, it's the greatest thing in the world to you. After a few months, a lot of that newness has worn off. Your menu can be a similar roller coaster of emotions. **Time to get your menu mojo back!**

FIRST THINGS FIRST

You must know the cost of every item on your menu (that means both food and beverages—no shortcuts here). **Not knowing your costs is not knowing your business.** I asked a recent audience (about 350 people) I was speaking to what *I thought* was a straightforward question: "How many people in the room know the cost of the items on your menu?" I was shocked to see only ten hands in the room rise. [Insert shaking head in disbelief here.]

With the advancement in technology, almost every point-of-sale system on the market has a food costing program built into the software. Every major broad line food distributor also has a food cost program that they offer to their customers. There is no excuse not to have a program that can help your nail your costs down. No excuses. If you have been slacking on updating your recipe costs for both the food and bar, then it's time to cowboy up and take some action.

DO YOUR RESEARCH

When you have been using the same menu for years you might be stuck in a little design rut, so fire up your internet and start stalking other restaurants! Not "get a restraining order" stalking, more like just checking out the competition.

I can't believe I am going to throw this out there, however, don't overlook Pinterest. Yes, the website has tons of samples of restaurant menus from around the world, and there are bound to be a few that spark some creative inspiration.

Jot down some notes and take in the look of some new ways to amp up your brand.

LESS IS MORE

Particularly when it comes to modern menu design, less is more. As a society, we have become a people of instant gratification. The younger generations are very used to having access to answers at their fingertips on just about any topic they want to inquire about. They move fast, and your menu needs to keep up. Drop some of the longwinded, drawn-out menu descriptions that are overused and overplayed.

How about "Seared to perfection"? Or the very popular, "A delightful balance of vodka, lemonade, and cardamom simple syrup." [Insert snoring sound here.]

Guests do love transparency on a menu, so be straightforward and give it to them:

The House Burger
8-ounce Sister's Ranch Grass-Fed Ground Beef + Red Curry Mayo + Sliced Bosque Farms Tomato + Organic Pea Tendrils

No need for menu fluff—be short and to the point. People don't read menus like they once did. They tend to scan them, so make it easy for them to find out what they need to know. Use fonts to simplify your menu like the examples below.

BE BOLD

A favorite Jedi Menu Mind Trick I use is called the **Bold** Word. Since people don't read menus and tend to scan over them, help them by **bolding** out **key**words that get attention.

Look at these two menu items:

Sweet Potato Calamari
Sweet Potato Flour Dusted Judith Point Calamari + peppadews + peanuts + red curry aioli
Sweet Potato **Calamari**

Sweet Potato Flour Dusted Judith Point Calamari + peppadews + peanuts + red curry aioli

Making it easy for your guests makes it easy for them to make a decision, and that is what your goal should be. Avoid the paradox of choice issue where they have so many choices that it increases anxiety.

You see it on the faces of guests who reach that point where they can't decide, which is called threshold.

They look confused or frustrated, and they will say something like, "Just give me a burger." The paradox of choice causes people to fall back to a decision that is easy, which means they'll miss out on your new Sweet Potato Calamari.

Look at your menu right now. Does it need to evolve? Maybe it's time for you to get out of your comfort zone and give your menu a new and improved look. Remember that insanity is doing the same thing over and over while expecting different results. Your menu is your number one marketing and profitability tool you have!

Treat it with some respect.

Advanced Jedi Menu Tricks: Brainwash Your Guests and Team on Your Menu

It's tough out there. More restaurants and bars open every year, making being unique a challenge. If you read the previous chapter that addressed how to shake up your menu design to give your sales a kick in the butt, you now might be asking, "What's next?"

Glad you asked. Now it's time to apply some real Jedi Mind Tricks to get everyone on board to maximize that nice, fresh menu design you created.

KEY #1: MANAGE YOUR ENERGY

Some universal laws must be obeyed. The first is that everything is energy. Everything. Even you. You are a bundle of energy that appears in human form. Some quantum physicists would go as far as saying you're an energy field existing in a larger energy field. That being said, know that energy is transferable. Energy is transferred whenever you interact with another person. Sometimes it's positive and other times negative.

Managing your energy to stay in the positive range is no easy task. There is a lot of negativity out there, and it's almost like you need to walk around with a protective force field to guard against it. When you want to influence another human being, your energy level needs to be higher than the person you are trying to influence. How much? Just about one to two levels higher. If your energy is too far above theirs, you will come across as being "too much."

It starts with self-awareness. Where is your energy level right now on a scale from 1-10 (10 being supercharged)? When you approach a guest, try to get a read on their energy level. Then, raise your energy to one level above theirs. Now you will have the power to influence their buying process.

KEY #2: MAKE SINCERE RECOMMENDATIONS

Menu choices and deciding on what to order can create anxiety in your guests. Offering many choices can be a bad thing sometimes. People don't want to make the wrong decision, so we tend to make the safe decision. That leads to stagnant sales.

You break free from this trap by making honest and sincere recommendations to help alleviate the pressure to decide. That requires you know two things:

Your favorite item on the menu in each category.

The most popular item in each category.

Personal recommendations are the stuff marketing gurus preach. Everyone trusts the inside tip from a friend. Facebook is filled with people asking their friends for recommendations. Tap into that need by offering up suggestions of items on the menu that you truly like. Now, it must be authentic or people will see right through your attempt to persuade them. Sincerity is paramount!

Telling them about the most popular items goes to social proof. We like the reassurance that others like it as well. Why do we buy toothpaste that 4 out of 5 dentists recommend? Social proof. Honestly, if you think about it, you have no clue who those dentists are! We gravitate towards social proof like a security blanket: it feels good even if it offers very little real security.

KEY #3: BACK IT WITH BODY LANGUAGE: 7-38-55

7-38-55. In communication, you should understand that words alone only make up 7 percent of how we communicate. Thirty-eight percent is the tone of voice, and a whopping 55 percent is non-verbal body language (Mehrabian, 1972). It is not what you say, but how you say it. Your body language speaks volumes for reinforcing the words you choose.

You say that the calamari is your favorite, yet your jaw tightens when you say it. They ask about what bourbon you recommend, and you look away while offering the highest-priced choice on the list. You might think you're being clever, but your body is saying something totally different than the words coming from your mouth.

Speak with authenticity and congruency in your body language. When your words and your non-verbals are aligned you will influence the items your guests buy.

KEY #4: FOCUS ON HOSPITALITY

Here's the real trick: Don't go for the big sales, go for the right sales! **Better to make recommendations that will enhance the guest experience than to rack up a big check.** People do know when you're manipulative rather than helpful. Make suggestions that fit the guest and come from the spirit of hospitality.

The word hospitality comes from the Latin *hospes*, which came from the word *hostis*, which originally meant "to have power." The words hospital, hospice, and hostel also come from the word "hospitality." It's all about giving personal care to people who are away from their homes. *Hospitality is about being a host to your guest in your establishment.*

Being a host is being committed to serving others. Many working in restaurants and bars have forgotten that. Stop trying to raise the check and instead focus on raising your level of hospitality. Do that, and you'll see that the sales follow.

The bonus is that sales will consistently increase as your level of hospitality increases.

The Art of the Simple Menu

In the world of restaurants and bars, there is nothing quite as important as your menu. It is part marketing tool, part profitability indicator, and all brand identity. Your menu is the one thing everyone who comes in contact with your concept is guaranteed to see.

Sadly, too many menus are written out from the ego. It is a statement of who you are. In a world vying for your attention, your menu can be a double-edged sword to get that attention.

Used properly, it can get you profits and a steady stream of patrons. Used foolishly it becomes a game of cat and mouse, with you being the poor mouse.

THE PROBLEM WITH EGO

Your ego is the brake that holds you back from getting the results you truly want. The ego tells you that you know enough, so you stop learning. The ego says your menu is awesome, so you ignore the data and keep driving ahead. Just remember that even those long roads in the desert have curves.

When your ego drives the menu, you become blind to the facts. Emotion is ego's second cousin and it rides shotgun on this trip. Maybe you have heard some of these sayings:

The guest doesn't get it.

My staff can't sell it.

It's my best seller (when the POS data clearly shows it's not).

I won't sacrifice my craft for people who don't get what I'm trying to do.

Yes, the ego says some batshit crazy things.

Once upon a time, there was a young chef who thought that his artistic integrity was everything. *What, you want the demi glacé on the side?* **No**. *You want to substitute sautéed spinach for haricot vert?* **Get out.**

One day the young chef was called into the owner's office to have a "little talk." It went something like this:

> *Owner:* You know, I think your food is amazing and so do many of our guests.

Young Chef: Thank you.

Owner: Here's the problem I have.

Young Chef (now getting nervous): What problem?

Owner: Well, you know how you won't make substitutions or allow guests to alter your dishes in any way?

Young Chef: Yes. The food was designed to be a perfect balance of texture and flavors. I even had the servers take the salt and pepper off the table because I saw the guests were seasoning the food without tasting it! Drives me crazy!

Owner: Yeah, well, you see, if people can't make changes to fit their needs, then they won't come back. If they don't come back, I won't be able to pay you.

Young Chef: So, you're saying this restaurant doesn't exist for my self-promotion but for the needs of the guests?

Owner: Yeah. Oh, and put the salt and pepper back on the table.

While the shocking revelation hit the young chef hard, it was a liberation in the sense that he learned the true meaning of hospitality that evening. It's about the other person, not you. ***That young chef never forgot that valuable lesson, and it's been said that he went on to become a restaurant coach and even wrote a few books (hint hint).***

THE ART OF SIMPLICITY

If you've never had the pleasure of eating at In-N-Out Burger, you are missing a perfect example of simplicity in action. The brand was founded in 1948 in Baldwin, California. The menu was created to get you in and out with your food in record time.

In 70 years, while prices have changed, the menu surprisingly has not changed very much. It still has just eight items.

Now, before you scoff or turn your nose up at the very small menu, take in the fact that, on average, each In-N-Out location takes in over $2M. Multiple that by 335 locations and you have an empire.

STOP ADDING TO YOUR MENU

You might be bored with your menu since you see it day after day. The temptation to change things that become repetitive is human nature. Here's a tip: **Don't fix what is not broken**!

You might be bored making that same Roasted Poblano Meatloaf or that Silver Coin Margarita. The real question you need to ask is: Are your guests bored with it? If sales are not declining, it isn't broken. Stop adding things to your menu that compete with your high-profit items.

When we give the guest too many options, they will experience anxiety about making the right choice. When people get confused about making the right choice, they fall back to the safe choice, which is usually the Caesar salad with chicken.

START TALKING AWAY ITEMS

It takes courage to go against your ego and strip away the fat from your menu. It's a challenge to suppress your ego and create a menu that serves your guests AND makes money.

Here are some wise words to place in your office when working on your next menu:

> *"Perfection is achieved, not when there is nothing more to add, but when there is nothing left to take away." —Antoine de Saint-Exupery*

When you can dial in your menu to where all items finally sell pretty evenly, then and only then will you have mastered the art of the simple menu. Until then, keep your eyes on the data, make adjustments frequently, and keep your ego locked in the back room.

You can let your ego out after work to get some fresh air, but don't feed it after midnight or bad things happen.

Trust me on that.

Is Your Restaurant Brand Sending Mixed Messages?

In the sea of restaurant options out there, does your brand stand out? So many fail to capture the attention of their guests and blend in with the masses. One of the main reasons for this is that they send mixed messages about who they are. Listen, when you're confused about who you are and what you stand for, how do you think your market will react to you? Lukewarm at best. Sure, new guests might stop in out of curiosity. If you don't deliver a solid message, they won't be back.

Let's explore some common mixed message mistakes and a three-step plan to correct course.

MENU CONFUSION

Your sign out front, your website, and Yelp listing all say you're an Italian restaurant. But when guests come in and see your menu you can tell by the look on their faces that they're confused. Asian Chicken Wings? Baja Fish Tacos? Bacon-Wrapped Filet with French Demi Glacé? Oh, and in the corner, four pasta dishes. Hmmm, what's going on here? You say Italian in all your marketing, but when your guests visit your restaurant, there are very few Italian options on the menu. Mixed message.

STAFF UNIFORMS

You say you're an upscale restaurant, and by judging by the menu prices online and the number of "$$$$" by your restaurant name on review sites, we believe you. But when guests arrive, they're greeted by a hostess wearing a sports jersey, jeans, flip-flops, and a nose ring so big they can't stop staring at it. A guest and their date are dressed for what they thought would be a high-end atmosphere, given the high prices. "Okay," they think, "We'll let this slide even though we may have overdressed." They're seated and try to settle in for the meal. Then they watch as a woman walking through the dining room wearing cutoff jean shorts and a tank top steps behind the bar. That's the bartender making the drinks! Mixed message.

BRAND IMAGE

So, dinner has gone well, and a manager stops by to give guests their card, a gesture intended to encourage future business and become a contact point. Nice job—well played. About 10 minutes later, another manager stops by the tables and hands out *their* business card. Only this time the card looks different. The same name of the restaurant but different colors, different fonts, different brand tagline. Confusing? Yes, and another mixed message.

We use the word "autonomy" often today. Autonomy can be both good and bad. The problem with autonomy as it relates to your brand image is guests experience mixed brand messages. When you allow your workers to take personal accountability and hold themselves accountable to your brand without having to micromanage them, that's good. When you allow them to add new items to the menu just because they want to build their reputation, allow the service team to dress however they like (even when what they choose to wear contradicts your brand), or allow managers to design their own "unique" business cards because they want to feel special, that's bad.

Too many restaurants allow their staffs to dictate the brand. **We live in a democracy, but when it comes to your brand, your money, your integrity, there can be only one voice:** <u>yours</u>.

HOW TO GET CONTROL OF YOUR BRAND: THE 3-STEP SOLUTION

We know what lands most restaurants into a funk of brand dilution: too much outside input and not enough inside input. When you set out on your path to creating your brand, you had a vision, a fire. It drove you and kept you awake at night. Maybe you don't feel that internal flame burn as hot as it once did. So, what is an owner or operator to do?

1. Be Crystal Clear

What's your brand identity? Who are you? What's your mission? Who do you want as guests? Who do you want as staff? Why do you do this day after day? Oh, and the answers for that last question must be more than just money or your brand will have a short shelf life. Please don't think that I'm saying making a profit is bad—it just can't be the all-consuming driving force as to why you do this if you're an operator.

These are questions that need to be answered, and you must write them down. Do you know the old saying that a verbal contract is not worth the paper it's written on? Well, that goes for your vision and core values for your restaurant as well! You must commit to writing those things down on paper and communicating them to your team and guests.

Contrary to the belief held by many, people can't read minds. You must be the megaphone for who you are, what you do, and why you do it! As the leader of a restaurant, you must become a culture advocate. Culture is created by design or by default. If you don't take part in creating and sculpting the culture of your brand, you can have faith that one will creep out of the primordial ooze and start to grow in your restaurant. Imagine the cult horror movie *The Blob* as an image of a culture gone bad.

When you've become clear on your brand message, you'll want to carve it into stone and bring it down from the mountain to present it to your guests and team like the tablets carried down by Moses himself. Yeah, **your brand message is non-negotiable!**

2. Be Obsessed with Consistency

Consistency makes or breaks restaurant brands. A comment made by people who stop visiting a restaurant is this: "Things just changed. They weren't the same anymore." Just like any relationship, when people (or brands) change, we lose trust and faith. Brand trust, also known as brand promise, is a sacred bond between the guest and the brand. Break it, and the road to healing and recovery will be slow and uphill. Just ask Chipotle…

Standardization is the key. Consistency is a promise that you want to honor with every ounce of your being and brand. Your internet presence, social media, how you answer the phone and greet guests, how drinks are made, how food is prepared, how you say goodbye… If you're not clear on everything that goes into operating your business and keeping your brand promise to your guests, get a pen and paper and write it all down. Remember that you absolutely *must* communicate your brand standards to the team.

Now, if you've allowed your team to become a democracy and the brand standards have slipped, it's time to snap everything back to where it belongs. Draw a line in the sand and remind the team that you're the boss, and you have clear standards. There's no debate; there are no substitutions, there is no compromise if someone wants to remain a member of the team!

When you come across team members who don't feel it's important to be consistent in delivering on your standards, it's your obligation to protect the brand and send them down the road to look for employment elsewhere. Oh, and before you even bother with the excuse that doing so will make you "short-staffed," answer this: What's worse, running short-staffed (which you can control, by the way) or running with a full team that's sabotaging your brand from the inside? Better to see the external wound and deal with it head on; it's internal bleeding that slowly kills restaurants. Remember that it's not the person you fail to hire that kills your brand; it's the person you fail to fire!

3. BE STICKY

What exactly is "stickiness?" It's when your brand has reached a point where it's the preferred choice in your market. That comes from practicing the previous two steps. Without a crystal-clear brand message and consistency in executing your brand promise, you will never become a sticky brand. Instead, that's a great way to become a brand most avoid or ridicule on the internet. Some say that any P.R. is good. Not true. Bad P.R. cuts a brand down in today's ultra-connected world.

Here's the real secret to becoming a sticky brand: It's not about *you* saying how great you are, it's about your *guests* saying how great you are!

Answer this question: Why should I drive to your restaurant?

The answer needs to be unique. It needs to stand out. It needs an emotional element. If you reply with "good food and service," remember that good is the standard today. Good is like getting a "C" on your report card. It's average, and being average isn't memorable or desirable if you want your brand to become sticky. Average isn't where you want to be in today's market. Average is a failing formula. Average, in a word, **sucks**.

So, take a long, hard look at what messages your restaurant brand is sending. Look at it through the eyes of your guests and try to see your brand as they see it. If you see different point of views, you're sending mixed messages that you need to clear up. It's not easy to be objective at times. It's not easy to take a hard look at your flaws. It's even harder to admit that you have flaws and need to make changes. That's why so many restaurants remain the same and eventually fade away.

If you want to grow your restaurant brand and move toward becoming sticky, you need to ask yourself hard questions and seek viable solutions.

*Accept that the definition of insanity
is repeating the same actions
over and over, expecting different
results—time to stop the insanity!*

10-Step Total Menu Makeover

Look at your menu. Go ahead, look at it as if you were casting your eyes upon it for the first time. Is it making a statement that supports your brand identity, or is it crying out for help? Being critical of your restaurant and brand can be downright impossible for some. It's so easy to point out the flaws in other restaurant menus instead of your own. Fight through the urge to resist criticizing your menu so you and your brand can grow.

Your menu is the one thing every guest is guaranteed to look at when they're in your restaurant. In today's world, they may even take a look at it before they step foot in your place. That's why it's so important for you to give it the full measure of respect it deserves. If this were a reality TV show called *Menu Makeovers*, there would be a requirement for you to design a new menu that could *also* act as an amazing calling card.

A brainstorming session is the first step toward making-over your menu. Break this session down into a couple of planning sessions. However, before you get started on any of these steps, check your ego at the door. Don't worry; you can pick it up later. However, you must be objective about what's best for the brand.

Get some blank paper, pencil, and tape. We're going to construct a visual mind map, a thought process, that will set you up for success. When you're ready, embark on the following ten steps.

1. THINK SEASONALLY

Just like we dress seasonally, we tend to eat seasonally. Of course, geography will play a role in this behavior, particularly if you live in a seasonally warm or cold climate. That being said, people who live in areas that don't get to experience changes in the season still crave seasonal foods. Pairing your creative juices with the seasons' traditional harvests or flavors will help you break this process down.

Look ahead to the next season for your menu planning. A huge reason a lot of menu makeovers fail is that the menu planning process isn't given the proper amount of time. Sure, you can roll out a new menu in a few days.

However, you wouldn't be doing justice to the entire process, or your guests. Let's slow down and do this right. Once you get the thought process mapped out, it will move a little faster the next time you decide to change the menu based on the season.

Okay, without overthinking, just write ideas down that relate to the next season. Let's say you're getting ready for summer. Brainstorm some ingredients related to *that* season. Notice that I mentioned just the ingredients and not the dishes. Let's really explore the flavors of the season first.

Here's a trick: Get a copy of either *Culinary Artistry* or *The Flavor Bible* by Andrew Dornenburg and Karen Page. They came up with a great way to list ingredients by season. Let's use their process as inspiration to get the brainstorming started.

Write down any seasonal ingredients that are going to be at their peak. So, if we were looking at summer, our list might include:
- Arugula
- Blackberries
- Salmon

We want to explore the flavors that represent your brand, as well. Everyone will tell you to "think outside the box," but when it comes to your brand, you want to stay within the box. Fusion cuisine quickly becomes *con*fusion cuisine when you start bouncing all around the globe with flavor profiles on your menu. If you're confused about who you are, how do you think your guest will feel?

Let's imagine that we're running a Pacific Rim concept in Southern California. Our flavor profiles could include:
- Thai
- Chinese
- Japanese
- Korean
- Pacific Northwest
- Southern California

Ingredients could include:
- Ginger
- Garlic
- Yuzu
- Gochujang
- Coffee

Now, we start formulating new menu ideas. Maybe from our list, we come up with:

Coffee & Blackberry Lacquered Salmon + Gochujang Brussel Sprouts + Baby Arugula + Yuzu Vinaigrette

We should also include any popular features that proved popular with guests that we offered over the last few months. Features are great ways to get feedback on future menu items. Here's one tip about features: make sure you have them worked-out and thought-out well in advance. Too many features are made up quickly without a lot of thought put into them. You need to approach features as "up-and-coming players" that could be added to your menu lineup if they perform well. Remember, half-assed efforts produce half-assed results.

When you have a list of menu items that could become part of your new menu, it's time for step two: a review of your current menu costs. You need to know where you've been to design a better menu.

2. MENU STRATIFICATION

If you have a modern POS system, you have access to what's known as a product mix report. This report is critical for menu development. Before we get too far into this step, you'll need to make sure that you have your current menu costed out completely. If you want to build a better menu and make more profits, you must know the cost of each menu item. There's no way around this—this is a non-negotiable. <u>If you don't know your costs, you don't know your business.</u>

Try not to only rely on popularity to decide which items should stay and go on a menu. You need to take into consideration the costs *and* popularity. *This is what's known as "menu stratification," and it comes complete with four categories:*

Stars: These are your most highly-profitable and highly-popular items, hence the name. **You always keep the stars.**

Plow horses: These items are low-profitability but highly-popular. Your guests love them. The problem is they don't make a lot of money for you. These menu items could easily become stars if they generated a little more profit. The best way to transform these into stars is to rework them by possibly changing out proteins or adjusting portion sizes to make the dishes more profitable while remaining highly-popular.

Puzzles: These items are highly-profitable yet low in popularity. These items could become stars if you sold more of them. Often these can increase in popularity by changing their descriptions or positioning on the menu.

Dogs: These items are lo- profitability and low-popularity. They don't sell and only cost you money. *Dogs always come off the menu, no matter what.* The problem with a lot of restaurants is that sometimes the dogs are favorites of the chef or owner. **Remember that menus need to be designed for profitability and popularity for the guest, not to feed the ego of the chef or owner.**

Sometimes a picture is worth 189 words:

Menu Engineering

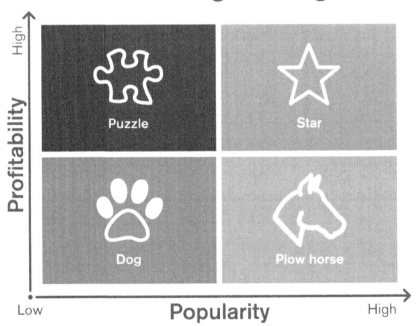

Source: Rewards Network, 2017

There are some cool spreadsheets on the market that can help you with stratification of your menu items. The team over at Toast POS has an easy one you can use, along with instructions on how to use it.

3. UPDATE COSTING

When it comes to menu design, it's easy to get caught up in the creative and fun stuff. It's exciting to brainstorm new menu ideas and explore new flavor profiles. Lest we forget, businesses exist to make a profit. Along with the fun comes the sometimes-dreaded operator tasks, like updating your food costs.

Most modern POS systems have an inventory and cost control feature built into their software.

There are also quite a few food cost programs on the market that you can use, like SimpleOrder, FusionPrep, CostGuard, Ctuit, SynergySuite, and Chefsheet. If you say you're not computer savvy with software, you can still use an Excel spreadsheet. Say you don't like Excel spreadsheets? Then you still have paper and a pen. So, you have no excuse not to calculate and maintain your food costs properly. And, don't forget to consider asking that team member who *is* great at computers for some help.

4. STATION FLOW

Here's an often-overlooked exercise during the menu design process. This tends to be neglected most by those who aren't chefs. You need to understand how many items are going to be prepared from each station in your kitchen. You might have a great list of menu items that you want to add to your new menu but, you need to see how much they're going to impact each station.

An easy way to do this is to look at every item on your menu and designate which station will be responsible for it. Total them up then take another look at the balance of the menu. Restaurants experience longer ticket times when stations get overloaded. If you have a menu with 46 total items and 24 of them come from the grill (and your grill is only 24 inches wide), you might have a problem. What if you have 12 sauté items on your menu and only four available burners in your kitchen? That could cause some problems and a backup on ticket times.

You need to seriously consider the workflow of the kitchen when plotting out the new menu. If you asked the team in the kitchen if they can handle it, of course, they're going to say they can because no one wants to lose their job. The problem will come during Friday night dinner service when the tickets are backed up and food is coming out more slowly than expected. Save yourself a headache (and heartache) by understanding and planning for the flow of the kitchen.

5. LAYOUT

You need to consider all options when it comes to the layout of your menu. Don't take the easy route during this step! Is your menu going to be one page or multiple pages? Letter size, legal size, or tabloid? It's kind of like the dilemma of Goldilocks and the Three Bears, too big, too small, just right.

Here are some things to consider before you get too far into menu layout:

- *People scan menus; they don't read them.* Please don't think you have to explain your brand story on the menu. Most people don't take the time to read it anyway; it just clutters up your overall menu flow.
- *The paradox of choice. Too many items or too many pages can be a little too much.* People do like having choices; that's true. However, when they're given too many choices, they have a difficult time making a decision, and they get frustrated. You can see this when you see a guest flipping back and forth in the menu to shake their head and say, "You know, I'll just have a burger." You just potentially lost a higher sale and a chance to showcase other amazing dishes.

Which is best for your brand? Get some samples and take them into your dining room to see how each one works in your space. If you have smaller tables, then having a large, tabloid-sized menu (11X17) might not be a good idea. While the look is important, so is the functionality of the layout. Is it easy for the guest to use?

6. COLOR

Another thing to consider is color. You need to consider the paper color and fonts (more on that next) you'll be using for your menu. Most menus are designed in the comfort of a well-lit office. You will need to take a sample out into the dining room to see what your menu looks like in "real-world" conditions. That means the corner table around 8:00 p.m. Can you read the menu? Don't force your guests to pull out their smartphones to read your menu.

Font color is important too, yet it's another option that many select by what looks "cool." Some colors don't work well on certain backgrounds. It doesn't matter if it's your favorite color—if you make it hard for guests to read, it's a bad choice.

7. FONT

When it comes to font selection, the same rules for color apply. Make it easy for guests to read instead of selecting a font based on what's cool. The best option is to choose a Serif font because the letters are familiar and distinct. Serif fonts are quite commonly used in popular media venues like books, newspapers, and magazines.

There are thousands of fonts that come in a wide variety of styles, some of which might be tempting like script, decorative, and grunge. For menus, stay away from these; they're hard to read at times, particularly if the font size is small.

Serif fonts (like Times New Roman and Garamond) have little lines at the end of each letter that assists the reader by guiding their eyes across the page. These little lines are referred to as serifs (yes, very clever). Using a Serif font helps the guest read the menu more effectively because there is less contrast between each letter, which can be distracting to the reader. Remember, we want to make reading the menu easy.

Sans serif fonts (like Helvetica) don't have serifs, hence the "sans." With very few exceptions, they're mono-weight, which means that every part of a letter is the same thickness. This style of font if good for item titles. Stay with Serif fonts for item descriptions.

8. MENU PSYCHOLOGY 101

To take this process to the next level, you'll want to know a few key menu psychology terms to ramp up your menu game.

Recency effect: This takes into account that most humans use short-term memory for a variety of daily tasks. It's easier to recall the events of yesterday than the events of the same day last year (unless it has a deep emotional trigger). The same applies to reading menus. Items at the top and bottom of columns tend to stick in the memory more. So, how can we use that? Simple—place your high-profit items at the top and the bottom of columns.

Semantic salience: See this symbol: $? Yeah, the dollar sign. It's probably one of your favorites. A study at Cornell University (Yang et al., 2009) has shown that diners spend more money when you take away that pesky little symbol. It seems that people have an association of pain when it comes to paying.

Priming or The Decoy Effect: This concept again primes the pain pump. You place a similar item with a higher in price right above one with a lower price. The higher-priced item primes the guest into perceiving the lower-priced item to be more of a bargain or deal. Example: You have a buffalo ribeye on the menu for $47. Below that, you have your regular ribeye priced at $35. Be prepared to sell a lot of *regular* ribeyes.

9. PRICING

Pricing is never an easy consideration. You need to consider three key factors when pricing out your menu: what the item cost to make; competition; and what your market will bear. Too many restaurants base their pricing solely on their competitors' prices. How do you know they're making money at their chosen price points? Have you costed out their menu or gotten your hands on their reports? I didn't think so.

A tale of two hamburgers. You can take a gourmet hamburger and sell it in Albuquerque, New Mexico, for $10. You can take that same hamburger 45 miles north to Santa Fe and sell that burger for $14. Why? Because in Santa Fe, the market can handle a $14 hamburger. Make sure to do a competitive price analysis of your market to avoid leaving money on the table.

10. PRINTING

Please, for the love of everything sacred in the restaurant industry, have your menus printed on quality paper using a quality printer. It's easy to understand that sometimes, budgets are tight. Your menu is your number one marketing tool and your calling card. Make sure it represents your brand 100 percent. It's so sad to see a menu that hasn't been given the proper respect it deserves. What does a menu printed on cheap printer paper from a home office printer say to guests?

If you're going to print your menus at least invest in a high-quality printer and high-quality paper. You can get great-looking results using thicker paper known as card stock. **A lot of time and energy goes into designing a menu that represents your brand—don't fall short of the finish line with poor-quality printing.**

Menu design can be an incredibly collaborative, creative, and fun project if you approach it as such. On the other hand, it can be frustrating, exhausting, and sometimes a real pain. It truly depends on your mindset and outlook.

Treat your menu with respect and it will go a long way toward building your brand and increasing your sales.

5 Down and Dirty Menu Tricks

When it comes to getting the most from your menu, how far would you push the edge? Would you make false claims? Would you say you use one brand yet really use a cheaper one?

Don't be so judgmental so fast—sometimes when things get desperate, people get desperate as well. Let's not go to that dark place so quickly. There are plenty of ways you can stimulate menu sales without going all-out crazy like *Breaking Bad's* Heisenberg.

The human mind is a fascinating thing. We can stimulate emotions with our mere thoughts. We can also be fooled quite easily. Now, what I'm talking about here is understanding and using the brain's loopholes to help us out. It's not sinister or evil if you play the psychological brain game *with* menu integrity.

What does that mean?

It means don't lie about ingredients. If you say you use San Marzano tomatoes in your signature sauce, use them. If you say you make your herb-infused vodka for that Martini you rave about, show them the slow-drip system that produces your infusion. If you say you have an 8-ounce beef tenderloin, don't tell your cooks to cut them to 7 ounces because the guests won't know the difference.

There are no shortcuts when it comes to your core values. Once you sell out, it's very difficult to come back. The sad thing is how cheaply most sell out for. Don't be that person!

So, what can you do? Here are five menu hacks that can keep your integrity intact and put more dollars in the bank.

1. PRIME THEM

Marketers take advantage of your subconscious all day long, attempting to highjack it. The image that keeps scrolling across your social media feed. That clever tune that you find yourself singing during the day. You are being *primed to buy* about 10,000 times a day.

When you hear marketers use the term "top of mind," what they're talking about is this concept of priming. Throw many subtle (yet direct) messages out there, and then ask for the sale.

That signature Brown Sugar & Coriander Beef Tenderloin you sell gets blasted (boosted) on all your social media feeds for a solid month with a short message: "You want me." You place a banner or poster at your front door of the same tenderloin with the message: "What are you waiting for?" Now the server comes to the table and mentions the beef tenderloin "will make you feel like you went to Heaven in one bite."

If you do that consistently, you'll see a dramatic increase in the sales mix for beef tenderloins. Repeat as needed to increase the sales of items you want sold.

2. MISDIRECTION

Magicians use this one all the time. You look one direction while they palm a coin or pull a card out from behind their back. Misdirection in restaurants and bars comes when a guest's attention is pulled away from one item to focus on another.

Your server walks up to the table asking for the cocktail order. One guest says that she's thinking of the

Silver Coin Margarita. Her attention is misdirected when the server uses their index finger to point to the Ancho Chile House-Infused Paloma. The server mentions that the bartenders use a slow-drip filtration system very similar to what they use in gourmet coffee shops, and then they point to it behind the bar.

Taking it further, your server adds that the bar staff also adds sliced ruby red grapefruits and herbs to give it a sweet heat flavor, unlike what they do at any other place. It's light, it's refreshing, and if the guest takes a sip and closes their eyes, they'll feel like they're walking along the beach in Cabo. Paloma sold.

3. PLAY ON SHORT-TERM MEMORY

The human brain is wired for survival. Knowing that the slow-moving animal behind that bush was a tiger that jumped out and ate your best friend is a good thing to etch into your memory bank. How the wiring works is good to know when brain-hacking your menu.

How can we use the memory loop to increase menu sales? Let's have a chat about the Recency Effect, also known as the Serial Position Effect.

This effect relates to a person's capacity to accurately recall items on a list and how that ability is dependent on the position of those items on that list. Most people, when asked to recount items from a list, will start with the last items first. This is the recency effect in action! These items are still fresh in their short-term memory, which makes them easier to recall. This can be amplified for your menu by listing the items you truly want to sell at the bottom of a column or by making it the second thing you recommend to a guest.

I call this the Rule of Two. You give them the option of *this* or *that*. It's very easy to implement and very effective.

Here's an example of the classic exchange when ordering a drink at a table:

Server: Would you like something from the bar?
Guest: I'll have a Vodka Tonic.
Server: What kind of vodka would you like?
Guest: What kind of vodka do you have?
[The server begins to recite the list of the 20 different vodkas you carry. Around number six the guest gets a distant look in their eyes. They've stopped listening.]

Here's an easier way to use the Rule of Two:

Server: Would you like something from the bar?
Guest: I'll have a Vodka Tonic.
Server: Grey Goose or Belvedere?

The cool trick is that most will order the second suggestion. Try it and do some field tests for yourself. Change up the order of which one you say second and see the difference in your sales.

4. SHARE A SECRET

Everyone likes an inside secret. Telling guests an item is your favorite or that it's the same item a local celebrity usually orders makes them feel like they're on the inside with the cool kids. We all want to belong and sharing something that may not be common knowledge builds rapport between you and the guests. Anything you can do to deepen rapport increases sales and tips.

Your servers should make eye contact and lean in towards the table like they're about to say something they don't want others to hear. **Sharing instead of reciting makes guest interaction special.**

"Okay, the burger is amazing by itself…but If you want a treat, let me get you a side of our red curry cheese sauce to dip into. It will change your life."

If you were to ask your team it's a sure bet that each member has a few sales techniques up their sleeves they use to sell your menu items. Maybe they change out the vodka in one Martini for the brand they prefer. Allow them to share that with their guests. Allow them to customize the experience to the individual and you'll have something very few restaurants, and bars have today: a reason to return.

5. AVOID SAYING NO

Yes, it should be common sense not to say no. Funny how common sense is not so common. Always look for ways to say yes.

Menus are filled with negative tones and all the things guests can't have:
- No substitutions.
- No split checks.
- No split plates.
- No. No. No.

The less accommodating your menu is, the more appealing a restaurant down the street starts looking.

Can guests be a pain in the ass? Of course—they're human. Humans tend to be that way when they have different expectations than your own. Making it your mission to tell people what they can and can't do via your menu is a one-way trip to a town called Frustrationville.

The problem with placing rules and restrictions on your menu is two-fold:
1. *Most people don't read the fine print on your menu.* Sorry to break this news to you but that mini novel you wrote on the back (or bottom) of your menu is rarely a focal point of interest for most guests.
2. *Words written on menus often lack tone or nuance.* It happens with the written word all the time. It's possible that the tone I intended for this chapter, and the one you're reading it in is different from one another. I can write the same paragraph, have it read by two different people, and get two different reactions to my words. Tone is powerful—it's an important aspect of how we communicate. When it's removed or misinterpreted, people put their tone behind the words, and that's when things can go badly.

Save the drama and headaches by training your team to be menu ambassadors. They should be thoroughly trained (and tested) to know <u>all the details</u> behind each menu item.

- Ingredients.
- Preparation.
- Common allergens.
- Suggestions for paired beverages.
- Suggestions to enhance the meal (up-selling).
- How to handle guest complaints professionally.

Not investing in training your team on your menu is a recipe for failure. Too many put in a lot of time and work into developing menu items and recipes that are meant to wow their guests only to drop the ball on the training end. <u>Your menu is only as good as the training behind it</u>.

Remember, your menu is your number one marketing and profitability tool. Treat it with respect and give your team the resources they need to succeed. You don't need tricks up your sleeve if you set yourself up for success from the start.

There are no shortcuts. You have to do the work—period.

.

Become a Badass (Putting the Lead in Leadership)

"You have enemies? Good. That means you've stood up for something, sometime in your life."

—Attributed to Winston Churchill

The 3 Big Problems with New Restaurant Managers

Managing a restaurant is not all sunshine and rainbows. *(Disclaimer: If you think it is ALL sunshine and rainbows, seek mental help immediately because you suffer from a condition called **delusion**.)* Many new managers find this out the hard way; sometimes through the lackluster results they get when taking control of the management wheel.

If you find yourself in a new management position, take notes. If you're reading this "for a friend," you should take notes and pass them along. Just remember that awareness precedes choice, choice precedes change. You have to realize that there's a problem before you can find a solution. Ignorance is not bliss, it's just ignorance and delusion (see the above note about delusion).

Restaurant success as a manager isn't that complex. Success does leave clues, and so does failure. Time to get out the pen and paper—we're going old school, so take notes!

Now, in this chapter, I'll drop you some not-so-subtle clues you might want to pay attention to. You can tell these clues by the tag #**WTSD**. It stands for **Write This Shit Down**!

These are the three biggest problems facing new managers:

THEY USE OUTDATED MANAGEMENT THEORIES (POOR MODELING)

Your early management style is a style-mashup of every supervisor you've had in your past. It's not good or bad; it's just naturally who we are: creatures that mimic the behavior of those we hang around with the most. It's like the cliques in high school: the athletes hang together, the band kids stick together, and so do the book-smart kids.

I hate to break this to you, but these cliques are a constant in your life, even as you get older. Your peer group largely determines your success level.

Sometimes you'll need to dump your current group if you want more success; water seeks its own level.

Your current management style is a product of your past. Now, if you were extremely lucky (like struck-by-lightning-twice-in-the-same-day lucky), you worked with exceptional leaders that developed your skills and made you a "natural." If you're like the majority, you endured some mental torture that would make waterboarding seem fun!

The most common and outdated management technique out there is "breaking them down to build them back up." Early in my chef career, I thought that was the way to do it. I learned the technique from the chef I worked for in high school—my father. He was a master of the break-you-down mindset. He just wasn't very good at putting people back together part (sounds like a lot of managers). I always wondered why we would have so many new people working at the restaurant. His common reply would be that "they weren't the right fit for the team." Hmmm...**delusion is a powerful mental drug that keeps us stuck in average.**

Solution: If this is your go-to tool for whipping your team into shape, stop immediately. You aren't building a better team; you're tearing your team apart. When I started to see the mass exits of people on my team when I became a chef and restaurant owner, I had a long talk with myself about getting better results.

I never liked it when my father did it to me, so why was I doing it to others? Answer: it was the only management technique I knew. I dropped that outdated tool and picked up a few new ones, like coaching and mentoring.

#WTSD: **You can hold up the standards in your restaurant without being a jerk. You can be firm without insulting people. You can be a leader and not an asshole boss.**

THEY DON'T COMMUNICATE

If you recognize problem number one above, number two is not far behind. We tend to either talk down to others or not communicate at all, assuming they "should know what to do." Well, I have good news and bad news.

Bad News: If they knew what to do, they would probably do it! If your team is not producing the results you want, your duty as a true leader is to keep training them (effectively and clearly) until they *do* know, and it becomes a habit. Does that mean train just until they get it right and say, "That's it, my job is done. They can do the task adequately."? No. Your duty as a leader is to train and train and train and train and train until they can't get it wrong.

How do you replace old habits?

#WTSD: **You keep on repeating the new habit with** *constant, steady pressure* **until the old habit doesn't show up anymore.**

Good News: You have the skill and the power to break old habits. It starts with changing your old habit of not training enough. Change starts with a change to ourselves.

Solution: Up your commitment to communicate more directly to your team. Passive-aggressive emails, text messages, notes in the logbook, or Post-It notes left on the cooler door aren't improving your results—they make your team avoid you. When you finally do speak to them, they have a look of terror on their faces because now you want to talk. Do this test: Walk up to a team member right now and say, "I'd like to talk to you in the office." Note the expression on their face. If they look petrified and their eyes got big...you are not communicating enough with your team. That changes today.

#WTSD: **Talk** <u>with</u> **your team, not** <u>down</u> **to your team.**

THEY THINK SUCCESS COMES FROM HARD WORK

Is success easy? Of course not. But it also doesn't have to be relentless 14- to 16-hour days sacrificing your life to the restaurant. Many new managers think that throwing more hours at their problems will fix them. That's not necessarily the case.

You are human and everyone has a personal limit on how long they can go. It's called internal kinetic energy (think of it as a battery). Some people have boundless energy and can go all day just like the Energizer Bunny! Some people put in two hours at work and start asking if they can take a break.

New managers think long hours are required to get respect.

#WTSD: **Working long hours in a restaurant is not a badge of honor, it's a mark of stupidity, poor planning, a lack of priorities, failure to develop your team, and a fear of saying no. The answer isn't more hours; it's less bullshit. It's facing the truth.**

Solution: Stop buying into the lie that success comes just from hard work. There are a lot of people who work extremely hard only to find that success looks like a mirage on the horizon—they keep chasing after it and never catch it. Success comes from knowing who you are and what you're great at doing. Build a team around you to complement your strengths and make up for your weaknesses. Being a leader is not about being the best at everything; it's about being the best at what you do best. If you suck at spreadsheets, hire someone who loves them and turn them loose! Stop wasting time doing things that do not match these three criteria:

1. Makes you better.
2. Makes your team better.
3. Makes your brand better.

Make yourself better by investing some time for self-care. That means taking some time each day to recharge yourself. Go to the gym, go for a walk, read a book, take 10 minutes to meditate.

#WTSD: **Prioritize your life properly: make time to take better care of yourself.**

Invest in your team members to help them develop and improve their skills. Host a workshop, and bring in a trainer, get your team access to some relevant online training, buy them a book, take them to a food show. Do something that shows your team you want them to grow and develop.

#WTSD: **Investing in your team's development will reduce your turnover.**

Improve your brand by staying on top of the numbers and knowing where your business is every day. You must keep your hands on the pulse of your business, and the heartbeat is found in your P&L. What are your operating costs? What are your food purchases for the week so far? Is anyone approaching overtime? If you don't know the answers to these simple questions, you can't make intelligent decisions that can improve your business.

#WTSD: **If you don't know your numbers, you are part of the problem in your restaurant. Be the solution by getting a grip on your day-to-day numbers.**

Restaurants become better when the people in them become better people. That starts with you as the owner, operator, or leader. Don't wait for things to happen, act, and make them happen.

Become the leader your team craves.

Stuck in a Leadership Rut? Here's How to Pull Yourself Out

Here you are running your restaurant. A leader, just living the dream... Right? Maybe it's not the dream you had. Perhaps some days it seems like a real nightmare that you can't wake up from.

What happened? How did you come to this point? It's quite simple.

You hit an obstacle you didn't know how to navigate, you tried using the skills you had to overcome it, and when that didn't work...you stopped. You threw up your hands and gave the universal signal that you'd had enough by saying these two fate-sealing words: "Screw this." (Or something graphic along that line.) It's tough to be a leader, and if anyone said it was easy, they probably tried to get you into their multilevel marketing scam, too.

Leadership isn't easy. It's a pain in the ass getting people to do things that most of the time they don't want to do. You try to motivate them. You encourage them. You say things like "nice job" or "way to go." Still, they seem to fall back into old habits and routines as soon as you stop watching them.

You scream up to the heavens for a break. You have bought so many books on becoming a leader that they pile up on your coffee table at home because you've read only the first chapter of each one. You might even start going to a medicine man for a magic talisman.

When things are not going your way, you can get desperate. When desperation doesn't work, you get angry. **When anger doesn't work, you give up.**

And now here you are, beaten down and questioning if you should've listened to your mother and gone to medical school. Yeah, it's a bitch when you seem to lose your leadership mojo. Let's get you out of this depressing funk you're in and get that magic back!

Sometimes the tactics that got you to the point where you are now aren't the same tactics that are going to carry you across the "leadership gap." Now, before you quip and say you don't have a leadership gap, let me assure you that every leader has one. *The denial of having a gap in your leadership skills is the first one!*

That edgy, aggressive tone and attitude, and your sheer willpower can get you past the others and into a leadership spot fast. But those same traits will have your team turning on you faster than hungry rats on a block of cheese! Time to back off the attitude and switch to some decaf herbal tea.

STEP ONE: IT'S NOT ABOUT YOU

This one is a hard one to swallow, particularly if the crowd around you has sung your praises and offered to write poems about your legendary leadership. The worst thing any leader can do is get a head (or ego) so big that others turn away and silently mouth the word "wow."

Your hard work may have raised you to the top but it's the team you build around you that will keep you there. People love to see a big, egocentric leader fall from the top—just look at any major news channel.

They cover those stories faster than a wildfire can spread.

Yes, you can take pride in your accomplishments. Just don't think you're the Lone Ranger doing it all by yourself. Even he had a sidekick. Restaurants and bars thrive when the team shares in the struggles, and the wins.

If you ask people to name someone they thought was an outstanding leader and what about that person made them outstanding, here's what they would say: "They made me feel like I was important."

Everyone has an innate need to feel appreciated. We all need to feel wanted and that we matter. Outstanding leaders go out of their way to make the team shine brighter than they do. If you're struggling to get your team to follow you, it's a simple fix: allow them to shine. Try a little less focus on yourself and a lot more on them.

STEP TWO: LET GO OF CONTROL (A LITTLE)

Another big leadership gap is the ability to let go of the metaphorical steering wheel on which you have a death grip. The white knuckles I see on your hands tell me you run your restaurant like Attila the Hun ran his army.

Stop watching *Game of Thrones* and thinking everyone on your team is conspiring to hurt your brand. If you truly and 100 percent think someone who works for you is going to sabotage your organization, why in the world do you keep them on your payroll?

This gap is mostly seen when leaders go from one location to two or more. You can't be everywhere all the time. You can try, but you'll soon find yourself in another bad situation called burnout. You're going to need to lighten up on the death grip and allow your team to carry the ball.

That doesn't mean letting go of the wheel completely. It means you need to set and standardize your expectations, so they know—without question or hesitation—what they need to do and exactly how to do it. And this is where many leaders go astray: they don't communicate clearly, consistently, and constantly. You need to do all three.

Be clear. Don't assume your employees know what you want. Spell out what's required of them. Write it down, verbalize it, and demonstrate the proper way.

Be consistent. Maintain the same story and standards. Changing how you do things every other day may be your prerogative as a leader, but it will drive your team bat-shit crazy. Most people like routine; they crave it.

Be constant. I know you told them once already. Most people need quite a few reminders before something sinks in. Here, you need to be like a broken record and say things over and over and over and over and over and over until it becomes an unconscious new behavior (*also known as a habit*).

STEP THREE: YOU GOTTA BELIEVE

Okay, you've toned down the ego and attitude. You've started to allow your team to take on more responsibilities. Now, it's time for the hardest part—you gotta believe in your brand and your team.

Trust doesn't come easy in our industry if you've been around for any amount of time, you surely have seen some shit that reality TV producers would love to film. Betrayal, stealing, fights, and enough drama to fill a couple hundred books. It's a wild ride at times. Along this journey, you've been taken advantage of and deceived quite a few times. You carry those emotional scars inside, and you've built a nice defense mechanism to cope: *you don't trust many people.*

When people have wronged you in the past, it says more about their poor character and low self-worth than it could ever say about your character. Why are you dragging around the painful, disturbing ghosts of the past? They're valuable lessons, but you only need to take what you've learned with you; leave behind the pain — time to leave the negativity in the past where it belongs.

People, for the most part, want to do a good job. They want responsibility (*at least some*). They want to take pride in what they do. When you don't trust them and micromanage them to death, you deny them the opportunity to grow. Lack of growth and appreciation are the two leading causes of turnover. They might say it's because the place down the street offered them more money, but the truth is they felt you didn't trust them, and they were being suffocated slowly by your constant verbal berating.

If you don't trust your team, you don't have a team. Instead, you have a bunch of mercenaries that job hop to the highest bidder. If you don't show them trust and loyalty first, they will never return it. Now, you can take the stand that they need to earn those things, and if that's your approach, let me ask you one simple question: "How's that working for you?" That's what I thought—not very well.

Change your attitude first. When you do that and remain committed to the new path, you'll see your team change too. How do you change a restaurant? It happens when the leader changes their attitude.

WATCH OUT FOR THE RUT

Everyone gets stuck in a rut at some point in their life. The difference between winners and losers is that winners realize they're in a rut and take immediate action to get out. Losers stay down there, wallowing in the rut. They whine, kick, and complain until that shallow rut has now become their grave. You see, what separates the two is only the depth.

Don't allow your leadership rut to become your leadership grave. Believe me when I warn you that there are plenty of ambitious people just waiting to start shoveling dirt on you if you stay down too long. Don't worry if they do because they'll soon be stuck in the same leadership rut.

The leadership bell tolls for us all at one time or another. Now that you are aware, you have the power to change the situation when it arises...if you so choose.

5 Traits of Great Leaders

Greatness is not something to take lightly. In the world of restaurants, it can be said that the majority only rise to the level of being good. In today's food industry, the last thing you want to be is just good.

Being good is a death sentence in a highly competitive market. Why do so many restaurants close? Being good plays a big part.

Another reason is lack of leadership. As the market reaches the saturation breaking point, we have started to serve our death sentence because we hired and promoted people into management roles that neither have the training nor the temperament to be leaders. Our industry is at a crossroads, and the solution is for people to step up, grab the wheel of leadership, and drive toward a promising future!

When you study restaurant leadership, you start to see there are common traits shared by great leaders. You might have some or all of these traits already. The lack of leadership afflicting the restaurant industry suggests, however, that you most likely lack at least a couple of these great leadership traits. Don't worry! It's never too late to adapt and learn. Admitting you have some work to do on yourself is a sign of strength.

1. ADAPTABILITY

The greatest human trait, in my opinion, is our ability to adapt. Adaptation is what took us from our primitive beginnings to our modern advancements. Adapting is natural, yet many seem to resist it. We seek comfort and routine, but for a restaurant leader, comfort is like a frog sitting in a room temperature pot of water on a burner that's slowly climbing in temperature. The frog gets comfortable, not realizing the danger it's in until it's too late and they become frog soup.

Great leaders stretch themselves first, then drive their team to become better. Failing to reach one's potential is the greatest waste in life. Leadership is about developing and playing to your natural strengths. Everyone has natural strengths, and leaders understand theirs, then position their teams around them to accent and enhance those strengths.

2. KAIZEN

After World War II, Japan was coming back from the devastation of their collapsed economy. An American named Dr. Deming came to their assistance, helping to get the country going again. He introduced a *concept of constant and never-ending improvement to the workforce*. That concept is known to the Japanese as *kaizen*.

The word has become a part of their culture and contributed to their return to economic stability. The Japanese technology and automotive industries, in particular, used the philosophy of Kaizen to dominate world markets.

Great leaders harness the same mindset to constantly look for opportunities to make small improvements to their teams, systems, and strategies, to stay ahead of the competition. Some people follow trends and those who *create* trends. Incorporating kaizen for your restaurant's culture is the best way to avoid complacency and mediocrity. Nothing good comes from being complacent.

3. COMMUNICATION

When you look at the heart of the problems, drama, and chaos that seem to infect our industry, you find that poor communication is the underlying issue. Great leaders always go out of their way to communicate with their teams and guests. Implied expectations are the downfall of most managers.

Does that mean great leaders repeat themselves over and over? Yes. Leadership requires constant, clear, and honest communication with those you serve in the position you hold.

4. PERSONAL ACCOUNTABILITY

It's hard to hold others accountable if you can't first hold yourself responsible. Great leaders truly understand that culture is the result of modeled behavior—their behavior. People are great mimics and are wired to behave like others. Collective consciousness, group-think, and the hive mindset are examples of how we model the behaviors of our coworkers and peers. Your team will imitate your behavior.

If you want to be a great leader, it all starts with accountability for your actions. Say you're going to do something, but you don't follow through? Your team remembers that. You say being punctual is important, yet you stroll in late pretty much every day? The lesson your team learns is that being on time isn't as important as you say it is, and the value of your word continuously diminishes.

Great leaders always hold themselves to higher standards than they do for others. How you behave, and act will become valuable examples for your team one way or another; you can be a leader to emulate or a fool to ignore. Your results depend on your actions, not just the words you say. Talk is truly cheap.

5. O.A.D. - OBSESSIVE ATTENTION TO DETAIL

To become outstanding—*and only 5 percent ever will*—you must sweat the small stuff. Obsession gets a bad reputation as something sinister. That perception is misguided. Properly channeled, obsession is akin to a light being transformed into a powerful laser.

You want to use the power of obsession to reach a higher level of development, and that requires you to have an O.A.D. Great leaders all have an **Obsessive Attention to Details**. They nurture a high sense of total situational awareness when it comes to their brands. "There's a water glass missing on table four." "The door to the private dining room has a scuff mark at the bottom." "The hostess seems preoccupied with something and isn't her normal cheerful self."

These little details, when stacked on top of one another, can create an outstanding guest experience. Being O.A.D. requires diligence and a constant scanning of the environment to ensure everything is how it must be. Standards are created to keep everyone dialed-in for consistent results. Great leaders notice variances in brand standards, and they speak up immediately to get the team back on track.

It's not very complicated to rise to the top of this industry because so many restaurants perform at an average level—it doesn't take much to pass them up. *Staying on top*, now that's a different story.

Remaining at the top once you've reached it is more a question of your character and ability to model the five traits that all outstanding leaders have in common.

The Vital Element Missing in Restaurant Leadership

The title on your business card may indicate that you're the leader and you may even truly see yourself as one, but the reality is often the opposite, unfortunately. We tend to think that being a leader is about the title or even tenure, but many people aren't the amazing leader they think they are.

There are a few important elements inherent to the title of leader; some are well known; others are elusive. The right combination will make a leader truly stand out. There's plenty of mediocrity floating around in the restaurant industry today. If you want to be a leader in your restaurant, aim to be outstanding.

SELF-AWARENESS

Many leaders are great at reading and understanding others. People skills are seen as a trait of a leader, and it's true—they're important. You need to be able to relate to others and inspire them to take action and grow.

The other side of the coin, however, is that many overlook the importance of self-awareness. Chinese philosopher Lao Tzu once said, "*Knowing others is intelligence; knowing yourself is true wisdom.*" You must know your strengths, weaknesses, and where the opportunity for personal growth lies.

I'm not going to let you forget that awareness precedes choice, choice precedes change. When you become self-aware, able to acknowledge your strengths—and what you suck at—you'll be in a position to make better choices. That has the potential to create positive change in your restaurant and your life.

TRUST

Few things destroy relationships faster than broken trust. Trust builds teams, period. If you don't trust your team, you don't have a team! What you have is a bunch of mercenaries who only look out for themselves. Without a team, what's the point of there being a leader?

The basis of trust is giving it freely. People usually rise to our level of expectations. If you don't trust them, they tend to let you down. They'll also come to be distrustful of *you*. **Trust lives in a realm of reciprocity—you only get it when you give it.**

FOCUS

The restaurant industry can be a whirlwind at times. The energy and excitement of service can become an addictive wave of endorphins that flood our senses. Many compare the rush of service to the stimulation provided by fast-paced video games. That rush can lead to desensitization for slower times.

Have you noticed that many of the mistakes you encounter occur when your restaurant is slow? Why do you think that is? It's partially due to leaders losing focus during slower times because things seem as though they're under control.

Think of it like this: If you were driving down the highway at 75 m.p.h. for an extended period and then entered a 55-m.p.h. Speed zone, you'd feel as though you were suddenly going very slowly. 55 m.p.h. isn't slow; the change in speed has caused a cognitive imbalance in your perception.

Leaders must always maintain focus and adjust the pace. True leaders kick up the team's energy to keep everyone on task and carry momentum through the slower times.

COMMUNICATION

As you've likely gathered by now, I believe that all business problems are people problems in disguise. I also believe that 99 percent of people problems in restaurants are communication problems. Communication is either poor or it's entirely lacking. *A true leader goes out of their way every day to communicate exactly what's expected of the team.*

Am I saying have you to be a broken record and repeat yourself over and over? Yes, you do, until your team can perform at the (hopefully incredibly high) level you've set. And once they've reached that level, you must keep preaching from your soap-box — Every – Single – Day.

True leaders never say, "Well, my team should just know that." If they knew it, they would do it. Assumption is the root cause of communication issues.

COURAGE TO BE THE LEADER

It takes courage to be a true leader. It's a humbling experience to step up and take personal accountability for your actions. It's brave to admit when you don't know something. It's rewarding when you can inspire others to change their lives. It's hard to stay true to your core values when others sell out their integrity.

Being a leader may not be financially rewarding. **Remember that being a leader isn't about a title; it's about action.** It's about taking conscious action to help another person become their best, while at the same time being *your* best!

What's the number one element missing in restaurant leadership today, you ask?

It's the raw courage needed to stand there and say, "I own this."

A True Leader Doesn't Wait to Change Their Restaurant

Every year it's the same story. Come January 1; things will be different! You'll make those changes you talked about endlessly last year. You've made a declaration to the world that this is your year, and you mean it this time. Again.

Here's the question: Why wait?

Oh, it's not the right time? The truth is that time isn't concerned with being convenient; it just keeps ticking away.

Do you need to pull a few things together first? Really? Like what? This stalling tactic is just a fancy version of the classic "I'll do it tomorrow" excuse. Of course, tomorrow will be so busy—because that's life— that you'll throw out that classic excuse again, pushing changes to tomorrow, again. And the tomorrow after that. And the one after that… again and again and again.

Stop making fucking excuses and move forward with the changes you know you need to make.

MARKET MORE

The longer you wait to up your marketing game, the harder it is to play the game. More and more new restaurants open every day, and that's competition. They don't want to play nice; they want to take your market share. The longer you wait to change and improve, the more market share you give away to your competitors. If your brand isn't top of mind with your guests, you'll soon be forgotten.

McDonald's is a well-known global brand. Do you see them stopping their marketing machine because everyone knows who they are by now? No way! They want those Golden Arches embedded deep inside your unconscious.

When you stop seeing McDonald's marketing campaigns, you can slow down because it will mean the world has ended. **Until then, press your marketing accelerator to the floor!**

How? Here are three short tips:

1. *Double-down on your posts.* Double the number of posts on social media for the next 30 days and see if you notice a difference.
2. *Boost your reach.* Social media platforms know they wield immense power for reaching the world, so they're constantly changing their algorithms to keep things exciting. (Basically, they change the rules just when you've figured them out.) You need to track which organic posts have resulted in the best reach and boost them to penetrate your market further.
3. *Play the trifecta.* You need to use at least three platforms to reach a wider market. Facebook is hot but it's just one of many. Look at your brand and consider Twitter, Instagram, Pinterest, and Snapchat. Think of it like a composed plate: you need an entree, a starch, and a vegetable to balance it out. It's the same for social media. One is your center of the plate and the other two are designed to support it.

KILL THE VAMPIRES

You see them, the negative energy vampires that are sucking the life out of your restaurant's culture. The A-level players loathe them because they have to pick up their slack. Guests cringe when they see them coming to their table to tell them about the terrible week they're having. You gasp when you see the paycheck you have to sign when all they've managed to do is cause drama. So, why tolerate them?

Will you be short staffed? Will you have to work their station? Are you afraid to let them go?

It's time to face all those fears because you created this situation when you failed to recruit consistently. You didn't become the recruitment machine you needed to be to build a pipeline of applicants, and now you're reduced to hiring out of desperation. You *never* want to hire only when you need to fill an empty spot—that's how you build a team of mostly C-level players.

#WTSD: **"What you put up with, you end up with."**

Time to get rid of those that are draining the life-blood from your restaurant.

ALL YOU NEED IS LOVE

Don't get all tearful just yet. This means that you must take care of yourself. There's a connection between your self-care and the energy in your restaurant. The hospitality business is all about being the consummate host (the word itself comes from "*hospes*," which means, you guessed it, "host"). We give so much to others in this business, yet we fail miserably at taking care of ourselves.

Most New Year's resolutions revolve around "finally getting in shape" or "joining a gym." Why wait?

Surely the gym in your neighborhood wouldn't turn you away, telling you to wait until next year to join.

There's no greater gift you can give to yourself, your family, your team, and your guests than the gift of self-care. What, no gym in your town? Surprise! Self-care is not just about the physical game. *It's even more critical to focus on your mental game!*

How? I'm glad you asked...

- Meditation (yes, there are mobile apps that make it easy)
- Reading (books or blog posts are a good start)
- Audiobooks (feed your mind)

Still want some exercise? Try these:

- Rebounders (these small trampolines are easy to set up in your house or apartment, no gym required)
- Walk (there's a big, beautiful world out there—you should check it out)

If you're looking at your goals for next year and they don't move you to take action *today*, I have some bad news for you—*they're not big enough*!

Big, audacious goals are required if you really want to be motivated to achieve them. Dig deeper and come up with a compelling goal that you can't resist. Avoid goals that you work toward simply out of a sense of obligation or that you only *think* you want. You need to crave accomplishing your goals like it's the last meal you'll ever have!

The power to change your restaurant isn't held captive by tomorrow or next year, it's in the actions you take today. Like, right now today!

3 Things to Never Say as a Restaurant Manager

We all get frustrated from time to time working in restaurants and bars. Emotions can run rampant, and things can escalate fairly quickly. If you've been in the industry for any amount of time (a veteran), you have surely heard a few things that would make some people do a double-take. I know I have.

Words have power. They can build a team or tear one apart. The sad thing is that sometimes damage happens so quickly it can have a ripple effect across your brand. Once those words leave your mouth and are spoken aloud, they tend to become a self-fulfilling prophecy. So, **watch what you say to your team because it tends to become a karma boomerang!**

Here are three things you should never say to your team:

"I HAVE TO DO IT ALL MYSELF."

Really? Do you have to do it all? People tend to make big claims that border on extremes. You've probably used a few other phrases that fit into this category as well. You "always" are late or you "never" clean up your station. When you shame people, you break trust, and without trust, you have no team.

If you keep telling your team that you have to do it all yourself, you will eventually make that prophecy come true. If you don't trust them to make and learn from mistakes, you have taken away a critical element of human nature—the ability to be fallible (and the powerful opportunity to learn).

We learn when we don't get it right the first few times, and for some people, the learning curve is even longer. Not everyone is a carbon copy of you, and that's a good thing. There's nothing scarier than everyone being the same. **Variety is the spice of life and the recipe for a dynamic team**. It's differences that build a high-performance team, not the similarities.

So, before you spew this saying out to your team, take a little reality check. You don't have to do it all yourself; you choose to do it because you lack trust in your team. Get over it and give your team some room to grow.

Now, with that also comes some responsibility on your end to coach, train, and set clear, defined expectations that can be measured. Without crystal-clear expectations you will not get the results you are seeking, and the statement, "I have to do it all myself," will resurface. *Stop it by being a leader and not a whiner about the standards you failed to set for your team.*

"HOW MANY TIMES DO I HAVE TO TELL YOU?"

This one is usually accompanied with either an exhale of frustration or an eye roll (sometimes both). Maybe they didn't understand the task at hand. The real question here is: Did you explain it or assume they knew how to do it? Assumptions consistently get us into trouble very quickly.

How many times have you hired a bartender and assumed they knew how to make drinks correctly? You start them off on a busy night, and you start getting complaints about some of the drinks. Yeah, they know how to make a Manhattan. They don't know *your* way to make one.

All business problems are people problems in disguise. Those people problems are 99 percent related to communication. It's your duty as an owner or leader in your restaurant or bar to communicate your core values, standards, and expectations (yes, not clearly stating expectations is a big contributor of communication problems).

Sometimes this problem is wrapped up in the generalization that your employees should know what you expect. Well, if they are not doing it the exact way you want it to be done, then they don't know! *They don't get it because you have not taken the time to explain it to them.* The time you take now will save you loads of time and frustration later.

The results you experience in your restaurant or bar are in direct proportion to the quality of your communication skills. That is not an exaggeration; it's the truth. If you want a better brand, become obsessed with communicating with your team better. **No bullshit, it's life changing.**

"I BUST MY ASS AROUND HERE."

Do you want some cheese to go with your whine? Seriously, your team does not want to hear about how hard *you think you work.*

You might be there long hours, however many of those hours are most likely not as "back busting" as you claim. When you really have nothing left, and you've truly pushed your body to the extreme, one of three things happen: you either pass out, you black out, or you die. If you do not experience one of those three, then you always have more to give.

People love to play the martyr and want sympathy from others. Here is an observation from 39 years in the industry: If you make it a point to tell others how hard you work, then chances are you are not working that hard. It's much like a magician who employs distraction: "Look over here, so you don't *really* see what I am doing." You tell others you are so busy, yet the results speak for themselves. Stop lying to yourself (and others) and do your job.

An adage of which you should be aware as an operator is Parkinson's Law, which states that work expands or contracts to meet time obligated. That means if most people are given a few tasks and 8 hours to accomplish them, they'll take the full 8 hours. If you give them the same tasks and only 6 hours to finish, they can usually get those things done in the time required. You're not managing your attention properly and end up getting pulled in so many directions that you *don't run your restaurant; it runs you.*

Once again, your team doesn't care how hard you think you work. They want a leader who is going to be out front, leading and setting the example without the whiny martyr tone.

AWARENESS PRECEDES CHOICE, CHOICE PRECEDES CHANGE

These statements are usually unleashed towards your team when your energy is low, and emotions run high. Everyone has natural energy peaks and valleys throughout the day. You need to become aware of these times throughout the day so you can be on guard for those moments when your energy is low, and the team comes around asking questions or venting about their day.

Yes, your team will sometimes vent about things that frustrate them. This is not the time for one-upmanship and launching into a rendition of, "You think that's bad, let me tell you about _____ [fill in the blank]". As a leader, your duty at times is to listen to your team and not always find an answer right away. A wise person once noticed that we have two ears and one mouth... *There might be a reason for that.*

Now, what do you do when you feel those emotions rising, and you know you're about to say something that you'll regret later? Here are a couple of solutions.

REMEMBER TO PAUSE AND PROCESS

Before one of the three problem phrases above slips out, you have a brief window of opportunity to shut your mouth and say nothing. Use a trigger phrase like "**pause and process.**" This little safety net of a saying can help you avoid situations in which you will need to apologize.

If you can avoid a problem by not saying anything, you should give it a try. There's nothing wrong with saying, "That's interesting. Please allow me some time to pause and process what you said."

CALL A TIME OUT

When emotions are running hot, it's a good idea to hold your hands up and give the sign for a time out. Say, "Can we take five minutes and think about this? I want to be able to give you my full attention."

Now, if the person is pushing you, call for a bathroom break! "Hey, can I use the restroom quickly and then we can discuss?" Unless the person is Hannibal Lecter, they most likely will allow you time to hit the restroom. Use the time to either really use the restroom or just throw some water on your face, take a few deep breaths, and get a grip on your emotions.

You are human and human beings are emotional creatures. Make sure that as a leade,r you are constantly striving to be in control of your emotions. Robert Greene, in his legendary book, *The 48 Laws of Power*, talks about controlling your emotions as a foundational element of power:

"The most important of these skills, and power's crucial foundation, is the ability to master your emotions. An emotional response to a situation is the single greatest barrier to power, a mistake that will cost you a lot more than any temporary satisfaction you might gain by expressing your feelings. Emotions cloud reason, and if you cannot see the situation clearly, you cannot prepare for and respond to it with any degree of control."

Get control of your emotions and your words before they cause havoc within your restaurant or bar. Avoid emotional reactions that cause you to lose credibility with your team.

Lose credibility, and it's game over.

5 Myths About Restaurant Leadership - Busted

You've made it to the top! Congratulations! Before you get too comfortable, let's see if your leadership game is on-point. *Being called* a leader and *being* a leader is, at times not one and the same. With so many restaurants opening each year, the strain on the labor pool is becoming an epidemic. We struggle to fill leadership positions, and one reason may be that we don't understand true leadership.

Undeclared expectations and undefined responsibilities are the most common culprits of this lack of understanding. We need to do a better job talking about what makes someone a true leader. There are a lot of myths out there about leadership. **To understand what leadership is** *we must understand what it is not.*

MYTH #1: LEADERSHIP IS A TITLE.

Truth: Leadership is not about the title—at all. True leadership is available to anyone. Too many people like to pull rank. It's the classic ego-driven mindset of "I'm the [insert job title here] and you're not!" This mindset creates fear and intimidation in a restaurant. Culture turns toxic, and people jump ship as soon as they find anything that appears to be better.

Leadership is about taking action and personal accountability. You can't sit on the sidelines, not playing in the game, hoping that you will somehow win. Leaders value action over words. How can you spot a leader? By the words they use. True leaders avoid statements that start with "they," "why," and "when." True leaders do not focus on blame or shame:

"*They're* stupid."

"Why don't *they* get it?"

"When will *they* start to follow the checklist I made?"

Ask questions that have a "poor me" attitude, and you'll get exactly what you ask for.

Instead, true leaders take personal accountability and ask questions like:

"What can *I* do to train my team better?"

"What can *I* do to clarify my expectations and standards?"

"What can *I* do to ensure the team understands and is appreciated for using, the checklists?"

Empower yourself and your team by stepping up and acting like a leader. **Leadership doesn't require a title.**

MYTH #2: LEADERSHIP IS LONELY.

Truth: It can be lonely if you're not a true leader. When some people think of leadership, they view it as a straight, vertical line with them at the top. They bark orders down the Leadership Line, and that militant chain of command flows from one person to the other, and vice versa. For leadership to grow in your culture, it needs to feed the Leadership Circle, not break it.

Leadership is about energy, and when you're the leader, you set the tone and fuel the energy of your culture. In the Leadership Circle, you're in the center, and your energy radiates outward, impacting everyone on your team. Communication flows openly and is transparent. The team trusts each other in the circle. They talk *with* each other, not *down* to each other as they do in the Leadership Line model).

Leaders that think it's lonely at the top choose to be isolated. They build mental barriers between themselves and their teams. People look to the leader for inspiration and the behaviors they must model. They won't be inspired or behave how you want them to if you play the martyr card and separate yourself from them by hiding in your office. Face-to-face time with your team transforms restaurants from mediocre to outstanding. Oh, and don't forget the power of expressing sincere thanks.

MYTH #3: LEADERSHIP IS NATURAL.

Truth: While some people take to the concept of leadership faster than others, no one is born with all the skills required to be a leader. Sometimes those with natural skills don't feel a need to develop and reach their highest potential.

Natural skills are, at times, a curse, because you become comfortable. You see some results and feel satisfied. True leaders are never content with where they are now—they have an unrelenting drive to learn, grow, and improve. In today's competitive market, becoming satisfied with the status quo is an invitation to mediocrity, the slow death of a restaurant.

In the martial arts, many see getting their first-degree black belt as the end goal. Once they reach that level, that's it—they know it all. Those people don't understand that obtaining that belt is a statement: now they're ready for the real learning to begin. The same goes for making it into a leadership role: now, the real work begins. True leaders don't rest on their laurels thinking, "they've made it" or "they've paid their dues," and it's time to kick-back.

Leadership is about constantly pushing to become the best version of yourself.

MYTH #4: LEADERSHIP IS HARD.

Truth: Leadership, particularly poor leadership, can certainly be challenging at times. No one ever said being a true leader was easy — this where the **5 Cs of leadership** come in.

Certainty: You must be 100 percent certain that you want to be the leader. Don't take the job for the money, take the job because you want to make an impact!

Clarity: You must set goals and have a crystal-clear vision of where you want the brand to go. It's like being dropped off in the middle of the forest with a map and compass but no destination in mind— you'll end up wandering. You need to know where you're going so you can create an action plan to get you there!

Confidence: Arrogance is different than confidence. One is internal; one is external. Confidence comes from your own beliefs that you can and will do the job. Arrogance is external and is all about boasting to others about your skills. One is all talk, and the other is all action. Choose wisely.

Conviction: There will be times when you question yourself and your goals. You'll be pushed to the point of quitting. Don't. You must get through the valleys if you want to make it to the summit of your goals.

Courage: You must be able to face your fears and hear hard truths. Remember that the truth will set you free, right after it first pisses you off. Face times of fear and doubt straight on with the one thing you have that no one can take from you: your inner strength.

Leadership is not hard; it requires focus and determination, setting goals, conviction, and courage to reach your goals. You've got this.... go out there and light the world on fire!!

MYTH #5: LEADERSHIP IS ABOUT HAVING ALL THE ANSWERS.

Truth: Leadership is never about having all the answers; it's about asking the **right questions**. If you find that you're always the smartest person in the room, you need a different room. Make sure you have people in your life who are a positive influence. Join a mastermind group. Get a mentor. Hire an executive coach. Read more books or listen to audiobooks. Commit to becoming a better person.

Many people think that once they reach the top of their organization, that's it. That's only true if your ambition is limited. True leadership thrives on growth, learning, and self-improvement. Some days you might experience significant growth. Other days, you may feel like you've only experienced a minuscule amount. Either way, you're still moving forward, always improving.

True leadership is about being honest. If you don't know something, admit that you don't know it. Then, search for the truth. Leaders gain more respect when they show that they're human. As mentioned before, it takes courage to be a leader and admit you may not have all the answers.

If you're currently a leader in your organization, take a hard look at these myths. They could be what's holding you back from reaching the next level; so, dump them. If you're not officially in a leadership role but aspire to be, what's stopping you? True leadership doesn't require a title; it only requires that you take personal accountability for your actions.

All you need to do is step up.

Stop Running Your Restaurant from the Rearview Mirror

When you look at your venue and your life, is your attention on the right things? Are you focusing on what's in front of you instead of looking behind you at all times?

Your mind does an incredible job of playing tricks on you. Even when you know your attention should be on the present so you can achieve in the future, your mind can draw you into replaying your past on a loop.

The mistakes you've made can become restless spirits that haunt you day after day. They make you question everything and turn your once confident behavior into a game of second-guessing.

Would have.

Could have.

Should have.

Living your life and running your restaurant by looking back constantly is never a good strategy. When the past pulls you backward, you lose your focus on the present and moving forward. You're stuck in a mental time warp where you replay scenarios and try to rethink what you should have done. The problem is that staying in the past makes you a prisoner. It doesn't matter what you do in your head; that past is not going to change.

Welcome to the land of suffering.

You suffer because you just won't let that shit go. So, why do we hold on to the past? There are a few reasons.

I was talking to a client the other day about holding on to the past even though they know it's not good for them. The past, even if it's painful, is comfortable. There's a saying that sums this up: **better the devil you know than the devil you don't**. Fear of the unknown is sometimes overwhelming to those who crave consistency in their lives.

Study human needs theory, and you'll see we all have six needs that must be fulfilled. These are not wants; they are *core needs*. Whether we achieve a happy outcome or make it a suffer fest is dependent on how we go about getting our needs met.

Here's a quick rundown of those six human needs:

1. *Certainty.* It's our need to feel in control and know what's coming next so we can feel secure. It's the need for basic comfort, the need to avoid pain and stress, and the need to create pleasure. Our need for certainty is a survival mechanism.

2. *Uncertainty.* While we want certainty, we also have a need for a little variety in life. It keeps us on our toes. Yes, life is paradoxical at times.

3. *Significance.* We all need to feel important, special, unique, or needed. Some bully others to feel significant, the wiser folks lift others as a leader or coach.

4. *Love and/or Connection.* This is like oxygen for the soul. We need love, and when we don't get it, we settle for its cousin: connection. That's why you have so many social media followers you don't know—you want to be connected.

5. *Growth.* Call it an evolutionary trait to evolve and adapt. Humans have an innate need to grow and become better. There's an old saying that if you're not growing, you're dying. #truth

6. *Contribution.* Giving back is the highest human need. People with this need see the "we" before the "me." It's also about sharing and having a purpose in your life.

The first four are your primary needs. The last two are higher-level needs. Everyone has the first four needs met one way or another; some get the last two. Those who are most fulfilled in life seek to grow and contribute. Most have that equation backwards, which is exactly why they get stuck running their restaurants while looking in the rearview mirror feeling frustrated, lonely, and stressed.

And if you think you don't have these human need cravings, bullshit. If you're human you have them; you want them, you *need* them. Clinging to the past is trying to meet two human needs: *certainty and connection.*

Certainty is comfortable. It like that favorite sweater you wear that has the holes in it. It's that movie you've watched 20 times and know the ending word for word because it still makes you feel good inside. We all crave the good old days. However, if you really sat down and honestly examined all the seconds from those good old days, you might be shocked to see that they weren't always so good. Many of those times sucked! Take a long, hard look back for a second, and it might not be the rose-colored world you once thought.

Connection is the strongest of human needs. We all want to connect to other people and feel like we matter. We want to feel like someone cares. You're hardwired for this from the time you're born. Infants who don't get enough tactile stimulation can die from a condition called Failure to Thrive (FTT; Jaffe, 2011).

We need human connections. Combine that with certainty, and it's a recipe to stay connected to people even though doing so may not be in your best interest. *You keep a person who impacts your life negatively around a little longer than you should. You smoke or drink, not because you want to but because you don't want to lose connection.* Don't make yourself suffer anymore. When you're around people in your personal and professional lives, make sure you **surround yourself with only those who elevate you**. Avoid the negative energy vampires at all costs!

Here a simple test to see if that person on your team or in your life is a good match: It's either a "Hell yes" or a "Hell no." Don't waste time or energy if you're somewhere in between!

When you focus too much on the past and all the things that could go wrong, you fail to operate your restaurant from growth and opportunity. Instead, you become obsessed with your past and not making the same mistakes. You don't take risks. You don't make the changes needed to rise above the competition. You end up losing it all.

The past needs to be put exactly where it belongs...*behind you.* When you focus on it too much, you lose the gift the current day offers. Try driving your car forward while only looking in your rearview mirror, and I think you'll get the picture: You're so focused on where you've been and what you've done (or haven't done) that you don't enjoy things that are happening now. You're so lost in the past that you can't see the opportunities in front of you (the future).

The past offers lessons. Take the lessons and leave the rest. Kylo Ren said it best to Rey in *Star Wars: The Last Jedi,* **"Let the past die. Kill it if you have to. That's the only way to become what you were meant to be."**

The past can be a powerful tool to run your restaurant (and your life) if you use it and don't allow it to use you. Rip down that rearview mirror, keep your eyes forward, and step on the damn accelerator!

The Dirty Dozen of Badass Leadership

By now you probably think I sound like a broken record. *You're not wrong.* I'm going to keep saying the same things until you start making some changes.

Let's talk one more time about leadership and how it's not a title. It's poetry in motion. It's integrity. It's all action. Everyone can be a leader. I'm going to repeat that: *Everyone can be a leader in your restaurant.*

Leadership is, at its core, about taking **personal accountability**. It's about doing exactly what you say you're going to do, no exceptions, no excuses. As soon as you start playing the excuse game, you drop from being a leader to being a victim. While we talk a lot about being a true leader at our restaurants and businesses, few achieve it.

Let's explore what it takes to become a true leader. If it's really what you desire, be the best version of you that you can be. That means **becoming a badass**.

1. DON'T ASK PEOPLE TO DO ANYTHING YOU WON'T OR CAN'T DO.

There is an old Sicilian saying that translates as, "Don't ask for what you can't take." As a leader, you need to take action every day. When you decide to be a leader, you step up to the big leagues and commit to playing the game at its highest level.

So, before you leap leadership, make sure you truly want it. Leadership *is* challenging, where the greatest challenge will come from within yourself. You need to be sure this is a path and a journey on which you want to embark. You need to take the time to reflect on your motivations for becoming a leader. Great leadership is born from the drive to serve others.

You need to be willing and able to roll up your sleeves and take on the same tasks you assign to your team members. Being a leader means leading. You lead by setting the example and remaining visible to your team. Leadership desires to be where the action is, not hiding in the office during peak service hours.

2. RESULTS ARE THE GOAL—<u>THE ONLY GOAL</u>.

Leaders don't worry about the clock. To them, time seems to stop because they're in the zone, the state in which they become laser focused on accomplishing tasks and time seems to fly by. Some people refer to it as a Zen-like experience: there's no past, no future, just the moment.

When you're the leader, you need to focus on getting results. Hours are arbitrary and aren't a measure of your ability to make things happen. You put in 12 hours or more a day? So what—did you get anything done? How did you move the business forward? How did you use your time? We all can *look* busy. The real question is, "What are you busy doing?"

3. YOU MUST HAVE INTEGRITY.

When you're a leader, your word is your bond with your team. Trust builds great teams and if it's lost, it's very hard to recover and rebuild. When you lack integrity, you lose respect. Lose that, and you'll find it very difficult to lead anyone.

You must make it your mission to do what you say you're going to do. There's no way around this as a leader. Telling the team one thing but doing something different sends mixed messages to your team. As the leader, they look to you and your actions as an example. If you're telling them to be on time and yet you're always strolling into work about 15 minutes late, you're sending mixed messages to your team.

4. YOU NEED A CONSISTENCY RECIPE.

Being average is just that, average. If you plotted out every restaurant in existence on a graph, you'd see a bell curve: most would fall into the middle or average. Let's be honest and admit that being in the middle sucks. There's more competition in the middle, and you'll have to fight every day to maintain your guests, your staff, and your mediocrity. **High turnover is a symptom of being average.** It starts with the leadership (*or lack of leadership*) in a restaurant. It happens because managers aren't consistent.

The number of restaurants that open each year, increasing the competition, make it crucial that you get a grip on consistency issues. This is where independent restaurants should take a lesson from their big chain counterparts. You must have systems in place that are clear, concise, easy to use, and teachable. Systems and standards are the two key ingredients in your consistency recipe. Most people understand the systems part—it's the standards part where most fall short.

"The greater danger for most of us lies not in setting our aim too high and falling short, but in setting our aim too low, and achieving our mark." —Michelangelo

True leaders set their standards high. The late Chef Charlie Trotter was an icon in this industry because of his high standards. His were so elevated that most people thought they were unrealistic, and he preferred it that way. Look at some of the amazing chefs today who spent time in Trotter's kitchen and excelled because of it: Graham Elliot, Giuseppe Tentori, Mindy Segal, Art Smith, Curtis Duffy, Matthias Merges, Michael Taus, Rick Tramonto, and Grant Achatz (to name a few). When you set your standards higher than you normally would, you raise the standards of those around you. Water does seek its own level, and if you want to be a real badass leader, you need badass standards.

"I have always looked at it this way: if you strive like crazy for perfection— an all-out assault on total perfection—at the very least, you will hit a high level of excellence, and then you might be able to sleep at night." —*Charlie Trotter*

5. YOU MUST MANAGE YOUR STATE.

State is energy—your energy. Just like in an atom, there are positive and negative charges. Whether you know it or not, as a leader, your energy has a great impact on your business. It always starts with the leader. If you come into work in a bad mood, you start looking for things to reinforce and fuel that bad mood. Energy begets energy. Negative thoughts crave more negativity and, on the flip-side, positive thoughts crave positivity. The problem comes when positive clashes with negative. It's sad to say, but most times the negative thoughts will overpower the positive.

Psychologists call this "negativity bias." The human brain is amazing and has evolved to fulfill one basic drive: survival. Negativity bias was built in so we would pass on our genetic code to further our lineage by naturally avoiding risk. So, most people are hardwired to be sensitive to bad news over good news. Knowing that you're wired this way is a good thing because now you can take steps to change.

Awareness precedes choice; choice precedes change.

Making sure your energy is on the positive side when you're at your restaurant is a key trait of badass leaders. They're consistently monitoring their state and adjusting to keep that energy elevated throughout the day.

How can you keep your state at its peak level?
- Exercise
- Eat better
- Listen to high-energy music
- Meditate
- Get a good night's sleep
- Maintain an attitude of positivity
- Focus on achievement

Leverage how your brain is wired to become sensitive to negative energy and be vigilant against it. Post signs in work areas and your office declaring, "NO Negativity." Become a seeker of the good and good things will come to you. The old saying, "Seek, and you shall find," is so very true. Stand guard over your state and work throughout the day to keep it up.

6. YOU NEED TO BE COMMITTED TO KAIZEN.

True leaders are committed to self-improvement. If leadership starts at the top and flows down, you're the source. When you improve and become your best self, you'll see your people rise in their skills too.

How many books do you read? Do you listen to audiobooks? Read any trade magazines? Dig through posts on Foodable™? Your dedication and the time you invest in yourself indicate more about your chances for success as a leader than you realize. If you think you can be a badass by just putting in your normal work hours, you're fooling yourself. Badass leadership is a dedication to the philosophy of kaizen. Improve yourself, and if you're a true leader, others around you will elevate their game.

7. WORK ON YOUR COMMUNICATION SKILLS.

Badass leaders articulate their visions, core values, and standards. They make it a daily ritual to talk to their teams. If you think that posting a memo on the wall telling the team your rules and policies is communicating...**you are part of the problem**.

True leaders communicate with authenticity and integrity. Don't be the manager or owner who makes all kinds of promises and never follows through. Your team wants a leader that backs up their words with actions.

Communication is a skill that can be learned. Yes, some people communicate easily and naturally. That doesn't mean they don't have to refine their skills of influence. Your goal in improving your communication skills is to be a positive influence on your team.

People are motivated by their reasons. For instance, if you want ultimate control, you can be a demanding jerk and talk down to your team. They'll comply with your berating demands ... for a while. Then you'll see the energy drain out of them. Some will become zombies, making no impact on the guest experience (or, more likely, seriously degrading it), and then your guests will find a place that delivers a superior experience to yours. If this business were just about food and beverage, people would eat and drink at home and save money.

They come for the experience you and your team deliver, so make it a <u>positively</u> *memorable one!*

8. SEEK TO UNDERSTAND YOURSELF FIRST, THEN OTHERS.

There are several behavioral surveys available on the market that can give you great insight into your key traits. The ProScan® Survey and DiSC® Profile are two very popular options available to businesses seeking to understand the behavioral matrix that makes us all so unique. Know your strengths. Know how you prefer to communicate. Know how you deal with stress. The ProScan® Survey and DiSC® Profile can give you that information, but you will want a qualified facilitator to explain the results to you, why they matter, and how you can use them.

Most managers are one-dimensional, which is great if everyone on their team is wired the same way. However, (and fortunately so) restaurant teams are diverse and are composed of staff with a wide range of personalities. When you understand and appreciate that fact, you take the first step to becoming a true badass leader.

When you understand and appreciate yourself *and* others, you can adjust your communication style to one that resonates with them. Most people are only aware of themselves, their wants and needs; uncovering how others process information is the key to true leadership.

9. KNOW THE DIFFERENCE BETWEEN CONFIDENCE AND COCKINESS.

This one is a challenge for many. It's a common roadblock for those seeking to make the jump from being a manager to becoming a badass leader.

So, what's the difference between confidence and cockiness?

Confidence: The **ability** to recognize when something isn't working and having the flexibility, courage, and knowledge to make adjustments. *Cockiness*: The **inability** to admit when something isn't working and repeating the same mistakes over and over because you're too stubborn to admit you're wrong (*or you are just blind to it*).

If that made you a little uncomfortable, good. That means you may realize you have a little more of one than the other. That realization means you understand you need to adjust. You can change with one simple decision: refusing to be that person any more.

10. LESS TALK, MORE ACTION.

Action is the cure for so many things in a restaurant. The laws of physics are very true: a body in motion stays in motion, and a body at rest sits in the office during service. Everyone talks a good game about being outstanding, pushing for excellence, and becoming legendary. Great visions. Great words. Meaningless without transforming those words into action. Talk is truly cheap in our industry because most are addicted to being average.

Write these three words down and post them where you can see them every day: "Deeds, not words."

When you take action, you create momentum, and that's powerful when applied properly. Tap into that power to not only get things started but keep them going.

> *"People often say motivation doesn't last. Well, neither does bathing— that's why we recommend it daily."* —*Zig Ziglar*

11. TAP INTO URGENCY.

The only thing you truly have any control of is *this moment*, right now. You don't have Doc Brown's DeLorean time machine to travel to the past or future to change things. The only thing you have an impact on is what you do today.

We talk a lot about having a sense of urgency in the restaurant business. We preach it to our teams to move forward and act with it. But how many among us demonstrate urgency themselves? A lot of managers are hypocrites. "Do as I say, not as I do," is the common theme. That goes back to integrity.

Without it; you'll never become a badass leader.

"The best time to plant a tree was 20 years ago. The second-best time is now."-Chinese proverb

Now has power. Use it and do one thing today for which your future self will be happy and grateful. **If you want to be a badass leader, become known for taking action, right now.**

12. EXPECT MORE FROM YOURSELF THAN OTHERS DO OF YOU.

What you put up with, you end up with, and that starts with you. You need to demand and expect more from yourself if you have any hope of becoming a badass leader.

Let's pull these 12 elements together. Just like a recipe, if you leave even one ingredient out, you'll get a different result.

Don't ask others to do what you wouldn't do. Results are what you get paid to produce. Your integrity is your code of honor. Always be consistent. You must manage your state. Commit to constant and never-ending improvement. Work on improving communication. Know your strengths. Avoid arrogance. Take action. Fine-tune your sense of urgency. And always expect more from yourself than others expect of you.

Use all of these in synergy and you'll be on your way to becoming a badass leader, in any restaurant. The skills you are developing are LIFE SKILLS, that can be applied anywhere, anytime. Go be your badass self!

5 Things Your Staff Wishes You'd Stop Doing

Being a leader in the restaurant business is far from easy. It's been said that it's somewhat like being a bull rider. Some days, you ride the bull, and other days the bull rides you!

Here you are still getting back out there day after day going for another round with the beast. You love the business deep down for all the good and bad that it offers. You even love that team you have that you complain about. What? Complain? Me? Yes, you.

Don't play innocent. Your love for your team is at times a torrid affair that has you watching episodes of Crime Scene Investigations (CSI) wondering how to dispose of the body. Well, here's some news you might not be aware of, your team probably has similar thoughts about you too! For all the good things you do as a leader, there is another list that your team keeps about all those other things they wish you would stop doing!

To keep your team from plotting your death, I'm going to share them with you now. Take this to heart or risk ending up as a missing person on the side of a milk carton!

YOU'RE LATE...*MORE THAN THEY ARE.*

Nothing worse in the eyes of your team than a hypocrite. They love it when you say one rule for them and do your own thing.... **not**! The days of "do what I say and not what I do" are gone. Leadership is about accountability, and that starts with personal accountability. That's you.

Your words and your actions must be aligned, or you risk being called an asshole. With the market saturated as it is, there are plenty of job openings in your market. Being a jerk is not conducive to attracting, hiring, or retaining top talent. Be a jerk, and you get the bottom feeders of the lob pool. Water does seek its own level.

Time to stop talking a good game with your team and step up to claim your spot as their leader. No more double talk, white lies, or straight up bullshit that you tell them why you can't do this or that. Sorry to break it to you...no one cares about your problems. They are too busy worrying about their problems. That's right; you are NOT special no matter what your mom said to you!

YOU PLAY FAVORITES....*EVEN THOUGH YOU SAY YOU DON'T.*

If anyone has children, you know where this is going. You always have a favorite team member. It's okay, it's natural.

The key is to be conscientious of this and not let it have a major impact on your effectiveness as a leader. The worst offense is the dreaded "double standard." You have one set of standards for the team, and you make (clear throat here) "exceptions" for your favorite.

Let's say that there is a hostess named Kayla, who is your favorite. She routinely walks into work 15-20 minutes late, and you never say a word to her. Sara, on the other hand, comes in one time 8 minutes late and you go into a 20-minute lecture about punctuality.

The downside of this behavior is the ripple effect it has on your culture. Soon Kayla is alienated by the team because she is one of your favorites. Kayla then loses the social connection with the team and becomes disengaged at work. Shortly after this happens, Kayla gives her notice to leave.

Great leaders are always aware of the social dynamics of their team.

YOU LEAVE WHEN IT GETS BUSY...*YOUR BANKER'S HOURS PISS THEM OFF.*

Yes, you have worked long and hard for your current executive position. Don't forget what got you there. It's not long hours and hard work; it was the way the team looked towards you as a leader! Allow me to digress on a little rant about "hard work": You are not paid to work hard; you are paid for the results and impact you have on the brand.

The saying that you've "paid your dues" is a warning sign you are about to discover mediocrity. Success is not a one-time payment. It's like rent, and that rent is due every damn day.

I know quite a few General Managers, Director of Operations, and Executive Chefs that work in restaurants serving lunch and dinner yet their hours are 8-4pm. Why? While paperwork is a big part of upper management, it's presence and visibility that separates managers from leaders. Without a leader, the team tends to do what they like. Being on the floor or in the kitchen during peak times is critical to team success. They need a leader to look up to.

Someone to keep them focused. Someone to keep the panic under control when the rush comes and all hell breaks loose!

If you're not the leader, then who? You might like this next statement. If you are not going to step out front and be a leader, then why does an owner need you? If you are not working with your team to develop them and make them better, you're deadweight on the payroll.

YOU HIDE IN THE OFFICE...*IT DOESN'T TAKE 8 HOURS TO WRITE A SCHEDULE.*

This one ties in closely to the one above. You can't hide in your office all day saying you're working on projects when you're just avoiding the team and the guests. Stop hiding from leadership and step into it! So many think (more like assume) that becoming a leader means less communication with the team and more time to kick back and dabble at work on the computer. Knock it off.

Is your team out there working to ensure the guests are ecstatic with the dining experience or maybe they aren't? You don't know what the pulse of your restaurant is if you sit in the office and allow things to happen organically. Outstanding service is not organic; it's carefully crafted, orchestrated, and rehearsed. With the market overflowing with restaurant options, you better be out training your competition. Failure to do so consistently puts your brand at risk!

If you want to see how effective you are, then start a time journal for a week. Just jot down everything you do the following week. If you are brutally honest with yourself, you are going to be quite shocked at the amount of time you spend on tasks that do not move your brand (or your life) forward. You spin round and round like a hamster running on a wheel. Eventually, you either burn yourself out or change jobs (either voluntary or involuntarily).

YOU'RE AFRAID TO FIRE THE SLACKERS.... *STEP UP AND BE THE DAMN LEADER.*

Right now, you have at least one person on your team that should be let go. Your team knows it too. By not stepping up and being the true leader, you create a tidal wave of negativity that runs through your culture.

The culture becomes toxic and selfish with every person looking out for their wellbeing. Toxic cultures suck! No one wants to be there. The team is constantly fighting amongst themselves. Guests might come in to watch the drama unfold before them like a real-life reality TV show!

So, why don't you fire these people? You're afraid, and that fear has you paralyzed from taking action. Being a leader means making tough decisions. It means facing fear and taking action in spite of it.

When you fail to act like the leader, you lose trust and respect from your team. Seriously, who wants to follow someone that can't make the right decisions for what is best for the brand? Oh, and if you can't manage your own life, do you think your team trusts you to run the restaurant. Being a leader means being a positive example. Is that fair? No. Is that how life is? Yes. Deal with it.

Now the final question that needs to be asked is, "What are you going to do with the information just presented to you?" Most will do nothing. I sense that you are not like most because you read to this part of the book. That shows character.

Now get out there and make the changes you need to get the restaurant you want.

How to Herd Cats: 7 Secrets to Getting the Restaurant You Want!

They say the restaurant and bar world can be a circus and they're right! At times, it seems like you are the ringmaster and you have three rings going at the same time: the lions, the tigers, and the bears...oh my! In the restaurant world that's the culinary team, the service team, and the bar team. *Sometimes getting everyone to work together is a lot like trying to herd cats.*

I'm not saying it's impossible, it's just a challenge at times. *Sometimes a very big challenge.* So, let's break out the catnip and get these animals to come together and sing Kumbaya! But before we do, let's clearly state the guidelines for herding cats:

1. **Cats don't like to be herded.**
2. **Cats prefer to herd themselves.**
3. **Cats understand that they sometimes need to be herded, but that doesn't make it easier.**
4. **Cats don't like being reminded that they are being herded.**
5. **Harsh herding has harsh consequences!**

The first step is to make a little change to *your* mindset. Yes, I know you thought this was going to be about how to change **them**! Sorry to disappoint you, we're going after the one person we can change, and that would be **you**! Contrary to popular opinion, your team is not the issue. **It's you.** Don't act shocked; you probably had some idea we were going to go there.

So, if you really want to herd cats, the trick is to be the ultra-alpha in the group. That means being the example that they *want* to follow. You don't chase cats or call out for them to come to you. Cats (and your team) tend to have a mind and personality that **does not** conform to obedience.

In your training to become a cat wrangler you're going to need to put on your big boy (or girl) pants and cowboy (or cowgirl) up! Where we are going there is only one course of action...become a better leader or get out of the business. Seriously, the industry is full of half-ass managers that just work the floor like the living dead. **If you want to get more out of your restaurant, your restaurant will want more from you!** It's a simple equation that many have completely ass backwards.

Before we get too far ahead of ourselves, let's break down the four levels of Cat Wrangling. Where are you?

Level One: Cat Fighter – you are in a constant battle with the team. You feel like you might get better results if you sprayed them in the face with a water bottle when they do things wrong (for the record **DO NOT** spray your team in the face with water). They secretly are plotting your demise by thinking they can get you to quit. They don't like you, and you don't like them. Every day is more about surviving the shift than guest satisfaction. You spend the majority of the shift hiding in the office where you feel safe. **Scaredy-cat.**

Level Two: Cat Nip – you decided to make everyone on the team your friend. Well, most of the people on the team. You quickly form little cliques with those you like and those that like you. After work, you tend to hang out for a drink or two (sometimes more). You're more of a buddy to them than an actual leader. You have so much fun that you forget that you are running a business and it shows in your profit and loss statement. The people who you are "friends" never get disciplined or written up. You and your "friends" drive away those you don't like with the excuse that they are not a "good fit" for the team. The restaurant is bleeding out, and soon you'll all be looking for a new restaurant to work at...*together of course.* **Bad cat.**

Level Three: **Jedi Cat Master** – you are in complete control and have tight reigns on the team. The force is strong in you! You rule like Darth Vader. You even had tried to use the force to choke a few of the team members (*yes, you were sad when it didn't work*). Rules are followed to the letter, and the team trembles in fear when you walk by. Fun? Oh, Hell NO! This is a business, and those that do not comply will be terminated with extreme prejudice. Mercy is for the weak! You must break them down and build them up...your way. You have a reputation for being a hard ass, and you like that. Granted, your turnover is so high that you keep the help wanted sign up all the time. You justify it with, "they weren't a good fit for **your** team." **Power hungry cat.**

Level Four: Master Cat Wrangler – you lead by example. You walk *and* talk about the core values your brand has, and you enjoy coming to work. You have high energy and the team respects you because you do what you say, how you said you'll do it when you said you would (*they call that integrity*). Your turnover is low, and your profits are high. You are the true definition of a true leader. You are running a successful restaurant, and you still have a life because you have a team around you that you trust to take care of business. **Respected cat.**

To get to the level of Master Cat Wrangler, you'll need to follow these 7 Secrets handed down from the wise cat herding masters who walked the trail before you. Failure to miss or forget a step could be dangerous for you. You never want a mob of angry cats (or your angry team) to turn on you. So, proceed with caution.

#1: STOP THE DRAMA - OH, THAT MEANS *YOUR* DRAMA!

People are attracted to drama for a variety of reasons. Perhaps seeing someone else have it worse off than you makes you feel okay about what is going on in your own life? Maybe they are addicted to the endorphins that are created when drama enters their day? Some want to feel important, and, out of a need to feel significant, they create drama?

Whatever the cause of the drama, here's a clue to stop it: **drama needs an audience!** If you don't participate and feed the fire that drama wants, it tends to fade away. *Yes, sometimes yelling and kicking on the way out.*

It's a safe bet that when you put a group of people together in a restaurant, there will be at least one person who is on the drama wagon. They like to stir things up and instigate the drama to keep what they think is normal. Addictions take many forms my friend and the addiction to drama is no different. It destroys cultures and slowly kills brands if left to roam your restaurant or bar.

Now, if you can't spot the drama creator in your restaurant, then you either don't have one, or <u>it's you</u>! If it is you, it's time to get into a quick **4 Step Drama-Free Program**!

1. **Admit** that you like drama.
2. **Commit** to stop causing drama.
3. **Tell** the team you are a drama addict and are on a recovery program.

4. **Pause and reframe**. Make a wristband or design a sign for your office to remind you to **STOP THE DRAMA!** When you have that old feeling starting to swell inside, you have about 5 seconds to stop it before that *crazy shit you say to create drama* comes rolling out of your mouth. Ask yourself this question: **Is what I am about to say going to improve the restaurant or my relationship with this person?** *If no, then just shut the hell up.*

Repeat as often as needed until you find your compulsion to create drama diminish.

#2: LEARN TO COMMUNICATE - YES, YOU'RE GOING TO NEED TO PLAY NICE

I don't care where in the world your restaurant or bar is located; **ALL BUSINESS PROBLEMS ARE** <u>PEOPLE PROBLEMS</u> **IN DISGUISE!** Now, the second part that goes along with that statement is: **ALL PEOPLE PROBLEMS ARE** <u>COMMUNICATION</u> **PROBLEMS!**

Those communication problems stem from just being a lazy manager. You know you should communicate better, yet you just take the easy out and fail to do it. That is being lazy whether you like to admit it or not. It's okay if you have been a little lazy about communicating with your team. We'll just keep it our dirty little secret.

Now it's time to change that.

To do this you will need to be honest with yourself on a few things:
- Do you have high standards?
- Do you know your core values?
- Do you like people?

Let's break each one down.

Do you have high standards? Saying you do **and** actually having them usually is the issue. When you have high standards, you are constantly telling, teaching, and preaching those standards day after day, year after year. You are a living example of the words you say and the actions you take. Yes, that's called integrity. Hypocrisy is an epidemic in the world; don't go there.

Do you know your core values? Not knowing this is like not knowing who you are! It's so fundamental and yet so often overlooked. If you do not know exactly what you stand for, then you are not a leader, you're just a sheep like the majority of the population that follows the crowd and never have an original idea. Know what the hell is important to you as a person, and then you can decide what is important to your brand. It all starts with you as the true leader; you need to uncover your values.

Do you like people? Piss poor communication comes from people who, at their core, really don't like people. It's cool if you don't. Just be honest and step away from management. Not everyone is made to be a leader and that's okay.

#3: BE AN EXAMPLE - THAT MEANS GET YOUR SHIT TOGETHER.

Now, if you decide that you want to follow the path of leadership, then it's time to step up and do what the fuck leaders do.... **lead by example**. You can't be a hypocrite. You can't fake being sincere to guests. You can't pretend to care about your team. Being a true leader means being authentic and transparent.

Leadership is taking care of two primary things:
- Yourself
- Your team

Yourself. Being a true leader means making sure you take care of you first. Stop playing the martyr and sacrificing your health. Think of it as the battery on your phone. If you went in to work with only a 25% charge and if you couldn't recharge your phone all day, how long would it last before it ran out of power? That's exactly what most do by not taking care of themselves. They go to work with little energy and run themselves into the ground. When you are low energy, you make bad decisions. You bark at your team. You do stupid shit.

Your team. After your internal battery is fully charged, it's time to focus on the energy of your team. Look at the culture in your restaurant like a big pipe that is standing up. At the top is the energy source (which is the leaders and owners) and that energy flows down along the pipe to the next level managers, shift leaders, hourly staff, and finally to the guests. I can tell pretty quickly exactly where the energy of the culture is being clogged up. It's sad to say that **8 out of 10 times it's towards the top**. If your energy is at a level 10 and your team is at a level 9, your guests will have an exceptional experience.... *guaranteed.*

#4: TRAIN LIKE YOUR LIFE DEPENDS ON IT - IT DOES!

The antidote for mediocrity is to be constantly training. Special operations teams in the military don't just train before a mission; they train every single day. There is a great saying in Latin: *Si vis pacem, para bellum,* which means, *"If you want peace, prepare for war."*

If you want to build a restaurant that stands out and get your team (the cats) heading in the same direction, then training is your crucible. Too many train to 'get it over with' after hiring and get people on the floor or in a station on the kitchen line. Major mistake.

You want to be the restaurant in your market that out-trains your competition! Hey, other restaurants might be able to knock off your food and decor, **don't let them out-train you**! Refuse to lose the training game. Be the place that never stops getting better by always, always, always training.

You can tell in a movie the actors who have practiced. They come across as believable. They come across as being real. They transfer emotions from the dialogue on paper to Oscar-worthy performances. Your restaurant can win that golden statue too if you are willing to put in the work to become so damn good that you stand out in your market with an extremely polished performance. You get that from training like your life depends on it.

#5: GIVE OUT SINCERE COMPLIMENTS - IT'S NOT GOING TO KILL YOU TO BE KIND.

Being the herd animals we are at heart; we also love a good old-fashioned pat on the back. Two of the most powerful words in the world are, "Thank you." The best thing is that those words are FREE, so give them away more often.

I'm not saying become a softy and give people a pass. I'm saying that being a true leader means being grateful to those around you. You must always remember to keep your team accountable and hold the line in the sand where the standards are. You can do that and not be an asshole (*it's true*). You can be firm and be respectful. You can be empathetic and respected. You can be the leader that they desire. You need to drop all the bullshit standing in your way!

What bullshit? Start with ego, pride, and denial. Those three are partners in crime at average restaurants to stir up the drama and start some shit. Don't let it happen in your restaurant. Take control by fostering an atmosphere where others feel appreciated and valued. It all starts with you saying a few words that are sincere and honest.

Sidebar: If you can't find anything nice to say to your team then why do you keep them around? Yes, they don't do everything right 100% of the time. Do you? It's easy to see the bad, try looking for the good for once.

#6: DON'T CROSS THE LINE - BE THEIR LEADER, NOT THEIR FRIEND!

A common problem for new leaders is making the "jump" from hourly team member to a salary position on the leadership team. This isn't a physical jump, it a mental leap. You are crossing an invisible line whether you know it or not. You'll develop faster when you realize that once you cross that line, there's no going back.

On the hourly side, you were one of the gang. You laughed and joked about things that now on the other side, you are responsible for. Who is the joke on now? That cushy and easy leadership role just took on an air of seriousness that you might not have expected. ***You have to hold people accountable!*** Don't reach for the brown paper bag and start hyperventilating yet.

To get more from life, you have to become more. Sometimes that means growing and shedding things, habits, and sometimes friends that are trying to keep you suppressed and not growing. That's the old you and that version of you gets you the same shit you have today. We all need growth. We all need a challenge. We all need some goal out in front of us, pulling us to it.

Leadership can be lonely; you'll need to understand and accept that. Being responsible and accountable is a tough job that many think they are ready for until the mantel of being a leader is thrust upon them. Some rise to this challenge. Others crumble under the weight of it. What you do depends on what drives you. I find that those that are just following the money, crumble. Those that want to have an impact and help others, thrive in a leadership role.

Don't be ashamed if your heart is not into being a leader. It's far better to pass on it if you are not committed to the challenge, then to accept the role and hate it.

#7: WATCH YOUR WORDS - DON'T THINK OF A PURPLE ELEPHANT.

Being a leader and a master cat herder means understanding the power of words. Words can pull people together. They can tear people apart. They start wars and they can build peace. How you use your words depends on your ability to be aware of how you use the three ways we communicate.

This is a game changer that you can use right away. In fact, I will go out on a limb to say that the words you use tell me all I need to know about the culture of your restaurant and the chance you have for long term success. Don't believe me? Let's test it...

Be honest. *Which word do you use the most?*

Customer or Guest

Staff or Team

Manager or Leader

No Problem or My Pleasure

Beware of these tricky words...

The But Eraser – there is a little know phenomenal effect that many are not aware of, and that is the power of the word **but**. You see, you can say something kind to start with, however, when you throw in the word **but** and follow up with something critical, all that was said before the word **but** gets mentally erased.

Example:

> *"Hey, great job on cleaning the walk-in,* **but** *next time make sure to sweep under the shelves too." What the team member hears is not what a great job they did. They hear that they* <u>suck</u> *at sweeping.*

It's far better to break down your conversations into two distinct parts so that the message does not get misrepresented.

> *"Let's make sure that when we sweep the walk-in that we get under the shelves* **because** *things tend to roll underneath and they can spoil easily.* **Thank you.** *Joe, you did a great job organizing the walk-in, and I* **appreciate** *the extra work you did. Keep it up!"*

On the second example, the message is clear, concise, and reinforced with power words (more on those in a minute).

The If, Then Deal Maker – Here is where many go wrong in that they want to trade a behavior for a consequence. It's basic terms this is called "horse-trading" and it a dangerous road to follow as a leader.

You set yourself up for short-term success and long-term failure because now you have conditioned the team like Pavlov's Dogs. They only respond when there is a reward for the behavior. This "what's in it for me" mindset is the beginning of a culture of entitlement. That is the beginning of the end of your business.

Example:

> *"Hey, Sara needs this Friday off.* **If** *you can work for her,* **I'll** *throw you an extra $40 in cash."*

This sets you up for a constant reward or bribe to get people to do things. If the reward or bribe isn't big enough, they will turn it down. The funny thing is that some managers get upset with the team member after they were the ones who started this barter system. You will find you have better results long term by reminding them of the core values and the team dynamics.

*"Can you work for Sara this Friday night? I know it's **not your normal night** to work. However, something came up, and she needs off. It would **truly help the team and our guests** if you could step in for her. I know that **family** is important to you, and this would be a great way to show Sara our **support**."*

POWER WORDS TO START USING TODAY

Now, there are certain words you want to throw around like confetti on New Year's Eve! These are known as power words and they can have a big impact on the attitude and therefore the performance of your team. **Use them often!**

Thank You – hands down these are the two most powerful words in the English language. When you are sincere and show an attitude of gratitude, your culture will become unstoppable. One of the greatest human needs we have is the need to feel appreciated.

Because – this one works because people want to understand the reason why. Sure, many in the world blindly follow anyone and do what they are told. However, if you are building an outstanding restaurant, you will not have many of those types working with you. High performers want to know the logic behind the requests, so make sure to give it to them.

My Pleasure – Chick-fil-A® is famous for using this saying to every guest, and there is a reason why they are consistently at the top of guest satisfaction surveys. You really cannot go wrong with being polite and friendly towards others in the hospitality industry. It's far better than the standard reply of "no problem." Why? Because **no problem** implies that there **is** a problem!

Their Name – there is nothing sweeter to a person than hearing their name. You want to use other people's names as often as you can to build rapport and show people that you care about them as a person.

"Words cannot move mountains, but they can move people to take action for a better life. Words can suppress or inspire you. Words can break people and they can build people. You have in your possession the most powerful tool to having a better relationship with your family, your team, your guests, and yourself... the words you use on a regular basis."

- Donald Burns, The Restaurant Coach™

Stop Marketing, Start Dominating

"A very wise man once taught me that the key to marketing is not what you say, but how well you can transfer emotion to your audience."

—Brian Lee

How to Market to Baby Boomers

Everyone talks about marketing to Millennials. What about the Baby Boomers? They're inclined to have more disposable income than younger generations and are loyal to brands they trust.

Any restaurant marketing plan needs to be balanced and reach out to multiple generations. So, who exactly are the Baby Boomers? Here's a quick reference:

- Baby boomers: born between 1946-1964
- Generation X: born between 1965-1980
- Millennials: born between 1981-2000

Baby Boomers prefer substance over flash. They don't jump when you pressure them to 'buy now' unlike the younger generations (limited time offers appeal to the younger generations due to FOMO, or "fear of missing out"); they're cautious. They use social media differently than younger generations. While Millennials are posting what they're eating for lunch, Baby Boomers are posting pictures of their grandkids.

To market effectively to Baby Boomers, you need to speak in a language they understand. Here are some tips to help. Since I'm one-year shy of being a Baby Boomer myself, these come from personal experience.

DON'T SAY THEY'RE OLD

If you're in your twenties, you might think that people over 50 are "old." That's one of the fastest ways to turn off this demographic. Baby Boomers see life after 50 as some of the best years of their lives! They tend to focus more on living a healthy lifestyle and enjoying their free time.

Healthy menu options, and cooking classes are perfect for Baby Boomers. At a recent cooking class at an upscale restaurant (that was charging $100 per person to attend), the class was sold out, and 80 percent of the people who attended were over 50 — not a bad way to fill up a slow evening at a restaurant, hint hint.

PLAY THE NOSTALGIA CARD

Nothing like a good emotional trigger or blast from the past to connect your brand to images or symbols from this demographics' youth. The '70s and '80s were good times for the Baby Boomers—remind them of that.

Do you have vintage menus from those eras that you could recreate? How about a theme night in your bar like *Saturday Night Fever* on a Monday? Try a play on brunch with Commodores-themed "Easy Like Sunday Morning" Mimosas. Sweet Tart Cosmos, anyone?

You can also create posters that leverage the nostalgia of popular movies from those days.

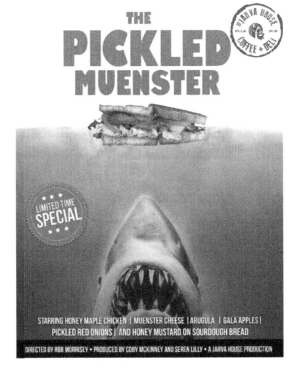

Source: Jahva House

Remember that marketing is, at its essence, all about triggering emotions. Tap into that, and you'll understand the world from their point of view, which will build rapport. In turn, rapport builds trust, and trust builds loyalty.

MARKET TO WHAT MATTERS TO THEM

With any marketing plan, you want to talk about what's important to the guest. Many get this backwards: when creating marketing content, they talk about what *they* feel is important. If you want to increase your marketing effectiveness, use the 80/20 Rule: 80 percent of your content should be about what interests your targets, 20 percent should be about your interests.

What do Baby Boomers care about? There are a few things that, when triggered, will cause them to give your marketing a second look.

> *Their grandkids:* These people light up with pride when they see their grandchildren and when anyone asks about them. Offering events that allow Baby Boomers to share time with their grandkids while enjoying your food is a great enticement. Host an afternoon *Alice in Wonderland* Tea Party. Try an afternoon circus theme featuring staff dressed like lions, tigers, and bears (oh my). What if their grandkids don't live close by? Create a promo entitled "Wish You Were Here" where you get a picture of them with a picture of their grandchild. You can bet that the smile on Boomers' faces will be priceless.
>
> *Healthy living:* Passing the age of 50 is a wakeup call for many people to start living a healthier lifestyle. Trends like the Keto Diet are gaining traction with Baby Boomers. The key is to avoid words like "diet" and "low carb." No one wants a reminder that they're on a diet (look at the first three letters of that word: "die"). Instead, use phrases like "heart-healthy" and "keto-friendly." Play to this demographics' desire for top-quality ingredients. Let them know if you offer things like Japanese Hokkaido A5 Wagyu, GMO-free products (better than just saying "No GMOs"), and whole grains (digestive health is important to Baby Boomers).
>
> *Value:* Hey, everyone likes a deal, and Baby Boomers are no exception. Restaurants like Bonefish Grill capture this demographic by providing a balance between high-end and value-priced seafood options. Boomers want flavor, however, they're not necessarily what I'd call adventurous. They like their classics served with a little twist. Kobe beef burgers with harissa ketchup, surf and turf with roasted

cashew butter, adult mac & cheese, and any twist on a classic Bloody Mary (like making yours with bacon—how can you go wrong with bacon?), are always a hit.

Breakfast: Baby Boomers love to eat breakfast. According to Technomic Inc., this generation spends more of the restaurant dollars on breakfast than any other demographic. If you can introduce new flavors that offer a twist while maintaining familiarity, you can bring them in with items like steak and eggs with lobster hollandaise, oatmeal crème brûlée, crawfish etouffee omelets, and a smoked salmon-scrambled egg breakfast.

Marketing to Baby Boomers should be a part of your business strategy. Once you get them through your doors, make sure your staff is trained properly to deal with them. Boomers are a little more traditional when it comes to manners, so little things like being polite, smiling, opening the door, handing them napkins, and saying "please" and "thank you," are very much appreciated by this generation.

Respect goes a long way toward making Baby Boomers loyal to your restaurant.

Make Your Restaurant Stand Out on Social Media

Look at your Facebook feed, and you'll see a world vying for your attention. The thing is, you're trying to capture the attention of your current guests and while also enticing new guests to come for a visit. Kind of a conundrum, right?

Throw TV and radio commercials on top of that, and you truly understand that we're all bombarded with marketing messages 24/7. We all want to be seen. We all want customers' attention. If you don't make an effort for your brand to compete for its share of attention out there, you'll be buried by your competitors.

So, how do you stand out? How do you get people to give your restaurant more than a fleeting glance? How do you make an impact in today's crowded marketing world?

Don't fret, below are a few tips to help your brand shine in the Digital Age!

1. STOP BEING BORING

It happens every day on the internet: a restaurant posts their daily special with a plea to come down today and try it, like a little bird begging for food. The problem is there are 1,000 other little birds in your market all chirping for the same thing. Your guests become desensitized to the same old marketing messages from your brand and everyone else's. You find yourself stuck in a marketing pattern that's failing to grab anyone's attention.

Have you even seen or been in a relationship that just seemed to lose that loving feeling? Of course. The only way to get that feeling back is to step up your action and fall back in love with your partner to get them to fall back in love with you. The same goes for your social media. **Stop being boring—care more about your posts.**

2. STOP PLAYING SMALL

Not wanting to get too far out there is understandable. Your natural inclination is likely to want to play it safe. When you play it safe, you're putting a restrictive muffler on your brand. It's like having a Porsche and only driving it at 35 m.p.h., *all the time*! Time to step on the accelerator if you want to leave Average City in the dust.

Maybe you operate a breakfast concept and keep posting the same pictures of your pancakes, omelets, and that famous Bloody Mary. Very nice. Very safe. [Insert snoring sound here.]

It's time for you to get in touch with your bolder side. Push the envelope and dip your toes outside of your comfort zone. That doesn't mean being offensive or tone deaf; it just means stepping things up to keep loyal and potential guests from scrolling past your posts or emails.

Radio shock jock Howard Stern built his brand by pushing the edge, often going right over it. Like him or hate him, one thing's certain: you know who he is. Shake up your brand a bit, and you can experience a similar boost in engagement.

If you want to take the brakes off your social media, you're going to have to get a little edgy. Check out this post from a pizza concept called Toppers:

3. Stop Fearing Negativity

Here's some bad news: When you put your brand out on the internet, not everyone in the world is going to like you. The more you disrupt the market, the more haters you'll attract.

Here's the good news: You want haters. When they start paying attention to your brand, it means you're shaking things up. Granted, some have a seemingly endless supply of hate to throw your way. Never mind them—they're overcompensating for their failures and being stuck in mediocrity. You might find that some are from a rival restaurant down the road or an employee who left on bad terms (when they steal steaks or money, you kinda need to terminate them). They'll strike back like most cowards do: from the shadows of the internet.

Embrace the haters, but don't let them trample you. Report their posts and block them, particularly if their rants are hateful or demeaning to your brand, team, followers, or anyone else. Oh, and don't take their venomous posts personally—that's what they want. Haters (or trolls) hope they can get you to come down to their level. Don't bother.

4. STOP BEING ONE-DIMENSIONAL

You probably have a Facebook page for your restaurant. You also need a presence on Twitter, Instagram, Snapchat, and LinkedIn. Why? Because your guests use those channels, too.

Once again, breaking free from the cult of the average restaurant requires you to learn how to use new tools. The beauty is that all those other social media platforms are free! The price of admission is a little time and effort. Compared to the monthly cost of a billboard to advertise, that's a sweet deal!

It's always shocking to see restaurants that have access to these free marketing tools spend thousands of dollars on billboards, radio, TV commercials, or full-page print ads instead. If they would spend half that amount on promoting social media posts, they could target the exact demographics and psychographics they desire. Perhaps some people like to see their faces up on billboards. Sadly, some egos need to be stroked.

5. STOP MAKING A RIPPLE.

How many times have you posted this week? Once? Three times? More? Whatever you think is effective isn't making the impact you think it is. You're throwing a rock into the ocean and think you're making a big splash. You might not be able to hear it, but the internet is laughing at you.

If you always do what you've done, you'll remain exactly where you are now. Habits make the person; your social media habits make marketing.

Here's your challenge: double-down on your social media posts. However often you're posting now, double it! If you're posting once a day, make that twice a day, across *all* your social media platforms. Do that for 60 days and then double-down again! If you're posting twice a day, ramp it up to four times on day sixty-one. You'll encounter a few people who say you're posting too much. Good—you'll never make waves if you play it safe or small, or avoid their negativity.

Here are some sad statistics on how often restaurants post only to Facebook:
- Only 22 percent have posted in the last ten days.
- Only 17 percent have posted in the last week.
- Only 9 percent have posted in the last 36 hours.

If your posting frequency resembles those stats, you need to take immediate action before your brand loses any more traction on social media. No excuses, just do it.

6. STOP BEING SELFISH

Maybe you have a legion of followers on social media. Good for you. How much time do you dedicate to engaging with them? Engagement is when you like other people's posts and carry on conversations through comments. The internet gave us an amazing tool to get our messages out there, but too often our communication is one-sided. Your message. Your restaurant. You, you, you.

Stop being selfish.

The secret to social media isn't much of a secret at all. It's about being social. It's about connecting with people. It's about sharing ideas. That means you're going to need to look past yourself and get involved in other people's interests. Share their posts. Like their pictures. Approach conversations as a two-way street. Oh, and please be sincere and authentic. When someone writes a great review about your restaurant, don't reply with a simple, "Thank you." That's the same as the hostess greeting guests at the door with the standard, "Just two?" You're better than that.

7. START BEING A LION

Here's a great story you might have heard before:

If you wake up and realize you're a gazelle, you know that your survival depends on your ability to outrun the slowest gazelle. You don't have to be the fastest; you don't have to outrun the lion, you have to be marginally faster than your average peers. When you have a gazelle's mindset, you're only thinking about doing the minimum to get by. You think you need to stay a few steps ahead of the slowest competitor. The gazelle lives through fear and only runs when the lion is chasing it. If you run your social media with a gazelle's mindset, you only take action or post when there's external motivation (*like pressure from a new restaurant opening down the street or if sales are slow*).

The lion realizes that if it wants to survive and feed its family, it must catch a gazelle. Every day, when the sun comes up, the lion starts chasing its goal. If you have a lion's mindset, you focus on your social media with a clear plan and you take action. You dominate your market with a consistent presence across all your social media profiles.

When the sun comes up, what do you do?

Do you run toward social media and keep your brand top of mind?

Or are you a gazelle afraid of its own shadow?

One gets dinner, the other becomes dinner to their competition.

Stop Competing and Start Standing-Out in Your Market

Do you have competition? Most would say yes. Many would argue that competition is healthy and good for your business. Your goal should never be to compete with others—it's a losing mindset that becomes a game of one-upmanship. Restaurants that compete get drawn into pricing wars, turning them into a commodity. Once you're classified as such, watch out—you might start to see profits slowly slip away as you give away more to "keep up with the Joneses."

Competition is for suckers.

Instead, you must aim to become outstanding. You want your brand to stand out and set the pace for competition, so every other restaurant in your market spends their time trying to catch you. It's always better to be the lead dog on a dogsled team.

So, how do you stop competing and start standing out? First, you'll need to get comfortable with being a little uncomfortable. When you're heading into new territory, there won't be any road signs to guide you. To get what you've never had before, you must be willing to do what you've never done before. That scares people. If you're a little scared right now, good. Being scared is the first step.

TELL THEM WHY YOU'RE DIFFERENT

Two pizza places operate in the same market. One is your typical cookie-cutter chain concept (no offense to chain concepts). They offer the standards at a very economical price point. These concepts have their niche, and they tend to dominate it.

Then there's Joe's Pizza, a local place that takes great pride in sourcing high-quality ingredients. They use local sausage made by a man down the street, basil grown in their hydroponic rooftop garden, and San Marzano tomatoes to make their sauce. Only the best for Joe's Pizza. When guests come in, they see a pizza that, on the surface, looks the same as the sausage pizza down the street at the chain concept. They can't justify the extra $2 for the pizza because they don't see the value or the difference since Joe has ignored Marketing 101. He hasn't made his unique selling proposition known. **If you're not consistently telling your guests why you're different, shame on you for assuming they know. They don't.**

Now, some guests won't care about your superior ingredients, and that's okay. They're not your ideal guests, and <u>you shouldn't try to be everything to everyone</u>. Some people want an economical price point. McDonald's tried to do the gourmet burger thing with an upscale attempt to market their Angus Premium Burger. It failed because that's not their niche. Find your niche and market the hell out of what makes you unique.

Joe would be smarter to stop competing against chain restaurants on price point. Instead, he should be obsessed with what he does have. He needs to market why he prefers the sausage from the local guy and why he decided to start his hydroponic herb garden.

TELL THEM WHY THEY SHOULD WORK WITH YOU

Many restaurant operators struggle with attracting talent. They put up the same help wanted ad as the other restaurants in their market and wonder why no one applies. As with the previous example, struggling operators haven't told people why their restaurant is different from all the others trying to hire them. Hey, the restaurant industry has a bad reputation for long hours, average pay, and very few benefits. What makes your restaurant and team different?

Don't just say what sets you apart with boring words. Show potential employees with video. Show them with testimonials from people who work there and let that authentic energy shine through. Show them how you encourage growth. Show them how joining your team is a wise move. Show them through video why you're the employer of choice.

Stop competing over hourly rates with other restaurants and show your culture. Inspire people to want to be a part of something bigger than just a restaurant. If you don't, you're just another restaurant that will pay them an hourly rate and be another dead-end job. No thanks.

You're going to have to overcome the negative perceptions about working in this industry if you hope to rise above the rest. You say you're different? Talk is cheap. Don't show them the money, show them your culture!

BE MORE AGGRESSIVE WITH MARKETING

So, how many times have you posted to Facebook recently? Can you do better than the statistics I shared in the previous chapter? Many restaurants fail to take social media seriously and play too small in their markets. They'll never dominate if they continue playing it safe and posting only a few times each week. The purpose of marketing is to keep your brand top of mind. With the amount of people on social media today, that means increasing posting frequency to stand out in a market.

Yes, it's scary to post more than you do now. Being scared and stepping outside of your comfort zone is good, remember?

It's time to ignore that little voice inside telling you this is all too much and instead tune into the voice that encourages you to own your market.

Are You a Red Ocean or Blue Ocean Restaurant?

In the market, you've probably sensed that the waters have changed. The easy pickings of yesterday have been replaced with a steady stream of more restaurants and bars opening in your market, taking your staff AND your guests.

The waters are red with blood from a saturated market that cannibalizes itself. You're in the category called "average" and that's the same as being a commodity. Welcome to what's known as the red ocean.

Out on the horizon, the water is calm and blue. There's little competition and there's plenty of staff and guests. You're now standing out in front, and you don't fear competition because you don't have much. Your brand is considered innovative and inspiring. Welcome to the blue ocean.

COMPETITION IS FOR SUCKERS

If you remember the bell curve in school; you know that most students fall into the C grade range. This is average. The problem is that average is the new standard and being average is also where all the competition is. The red ocean is full of other sharks just looking to gobble up your staff and guests. They entice your staff with a few dollars more per hour, or they offer guests discounts for food and drink.

When you're in the red ocean, you fight back by playing the "I'll-see-your-move-and-go-one-better" game. It's a keeping up with the Joneses mentality that is very similar to what psychologists call the hedonic treadmill. For instance, your competition offers a 5 for $5 happy hour promotion and you counter with a 4 for $4 menu.

The red ocean is laced with average brands that would rather give everything away just to beat the others. This is very similar to the bucket of crabs' mentality: They never put a lid on a bucket of crabs because as soon as one gets above the other, another crab grabs it and pulls it back down.

In the red ocean, you want your slice of the pie (market), and you fight for table scraps. The staff makes the rounds from one red ocean restaurant to another. Guests are more loyal to the best deal than the actual brand, so you compete.

GETTING TO THE BLUE OCEAN

Looking at the bell curve again, we find the straight-A students. These restaurants and bars are the venues the average admire. They don't follow trends, they set trends. C students look at the A students as smarter and *just* gifted. The truth is that they work harder and are more consistent.

C students and average restaurants throw in the towel way too easily, accepting where they are as the way it is. To make it to the blue ocean restaurant waters, you need to change your mindset. Becoming a blue ocean restaurant takes a renewed commitment to stand out and establish your brand as the leader in your market! How?

Revisit Your Core Values

If you've never explored your core values (what you stand for), now is the time. Knowing your core values, and exactly who you are as a brand, is the first step to swimming out of the red ocean.

People identify with brands that align with their own set of core values. How will you attract better talent and guests without knowing what you believe in? You can't.

Create the Cult in Culture!

In your market right now, some restaurants and bars are very similar to yours. I hate to be the bearer of bad news...*you're not as special as you think.*

- You can buy the same food for vendors.
- You can hire from the same labor pool.
- You can market to the same guests.

So why do some standout and others stay stuck in the middle of the Red Ocean? It all comes down to culture. While menus can be copied, service models can be replicated. Concepts can be knocked off. **Culture is impossible to imitate.**

Why? Because culture is a living thing that is feed by the energy, core values, and vision of the leader. Culture at its essence is cultivated. It's nurtured. It's tended to like a garden. If you fail to care for your culture, it is quickly overrun with negative energy, bad behavior, and becomes a pit of despair for a poor guest experience. Just like all living things, what you feed it matters.

What to feed your culture:

There is a couple of immediate things you can do to cultivate your culture starting today! The key is to be consistent when you start down this path. Oh, and fair warning: if you have neglected your culture for a while, it's going to take some time to get it back on track. Be patient and stay the course.

Bring back appreciation. If you look at studies why people leave companies, the main reason it's not money. It's because they did not feel appreciated. This is such an easy fix that you have no excuse to start showing more appreciation to your team immediately (well unless you are just an asshole). If you are new to the appreciation game, start with something easy....say "thank you." Probably two of the most powerful words in the world are thank you. Commit not to leave your restaurant or bar without saying those words to every member of your team.

Make a virtual water cooler. We are at our core heard animals. We come together to form communities and share in the bounty that comes from that connection. We all want to connect with other people. It's hard-wired into your DNA, and unless you have a psychological issue (like being a sociopath), you crave to be connected to others.

Traditional workplaces have the water cooler or break room to get together and share stories or catch up with each other. In the restaurant and bar world, that can be a little more difficult. Why not make it easy for your team to bond by setting up a private Facebook group just for your team? It becomes your virtual water cooler for social interaction! Celebrate birthdays, anniversaries, kids, sports, share recipes, or whatever else you want. You're only limited by your imagination and creativity. Of course, being on a social media platform, you'll want to establish some firm guidelines and policies about appropriate and inappropriate posts. Keep it focused, keep it positive, and keep it fun so your team will want to go and share their life with the team.

Culture is the social glue that keeps teams together long term!

BE WHERE YOUR GUESTS WANT YOU TO BE

Uber Eats is not going away anytime soon. The desires of the market changes (sometimes very quickly) and those that adapt will get a piece of that market share. Being the last restaurant in your market to jump on a trend is not a good market position to be in. Better to be the leader than a follower.

Love it or hate it, third-party delivery services are what guests want. You can jump in on this or lose market share to those that already have adapted. Just remember that to take no action is an action...it's just not smart action.

You want to focus your brand (if applicable) to the keyword: convenience. That's where the most opportunity for growth is this year. Third party apps, curbside pickup, or drop-n-go catering are a great way to increase sales.

Gen Z and the Millennials love to stay in, order food, and stream movies from Netflix, Hulu, and iTunes. This is where your current market is residing at home. To not offer solutions that fulfill their needs, you are missing out. Granted if you are a microbrewery, delivering beer might be a legal issue in your market, so why no push curbside pickup and take a growler home? House tap cocktails are another option for filling up a growler. There is a restaurant near me that has a killer Paloma on tap! I'm not a beer guy. However, tequila is right up my alley!

Start Story Marketing

Everyone has a story behind their restaurant. It doesn't matter if you're a family-owned business now run by the great-grandchildren, a lawyer who decided he hated practice law and wanted to follow his dream to be a chef or the mom who wanted to start a gluten-free line of entrees for home meal replacement. We all have a story to tell.

The sad thing is that most restaurants and bars fail to tell their story. They think they need to promote their food and beverage. And while that is a good thing to market, it has not nearly the power of a good story. Just look at the movies you love. The chances are high that you loved the story it told and not just the big car chase scene three fourths the way through. Storytelling invokes emotions and marketing is all about stirring up emotions.

When you fall to trigger a response in your marketing you are failing to connect with your target demographic (ideal guest), you not marketing now.... you're just making noise. There is plenty of noise on social media. Be clear and concise when telling your story. Oh, and don't get too wrapped up that the video of the post is not perfect. Perfection is unattainable. It's far better to throw some video out there and refine your skills as you go on, then be too afraid to post something because your concerned about what others might think. The key is to get started. Turn that damn camera around and share your story!

Go Beyond the Average

Setting yourself up to break free from the red ocean also requires you to do things others don't (or won't). Burger restaurants are a dime a dozen these days. Most restaurants and bars have at least a version of a burger featured on their menu. How do you go beyond the norm?

- *Maybe it's grass-fed beef cooked in organic ghee?*
- *A signature burger sauce that is classified as a "secret"?*
- *Maybe unique milkshakes that use real ice cream and local heavy cream from a nearby dairy?*
- *Maybe some your signature cocktails are made with your own burnt orange simple syrup?*

You can blend in or you can stand out—it's your choice.

Think of Your Menu Like a Bikini

There is an old joke that goes, "Everyone can wear a bikini at the beach, but not everyone should." The same goes for your menu. Granted, with the inventory you have in your business right now, you could create a couple of thousand menu items if you sat down and thought about it. But why? To show off how creative you are? I hate to tell you this, most of your guests do not care how creative you are. That Cabernet poached pear with Gorgonzola ice cream sounds cool, but can you sell enough to justify it a place on your menu?

Stop being creative to be creative. Be outstanding at dialing in the flavor profiles and then execution of the dish (or cocktail) consistently! Too many restaurants and bars create their menu around their egos and not what is best for the guest. Hey, if you are Grant Achatz then, by all means, push the edge on culinary and beverage innovation. There are around 2% of chefs and mixologist in the world that can command the prices to be creative at that level. The rest of the industry should focus on being the best they can be in their market.

You become the best with **consistency** in both product and service. That comes from becoming obsessed with training and becoming your best! Remember that restaurants only become better when the people in them become better people! That starts with you becoming better. That also starts with getting your ego under control and creating a menu that is a reflection of your brand!

Do the Work

Getting to the blue ocean requires dedication and total commitment. You can't go half-ass on this. You must be willing to dig down and take accountability for everything that occurs in your restaurant.

- *Are you holding onto lazy and incompetent staff?* **Get rid of them!**
- *Not sure what everything on your menu costs?* **Time to update your recipe cards!**
- *Marketing now and then?* **Double-down and increase your posts to keep your brand positioned as top-of-mind! Start using video to tell your story!**

Become Obsessed with the Details

Getting to the blue ocean also requires you to develop some O.A.D. or **Obsessive Attention to Details**. Re-examine everything from how your team answers the phone to packing a meal for delivery. The devil is in the details, and it's *so* true.

What separates Apple from other phones on the market is the extreme detail that goes into everything that makes the guest experience memorable. They purposely designed the box your new iPhone comes in to open in 7 seconds to increase the feeling of anticipation. They want to create positive emotions around their product, thus increasing the emotional bond between brand and user.

Only around 5 percent of all restaurants and bars will reach the blue ocean waters. The number one reason they fail to reach their destination is they give up when the going gets tough. When you truly want something, you put all you can into it—your heart and soul. Don't sell yourself short anymore.

Don't waste one more day competing with others. Make a stand to do more than only own the market—dominate it!

"If any of my competitors were drowning, I'd stick a hose in their mouth and turn on the water. It is ridiculous to call this an industry. This is not. This is rat eat rat, dog eat dog. I'll kill 'em, and I'm going to kill 'em before they kill me. You're talking about the American way - of survival of the fittest." —*Ray Kroc*

Is that a little brutal to say?
Maybe.
Is it required to get to the blue ocean?

Definitely.

4 Marketing Myths You Need to Abandon

"Drive traffic."

"Get butts in seats."

"Be top of mind."

Do any of these marketing terms sound familiar? They should because the marketing gurus throw them out all day long attempting to get you to try their systems.

Marketing your restaurant or bar is not as complicated as they would like you to believe. Is it a challenge to stand out in a crowded market? Yes. Is there a secret combination that will turn your restaurant marketing into a gold mine? No.

The situation is similar to the diet gurus who possess "the secret" to losing weight. There isn't a secret at all. Eat less food and burn more calories each day. Get in some exercise. Be conscious of the crap you eat and drink. Not a big secret. Marketing is a lot like that: awareness, logic, tenacity.

Let's break down four common marketing myths and the truths behind them.

MYTH #1: IT TAKES A LOT OF MONEY TO MARKET EFFECTIVELY.

This one comes from those marketing agencies that are trying to sell you their services. For a couple of thousand dollars a month they'll post to your social media accounts, so traffic becomes a river carrying new guests to your door. If only that were true.

Throwing more money at a problem like lack of traffic doesn't mean you're going to get a return on that investment. Yes, posting consistently is a good move, and they'll make sure you have a steady stream of generic content floating around your social media pages. Just remember that even a broken watch is right twice a day. The shotgun marketing strategy is as outdated as ads in the Yellow Pages.

Truth: While the Internet is a crowded place, you don't need a lot of money to make noise. You need to know how to *make noise that will get people's attention.* That requires you to be creative, courageous, and a little weird. Yes, being weird sells.

Example: You could post the standard (which means *boring*) stock photo of chicken wings, and a pint of beer saying, "Come on down for $1.00 wings and $2.00 draft beers."

Or you could make a fun video clip using time lapse of a person throwing down a frosty cold one and eating two dozen wings with the pile of bones stacking up on the table. Caption the video, **"Become a wing warrior!"** Does that make you smile? Your potential guests are smiling too, and now they are curious and interested in trying your wings with that frosty beer. Yum.

Or how about a slow-motion video of a woman or man seductively eating a jumbo wing with sauce running down their fingers and chin. They slowly lick the tip of each finger with an extended tongue like Gene Simmons from the iconic rock band KISS. All you would need to say is, **"Come get some"**. Do you want some of that? So do your potential guests.

Which do you think will get people in the door? There is one way to find out...try them both! Here's the real bonus: No need to bribe people with discounts if your marketing is clever and a little edgy. How do you know you're edgy? If it makes you feel a little outside your comfort zone, you should be there.

MYTH #2: MARKETING CREATES YOUR BRAND.

Marketing doesn't create your brand any more than your logo or tagline does. It's the biggest lie out there. Marketing is just a messenger for your brand. Sorry, but no amount of marketing will make up for a bad brand. Your brand is a combination of core values, purpose, and emotions. Those things are translated through the products you offer on your menu, and the hospitality conveyed through your crafted guest experience.

Truth: Marketing (done correctly) *accentuates* your brand; it doesn't *replace* your brand. If you don't know what your brand stands for (a brand is an extension of the founder's values), you won't be able to relay it, and then why anyone would want to listen to your marketing message? They won't, and that's why most marketing fails. This concept can be seen in the work of Simon Sinek whose bestselling book *Start with Why* breaks down the essence of what all great brands know: **People don't buy what you do, they buy why you do it!**

Most marketing focuses on the product or the "what." Few ever come close to talking about people and emotions, the "why." One simple change in your marketing content will be life changing for the direction and effectiveness of your marketing. **Start with why you do it**!

MYTH #3: MARKET TODAY, GET BUSINESS TOMORROW.

If only it were that easy. Sadly, marketing is a lot like online dating—you'll need to kiss a lot of frogs before you find your prince or princess. Marketing is far from a get-traffic-fast system. The most common myth is, "If you post it, they will come." Not exactly.

According to the American Marketing Association, the average consumer is exposed to up to 10,000 brand messages a day. *Ten thousand*! Now combine that with the 60,000 thoughts that neuroscientists say float around your head each day. Do you still wonder why no one likes your boring posts on Facebook or jumps in their car immediately to head down for that special you just posted? *(Note: If you still do wonder, please re-read myth #1.)*

Truth: Marketing needs to be thought of like planting seeds now for the harvest later. You plant now, nurture and care for it every day, then reap the bounty later.

Plant: Post today and *every* day. Please don't think that posting once a week is having an impact on your marketing efforts. That would be like going to the ocean, throwing in a pebble, and expecting a tidal wave to occur. It's not going to happen.

Nurture: Engage and comment when people like your posts. People have a human need to be appreciated, so share some love in your marketing. The secret to social media is being *social*. I know— not really a big secret, yet it's a component many leave out of their marketing plan.

Reap: Always look for returns on your marketing efforts to pay off about 30 to 60 days later. Yeah, I know—it sucks. However, you need to build up some marketing equity in your market before people will start to respond to your efforts. Before you reach critical mass, and the momentum continues.

Is it fair? No.
Is that the way it is? Yes.

MYTH #4: ALL YOU NEED IS FACEBOOK TO MARKET TODAY.

To bust this myth allow me to throw out two words for you: Cambridge Analytics. That mishap changed the smooth sailing you've been experiencing with Facebook for the past several years. Yes, Facebook is still a great way to spread your brand message and market. However, they also have made (and will continue to make) rapid changes to show the public (that means shareholders) that your data is safe.

They're already putting restrictions on how third-party apps can access information.

Should you worry? No.
Should you be concerned? Yes.

Truth: If you've thrown all your proverbial marketing eggs into the Facebook basket, it's time to take some out and diversify your marketing portfolio. Instagram is hot (even though Facebook owns it) and a great avenue for creative restaurant brands to share their messages through live streaming and stories (IGTV). The new IGTV looks like a great way to showcase who your brand is through longer-format video.

Don't forget the old-fashioned email blasts! Most modern point-of-sale systems today capture emails when guests place orders or make reservations at your restaurant. Is email as great as it once was? Sadly, no: too many people's inboxes have become littered with spam. However, marketing emails still get through to some. **If you're clever with your headline writing, you can get people to open your emails.**

If you haven't noticed the breadcrumbs dropped throughout this section... **video is the only way to grab the attention of today's guest**. People love video! Don't believe it? Look at these facts:

The total number of people who use YouTube: 1,300,000,000.

- 300 hours of video are uploaded to YouTube every minute.
- Almost 5 billion videos are watched on YouTube every single day.
- YouTube gets over 30 million visitors per day.

Damn, break out the smartphone and get going!

Here are two tips to make your video content stand out:

1. *Be transparent.* Consumers want to see the real people behind the brand. Take them on a tour of how to use a cold-drip coffee system to infuse your signature vodka for your award-winning Martini. How about filming your trip and conversation with a local farmer from whom you get your tomatoes?

2. *Give away some good stuff.* I'm not saying to give away all your secrets. However, share your famous Bolognese recipe that your great

grandmother taught you with your followers. Sharing the story behind the recipe is more important than the recipe itself! People love a great story. Take comfort that most people will appreciate your openness to share recipes and don't always have the time or ingredients to make it at home, so they'll still come down to your business. And let's be honest, some of your followers are just too lazy to try recreating your recipe at home. Marketing loves to exploit the duality of human behavior.

Becoming better at marketing your restaurant or bar starts with breaking free from the bullshit and heading for the truth. You now have four myths busted wide open and a few solutions to solve them.

Are you the kind of person to take action, or the kind who likes to keep doing the same things expecting different results?

Mindset is Your Secret Weapon

"Impossible is just a big word thrown around by small men who find it easier to live in the world they've been given than to explore the power they have to change it. Impossible is not a fact. It's an opinion. Impossible is not a declaration. It's a dare. Impossible is potential. Impossible is temporary. Impossible is nothing."

Muhammad Ali

Pararescue Mind Games

January 1984, San Antonio, TX
Pararescue O.L.J. (Operating Location J)
Week 8 of Indoctrination Training Phase (Indoc)

The team has been whittled down from 83 to 20. Still too many to send down to Pararescue Pipeline School, which includes S.E.R.E., Airborne, H.A.L.O., Special Forces Combat Diver, Paramedic, Aircrew, and Tactical Ops. Even with all that still pending, the cadre (instructors) think of ways to push the team even further (like along the lines of "Let's turn off the heater in the pool.")

A big part of Pararescue training is pool work. Water confidence exercises like bobbing, buddy breathing, underwater knot-tying, and crossovers are very common. You must be comfortable and calm under pressure to survive in a combat rescue scenario. Panic, and you make mistakes. Mistakes in combat get you or your fellow servicemen killed. Better the cadre finds out now whether you can handle the stress.

Believe or not, San Antonio gets a little chilly in the winter. With time at the Indoctrination Course coming to an end, the cadre had to play the mind game card.

ICE IN THE POOL

The start of pool training often starts with a distance fin swim. You wear a Speedo swimsuit (don't judge) and you're given scuba fins and a mask. The Olympic-sized outdoor pool has swim lanes, you get in, and you go! This day would be a little different.

When we arrived at the pool, the cadre had some bad news. The heater for the pool was broken, but we'd still have to swim. With the winter air crisp and cold, we got ready for the distance swim. A year later, we found out that the heater wasn't broken; it was turned off to put extra stress on the team. One of the cadres even went so far as to throw a couple of buckets of ice into the pool to accent the situation and kick the mind game up a notch. Before we even felt the brisk water, some of the class was already letting the idea of cold water get to them.

When shit starts flying sideways, people usually first quit in their minds. Special Ops teams call this the 40% Rule, which means you usually hit mental resistance at about 40% of your capacity—and that's where most people quit. You always have more inside of you than you think. We quit in our heads, and the body follows. You talk yourself out of it when you still have 60% left in the tank.

Guys were already talking about how much it was going to suck. Some guys got out Vaseline and smeared thin layers onto their skin to insulate themselves and keep warm. Others were given wetsuit headpieces to fight the cold. A few of us just said, "Fuck it." We planned to swim at our normal pace to keep us warm once we got going.

The water was the coldest I've ever felt in my life. My body went into shock briefly as the blood flowed from my extremities to keep my heart going. That's the first sign of hypothermia. I knew I had to get swimming or my legs and arms would seize up. Cold water has an almost thick feeling to it, much like you would think swimming in a large slushy pond would be. I could feel my legs getting numb, but I pushed on. I just had to get to my normal pace, and my body would heat up.

When I swim, it's very much a meditative act because all I hear is the sound in my head. Here, self-talk is critical to success. If you start to even *entertain the idea of quitting, you end up quitting*. I had to stay focused on pace and tempo. No time for negative thoughts or letting the temperature of the pool get in my head (figuratively and literally, now that I think about it).

I kicked faster and pushed off the wall harder on my flip turn. Keep going. Keep kicking. Control your breathing. Stay focused.

It worked.

Before I knew it, I had done my 60 laps. My hands and feet were numb. I looked around and saw that seven guys had taken S.I.E. (Self-Initiated Elimination). They quit, and I was shocked. They pushed through to the last week of Indoc Training just before entering the Pararescue Pipeline School only to give up.

It's easy to stay motivated when things are going your way. It's easy to smile when you have money in the bank. It's easy to be in love when you're not fighting or arguing with your significant other. Easy is the path of least resistance. But easy doesn't get you an outstanding life. Why? Because easy doesn't last.

Life is going to fuck with you as the cadres fucked with our heads. Some of the guys bought into the bullshit and let it take them down. The mental game of life serves one purpose: to make you adapt and evolve. It's part of your genetic makeup! Humans are built to adapt. It's the law of evolution, those who fail to adapt become extinct. Worse than becoming extinct is to become complacent and average. You didn't buy this book to find a formula that would allow you to stay where you are! You want it all.

I'm going to share with you, for the first time, how to finally get what you want in life. *Ready?*

You need to ask yourself a better question that drives your day.

In performance psychology, there's a concept known as "implementation intentions." I know it sounds fancy, but it's the same technique that has been used by Special Forces Operatives for decades. It's also known as **contingency planning** or the "if-then" framework.

For a better definition, let's go to Wikipedia:

> "*People generally have positive intentions, but often fail to act on them. The question is how to ensure that the set goal intentions will reliably lead to the desired goal-directed behaviors and subsequent attainment of those goals. Implementation intentions offer a practical solution for such a problem.*
>
> "*Achieving one's goals requires that certain goal-directed behaviors be instituted, but people are often unsuccessful in either initiating or maintaining these behaviors. The problems of initiating and maintaining goal-directed behavior can be addressed by using the implementation intention process. This if-then plan is a very specific approach as compared to goal intentions. A goal intention may be phrased in the following way: "I want to reach X!" Implementation intentions, on the other hand, are much more specific and seek to connect a future critical situation (an opportunity for goal attainment) with a specific goal-directed behavior, thereby leading to what could be called automatization in goal attainment. They are often phrased in the following way: "When situation X arises, I will perform response Y!" Where goal intentions are more general and abstract, implementation intentions are much more concrete and procedural.*
>
> "*Having formed a concrete plan involving a specific situation, this situation then becomes mentally represented and activated, leading to better perception, attention and memory concerning the critical situation. As a result, the chosen goal-directed behavior (the then-part of the plan) will be performed automatically and efficiently, without conscious effort. The automatization*

of the behavior in response to the future situation or cue, removes all hesitation and deliberation on the part of the decision maker when such a critical situation arises. This also has the effect of freeing cognitive resources for other mental processing tasks, and also for avoiding goal-threatening distractions or competing goals. It is also assumed that an implementation intention, once set, will continue operating non-consciously. This process is called strategic automaticity.

"The strength of commitment related to both the plan set and the goal is very important for the implementation intention to have an effect on people's behavior. Without commitment, an implementation intention will hardly have any effect on goal-directed behavior.

In the phase model of action, the use of implementation intention takes place in the post-decisional phase (implemental mindset, volition is the driving force of action) which follows the predecisional phase (deliberative mindset, motivation is the driving force of setting goals).[9] In the implemental mindset, a person is already committed to a goal and an implementation intention can be a good strategy to reach this goal.

"The basic structure of an implementation intention is as follows:

"IF *{situation}* **THEN** *I will {behavior}* "

For your driving question, I want you to use this: *Will it make the restaurant better?*

Using the if-then model, you would use this driving question to answer common scenarios:

If I stay out late [if], then go to work tired [then], will it make the restaurant better?

No. Lack of sleep will make me edgy and not as productive as I could be.

If I train my team every day [if] and it helps them increase sales [then], will it make the restaurant better?

Yes. Consistent training gives people confidence. Confident people are happier, and happier people sell more.

The key is to remember that there are solutions to every problem. Sometimes, you just can't see the solution because you're stuck in a mindset that isn't serving you. To break free, you must change how you look at the problem and change your attitude about finding a solution.

Sidebar: The problem is not the real problem, it's the **meaning you give the problem. Being flexible and open-minded is paramount to finding creative solutions.*

Don't accept other people's opinions that "it can't be done" or "it won't work." Just because they haven't done it, <u>doesn't mean you can't</u>. People will try to get you to be "reasonable." The last thing you want to be is reasonable when you're going after the life you want. "Easy like Sunday morning" are the lyrics to a Commodores song—fuck that!

Say NO to mediocrity.

Say NO to complacency.

Say YES to getting everything you want.

Will the Real Leader Please Stand Up?

Manager.

Leader.

Two words are thrown around our industry as if they're the same. Let me be clear that they are *not*. They aren't even close to the same—one works on push and the other pull.

Don't misunderstand; there are times you need to push people to get things done. For those times, the role of the manager is appropriate. However, if you want to break free from the cult of average and take your restaurant to the highest level, the real leader must stand up.

Leaders pull people forward by being the example, a *positive* example. You can't sit on the sidelines and bark orders. In simple terms, leaders lead the vision; managers manage the shift.

How do you step up to be the leader? These five steps you can get you going in the right direction.

1. CONTROL YOUR EMOTIONS TO INFLUENCE THE EMOTIONS IN OTHERS

You must understand that your restaurant reflects your leadership. Do you know that old saying that shit rolls downhill? That translates to restaurants: how you feel and how you act will flow down to your team.

If you're stressed and nervous, your team will be as well. When you stepped into the role of leadership, you were placed underneath a huge, glaring spotlight. Leadership comes with responsibilities you may not have considered. Managing your emotions and energy is one such responsibility that perhaps no one told you about before you took on the leadership mantle.

At our essence, we're social creatures that copy and mimic the behavior of leaders, good, bad, and ugly. Are you constantly upset that people show up for work late? Are you punctual yourself? **You can't expect more from your team than you do from yourself**. Well, you can, it just never ends well.

2. TAKE CARE OF YOURSELF

The restaurant industry can be brutal, physically and mentally. You might think that you're young and you can take it, but the body has limitations. Push yourself too hard for too long without proper self-care, and you'll quickly discover how brutal leading a restaurant can be.

Long-term success in this business means caring for your mind and body like a professional athlete. You're a professional. Start acting like it. Go to the gym and exercise. Sign up for a yoga class. Do something that will push your body to adapt and grow stronger. Too many people sacrifice their bodies for work. The stronger your body is, the more endurance and energy you'll have.

Make sure to eat better. I never fail to see the irony in someone working in the food business who has terrible eating habits. They're surrounded by food! Not eating healthier (or at all) is the behavior of a martyr just aching to say, "I worked all day and didn't eat." Please, don't behave like that. Here's a quarter, call someone who gives a shit. If your excuse is that you don't like the food at your restaurant, why do you work there? If you have dietary or budget concerns, pack some food.

Oh, and take a few minutes to eat at a table or sit in a chair to consume your food. You don't need to stand over a garbage can, shoveling cold food out of a deli cup into your mouth like it's the last meal you'll ever have. Sit down and enjoy your food like a dignified human.

Train your brain, too. Just like you need to push your body to become a world-class athlete, you must also condition your mind. Reading blogs, books, and industry magazines are a great start. Don't limit yourself to just restaurant topics. Be open to other life interests as well, like art, social science, philosophy, poetry, and classic literature. You might be surprised that something you learn elsewhere applies to the restaurant. Don't like to read? Get audiobooks or tune into YouTube. There's no excuse for not learning when you have a world of information available at your convenience, at your fingertips.

3. FOCUS ON THE POSITIVE

What's wrong is always available. So is *what's right*. You must be aware of a condition known as "negativity bias." Humans are wired to adapt and survive. Self-preservation kept your ancestors from being eaten by dangerous animals and engaging in activities that would get them killed. We still have that drive embedded deeply in our brains. Have you ever seen someone freeze like a deer in headlights? That's a prime example.

You might like to think that you look for the good in your restaurant. If so, you're one of the few. We tend to notice the things that aren't right with our world. Most people tend to focus on what's wrong in their restaurants and, sadly, with that as their sole focus, they get more of the same.

Try looking for and noticing all the things that are going right in your restaurant. Try that approach for a week. Negativity is like a dark, stormy cloud that hangs heavy in a restaurant and pollutes the culture. If you have a toxic culture, a sure symptom is negativity bias. I'm not asking you to become a Pollyanna, being ridiculously optimistic by living in denial. If something is wrong, accept it—but seek positive ways to make corrections and move forward. Negativity is like strapping on 100-pound lead boots and trying to dunk a basketball. Good luck with that, even if you are Michael Jordan.

4. JUST BE YOURSELF

Some people think they can act a certain way and be effective. You'll never get to the top of your game pretending to be someone or something you're not. Going through the motions rather than putting in real effort won't get you what you want.

A great example of acting like a leader is yelling at team members. People who behave this way are engaging in an embarrassing caricature of leadership. You don't need to yell to get your point across. Amateurs raise their voices—professionals improve their communication skills.

Being yourself, the real you is the only way to ascend into true leadership. This involves being authentic and vulnerable. Those two words can cause many to have that aforementioned "deer in headlights" look! Take a deep breath; it's not as frightening as you think.

Being authentic is just being you. Super easy, right? Now, if you worry that your team and guests may not like the real you, I have a question: Have you ever tried showing anyone the real you? You can succeed as a leader by being yourself.

Being vulnerable doesn't mean being weak, and letting people take advantage of you. It means being open to discussing things with sympathy and empathy. You've been there yourself. You can relate. You understand. Sympathy and empathy are elements of vulnerability. Empathy is the ability to understand what someone is feeling, either because you've gone through something similar or can imagine what they're experiencing. Sympathy is acknowledging a person's hardship and letting them know that you care.

Both are important; just don't get distracted from your role as a leader by being *too* empathetic.

5. ASK, DON'T ORDER

True leaders understand that influence skills are paramount to success. Influence is built by harnessing the power of a few key ingredients.

Respect

Many leaders assume that their role requires them to be a jerk. They feel their team needs to fear them. They bark orders and try to make team members bend to their will. That may have worked in the '70s, but in 2019, it's a sure-fire way to earn a high turnover rate.

Lead like that, and you'll spend more time placing help-wanted ads and interviewing very few high-quality candidates because word will get out that you're an unpleasant person and your restaurant is a bad place to work. Respect is not achieved by demand—you earn it from your team by proving you deserve it. Nothing is given to anyone in the restaurant world. You'll have to fight tooth and nail to become (and remain) a leader. Leadership isn't a title; it's the actions you take every day for your team and your guests. Notice that order: **your team before your guests**. Show your team respect and not only will they return it to you (that's basic reciprocity), they'll give it to your guests.

Trust

This is the element that makes or breaks teams. Leaders understand the importance of trust and work diligently to maintain it with their team. You must trust your team to do what you expect, which means having authentic conversations about expectations and then allow them to do their jobs. If you find yourself needing to micromanage or bug your team constantly to get things done, you either don't trust them, or you might have the wrong person on your team. Trust them, train them, declare your standards, and then allow them to shine. You must also demonstrate integrity through your words and actions. No one trusts a hypocrite.

Requests

Which of these sounds more likely to get the team to act?

1. "You need to wipe the booths down after every guest leaves. If you don't, I'll have to write you up."

2. "I have a request. It's important to make sure we're always ready for the next guest. So, I'm requesting that you stay diligent on keeping the booths wiped down as soon as the guests get up. Can you help me with that?"

A simple key to influencing your staff: ask. That's all. Ask with clear directions, expectations, and reasons why. People who do things without having a "why" only comply out of fear. People who understand the why behind a request will commit to keeping the standards.

If you've been vacillating between being a manager and being a leader, it's time to take a stand. Step up and be the leader your team wants and needs.

Be Unfuckwithable

You never know where inspiration can come from. That is why active listening and having situational awareness is critical to your growth as a leader. About a year ago, I was in a meeting of a high-level mastermind group I belong to (*a group of restaurant consultants and thought leaders*), and I heard these intriguing words: **Be Unfuckwithable!**

I immediately resonated with the phrase. I set about to find a definition and a way to incorporate that into my coaching practice and personal life.

It all comes down to your relationship with yourself and all the little "sub-selves" inside you. If you can master this concept, you'll break free to the other side of life! This is the barrier holding you back, stuck and in pain.

Life is a firestorm at times. As more shit comes up, challenging you, the flames rise and often block your view of the other side. This is where faith comes into play. You'll also need to connect with your five selves, the selves that serve as your compass to become *Unfuckwithable*. Time to look Toto in the eyes, click your fucking heels, and say, *"I don't think we're in mediocrity anymore!"*

THE FIVE SELVES YOU *NEED* TO *BE* UNFUCKWITHABLE

Let me start with this: You need *all* 5 of these to be Unfuckwithable. They aren't just nice to have—*you need to own these five selves and protect them with everything you have.*

The Three Agents of Personal Doom (Negativity, Complacency, and Mediocrity) will come for your five selves and try to take them from you. You must do everything in your power to prevent this. The quality of your life depends on protecting your five selves!

1. SELF-CONFIDENCE: BELIEF IN YOUR ABILITIES

For most, this one is easy, particularly if you've been in the business for a decent amount of time. You don't last in the restaurant business for a long time if you suck or don't believe in your abilities!

Now, self-confidence is different than being cocky. Self-confidence is quiet and takes action without fanfare. Cockiness is brash, crude, and seeks attention. The problem is that cocky people usually aren't as good at what they do as they think. Self-confident people know they're good and don't have to prove it to anyone because their results speak for themselves. Your goal should always be to have your results do the talking.

> *"Those who know, do not speak. Those who speak, do not know."*
> —*Lao Tzu*

2. SELF-WORTH: BELIEVE YOU DESERVE

Here's where things start to go wrong for many. While we may be rich in self-confidence, we may also be broke when it comes to self-worth. If you don't think you deserve success, your self-worth is low. Problems arise when we make our way up the ladder of success, and our poor self-worth starts ringing the alarm that we don't deserve it. Next, we subconsciously sabotage ourselves and drop back down to where we "should" be. It's a lot like a thermostat set to maintain a specific temperature. You have subconscious mental set-points, too.

Those with poor self-worth have, unfortunately, bought into a bullshit belief. Quite commonly, this buy-in occurs in our youth. Someone tells us that we're "not good enough" or "won't amount to much," and that bullshit plays like a broken record in our heads. Stop letting the past control your future. It's time to toss that old record and play a new one: You are worthy. You are valuable. You do matter. You are important.

3. SELF-ACCEPTANCE: UNDERSTAND THINGS JUST *ARE*

Nothing is good or bad until you attach meaning. Shit is going to happen during your life and, you need to be able to separate what each event means to you. A bird flies over you and shits on your head. You can look at that event as the universe telling you that you suck, or you can decide that it's just bad timing (wrong place, wrong time). Things don't happen *to* you if you want to **Be Unfuckwithable**—you make things happen *for yourself*.

When you find your mind spinning out of control with meaningless bullshit, you need to ask yourself more empowering questions. No, not, "Why does this shit always happen to me?" Instead try, "What else could this mean?" Or, "What can I learn from this?" Then search for at least three positive meanings for what happened. Yes, *three* positive meanings. This will prove to be a challenge because your mind tends to gravitate towards negativity. That bias is the default setting for most humans. So, break free from the bullshit holding you back. Come up with better meanings to events in your life and realize that no, things aren't always your fault.

4. SELF-COMPASSION: FORGIVE YOURSELF AND LOVE WHO YOU ARE

"Forgiveness means giving up all hope for a better past." —Attribution unclear

You must let the past die. You must bury the pain and let it go, or it will haunt your every fucking moment until it consumes you. You are human. Humans are fallible. We make mistakes. We say the wrong things. We cause pain to others, sometimes without realizing it. Unless you're an asshole who enjoys bringing misery to others, you're a good person. You need to forgive yourself. It's impossible to reach Unfuckwithable status if you're full of self-pity and victim thinking.

Start by forgiving yourself. Then forgive others who have wronged or hurt you. Holding onto hate and anger eats away at you from the inside, and manifests poorly in your outward behavior and actions. It's hard to hold opposing energies in your body. Replace the negative with the positive. Let go of the hate and replace it with love. Not to get all sentimental or mushy here, but you need to love yourself.

Self-love is the only true love there is. It starts with you. Your capacity to love others depends on your capacity to love yourself! No bullshit. You can't give to others what you can't give to yourself. Honestly, I struggled with self-love for years. I sought love from outside sources and validation. It never was enough because I didn't have self-love, and all I was doing was filling up an empty heart with outside "love." It didn't last until I learned first to have more compassion and love for myself.

5. SELF-CONTROL: DO WHAT YOU NEED TO DO

The last of the five selves is the hardest one to maintain. Why? Because there are so many distractions trying to steal your attention.

Gotta look at Facebook.

Need to hop onto Instagram.

My friend sent me a link to a YouTube video—better click it before I forget.

What's happening on Twitter?

Every second of every day, your self-control is doing battle with the outside world for the most precious things you own: your time and attention.

Remember that time is not money; money is money. You can make more money—you can't make more time.

Self-control and **discipline** are required if you want to reach Unfuckwithable status! You can't get there without them. Discipline is doing the right thing even if you don't want to. It's saying "fuck you" to distraction and "fuck yes" to the life you truly want. Temptations are bombarding you all day long, so you better have a plan to deal with them before they shove you into the quicksand of time management.

In case you forgot, I think time management is bullshit. You don't control time; you only control where you focus your attention.

If you've read my booklet *Outstanding Mindset*, you know I believe that how you structure your day is crucial to getting shit done. I use that system religiously, and so do my clients. You must have a solid routine that puts you in the right frame of mind **every day**. And, you must be crystal clear to yourself about your objectives for the day (I call them the Big Three). Without a plan, you're vulnerable to the demands and distractions that life throws at you. Come up with a plan and stay the course. You must be a little selfish with your time and attention to ensure you do what you must move your life and restaurant forward.

THE FLIP SIDE: THE FOUR SELVES TO AVOID

Now you know the power of the five selves and why they're crucial to your quest to **Be Unfuckwithable**.

Standing in your way, however, are the enemies you and your five selves will face on that quest: The Four Selves of Your Personal Apocalypse. So many with potential have fallen prey to these manipulative, emotional creatures that thrive on your downfall. *Know them so you can avoid them!*

1. SELF-DOUBT: LACKING FAITH IN YOURSELF

Second-guessing yourself is natural at times. When it holds you hostage and keeps you from taking action, it's a paralyzing monster. Self-doubt comes from that same voice that questions your self-worth. It's that wounded child in you that thinks it's protecting you. It's not—it's keeping you stuck in complacency and mediocrity. Self-doubt lives in your comfort zone. Stop thinking of your comfort zone as a place of comfort and see it for what it is: a place that causes you pain.

Nothing great ever originates from that cozy place where you don't challenge yourself to improve and achieve success. In your comfort zone, you sit back, becoming jealous and resentful while you watch others reach their goals. That could be *you* attaining success—you need to drop the limiting beliefs that hold you down. Breaking free comes from one simple declaration: **NO MORE!**

2. SELF-DECEPTION: LYING TO YOURSELF

The greatest lies we tell are the ones we tell ourselves. It's true. You're a master at self-deception. You are adept at talking yourself into or out of anything! You have an entire league of misery living in your head telling you why you can't do the things that will improve you and your restaurant. Stop listing to them and start searching for the truth.

The truth is truly out there if (*and only if*) you're bold enough to look at it and accept it. The truth isn't some shady used car salesperson willing to say anything to get you to buy a lemon. The truth…*just…is*. Ignore the bullshit narrative the voices in your head tell you; they're keeping you from seeing the truth. They say the truth will set you free, but first it will piss you off, and they're right. After you get over being pissed off, you'll see the situation for what it truly is.

3. SELF-PITY: THINKING LIKE A VICTIM

Poor you. Things don't seem to go right for you. Why don't you take it easy? Have some milk and cookies.

Yeah, that victim bullshit doesn't fly with me. If you want to play the victim, stand in line with the other 95 percent of the population that thinks the world is doing them wrong. Winners, those who become **Unfuckwithable**, don't play the victim, ever! They take personal accountability for everything in their lives!

You *own* you! That means your thoughts, your actions, and your results are yours and yours alone. No whiners here. Losers whine about how unfair life is. Believe me when I tell you that life isn't out to get you. If your restaurant and life aren't 100 percent the way you want them, you're the only one to blame.

To **Be Unfuckwithable** means, you step up and take charge of your life. It means not settling for less than you're capable of achieving. It means giving 100 percent every time and every day! Oh, and for the sake of not driving me crazy, stop saying you "give 110 percent." You only have 100 percent to give and honestly, if people would give 80 percent they would be astonished by the results!

4. SELF-CENTEREDNESS: MAKING EVERYTHING ABOUT *YOU*

Not to be the bearer of bad news but you can't **Be Unfuckwithable** if you don't contribute to the world and have an impact on others. Being self-centered causes the world to turn against you because you're only looking out for yourself. In the social hierarchy that we dwell in, *we elevate to higher levels by lifting others up and not just ourselves.*

You will never reach the top of your game without building deep and lasting relationships with other people. Your team, your family, and your friends need to know you're looking out for them. In the movies we root for the hero who helps others become *their* best and overcome life challenges. We despise the villains who betray others for self-centered gain. Life does imitate the movies because the stories come from real human emotions and experiences.

It's not about you; it's about what you can do for others. To **Be Unfuckwithable,** you must understand that the value you provide to others *is* everything! Those who survive get paid by the hour. Those who thrive get paid according to how valuable they are to others. If you want more, you must become more valuable.

FINAL THOUGHTS ON BEING UNFUCKWITHABLE

Time is NOT on Your Side

Coach Obvious here, throwing this in your face: You're going to die one day. Yeah, I know—you want to thank me for that fucking uplifting pep talk. Well, it *is* a pep talk. I don't want you to waste another day being fuck**WITH**able. You need a wakeup call—the only way to get what the fuck you want with the precious time you have left is to **Be Unfuckwithable**! It's the cure for being average and the key component to getting the life you want.

Now, to get where you need to be, we're going to need to make one last stop...

Tap into Your Dark Side to Be Unfuckwithable

Bruce Wayne has Batman. Clark Kent has Superman. Bruce Banner has The Hulk. Kobe Bryant has the Black Mamba. How about you? Do you have an alter ego you can channel to elevate your leadership to the elite level?

You should.

To find it, we're going to need to take a trip to your dark side. Don't think you have a dark side? Let me assure you that everybody has one. Think about the things you crave, the things you lust after, the secrets you keep hidden deep, deep inside. That energy comes from your dark side. The problem is that your entire life you've been told those feelings are bad, so you locked them away and hid them from the world.

That's a mistake: they're the key to leadership success. It's time to tap into that power and harness it so you can become the badass leader you truly are.

Your Dark Side Doesn't Have to Be Bad

Just because it's called your dark side doesn't mean it has to be dark, per se. Batman fought against injustice even though he lived a dark life, so maybe you prefer to call it your "**alter ego.**" It's that part of you that comes out when you need an edge. Most of the time it sits quietly in the background not causing any problems.

But you need it to surface because your alter ego is your true self. It's the person who doesn't give a shit about what others think. **Its purpose is to protect you, and its mission is to win**. You probably shut it down when those around you (*usually family and friends*) told you things like:

"You can't say that."

"Don't do that."

"Be good."

"Stop causing trouble."

"Behave."

"Don't make a big deal of it."

"Why can't you be like _____."

You've been trained like Pavlov's dogs to push that alter ego to the back. Instead, another persona you've adopted for everyday life comes to the front. That's not the real you, that's the "surface" you. Deep inside *is* the real you, just waiting to come out.

The real you is powerful. It's exacting. It's strategic. It's honest. It's driven. It wants to succeed, and it doesn't accept failure.

It's not evil; it's merciful.

It's not cruel; it's fair.

It's not hateful; it's compassionate.

HOW TO RELEASE THE REAL YOU

Now that you know the truth about the real you, how do you bring it back to the spotlight? The first step is to be honest with yourself.

Think about this: What would it feel like to let go of all the bullshit, all the external pressures, every false expectation, and just be yourself?

It's fucking freedom.

To get there you need to trust the voice inside you, the raw instinct that knows you best. For years you've suppressed that person to conform and be who others said you should be, **who you thought you** <u>had</u> **to be**. Unfuckwithable leaders know exactly who they are and the things at which they excel. They don't bullshit others; they stare straight at the truth; they move forward without wondering what others think. *They own their shit…all of it.*

Chef Lee Hefter (a partner at Wolfgang Puck) was asked once by food editors at a press shoot to make a statement about his food. His reply was just one sentence, *"I make my statement on the plate."*

Boom. That's being **Unfuckwithable**.

Not sure if you're there yet? How about a simple scale to determine where you are?

> *Supervisor:* You need to be told what to do and when to do it. You don't take any chances—playing it safe is your way of life. You don't confront people, and you fly below the radar to avoid making people upset. You care about what everyone thinks of you.
>
> *Manager:* You tell people what to do even if you don't do it yourself. You run around most of the shift, putting out fires, so you feel important. You never have time for the important tasks because you're just too busy *looking* busy. You talk *down to* your staff instead of *to* your staff. You get a buzz off the high of being the boss. You're more concerned about yourself than the team or the brand.
>
> *Unfuckwithable Leader:* You lead by example and live the core values you talk about. You take personal accountability for everything in your life. You don't wait for things to happen; you *make* things happen. You coach and train your team constantly and consistently, and you're always looking for ways to improve yourself. You don't worry about what others think of you because you're confident in your abilities. You put the team and brand before your personal agenda.

Be honest, which one are you?

It's not too late to become an **Unfuckwithable** leader. You need to stop pretending to be someone you're not. Time to suppress the outside input and listen to that inner voice that pushes its finger in your back and tells you to do it. Time to unleash your true self and drop the mask you've been wearing for so long.

Your alter ego is your true self. You've done such a good job wearing the mask of who you think you need to be that you've likely forgotten who you really are. In coaching, I use a behavior survey tool (The ProScan® Survey) to assess your natural strengths. The tool shows who you're pretending to be in the world—*it reveals your mask.* The goal of coaching is to get you to drop the bullshit, put down the mask, and be who you truly are.

St. Catherine of Siena summed it up best: ***"Be who you were meant to be and you will set the world on fire."***

It's time for your true identity to come forward from the shadows and take charge.

Be who you have always been.

You're Unfuckwithable—don't forget that.

3 Signs the Restaurant Industry is the Business for You

We've all had times during which we've questioned ourselves, particularly those of us who work in the restaurant industry. Some call it burnout. Some call it a sign to get out. In reality, the issue is that you've disconnected with the driving force that sustains you. That force is still there; it's just taking a nap.

Let's rekindle your love of this industry and your restaurant. Let's re-ignite that fire deep down inside and get it roaring again.

Quitting is easy. It's easy to say, "I'm just not right for this industry." That's the coward's way out. The fact that you're reading this tells me you truly love the chaos and intensity of this roller coaster industry. *You need to remember why you love it.*

PEOPLE FUEL YOU

We're drawn to the restaurant industry because we thrive on the energy we feel when we're around other people. You probably sense a magnetic quality about yourself that you can't quite put your finger on. We're wired in our DNA to be social creatures. Human beings gather for the common good of the collective. We have families, feel connections to neighborhoods, build cities, and go to restaurants to share life.

Breaking bread traditionally signifies trust, confidence, brotherhood, and comfort with other people. It is a way of celebrating our ability to come together as one. No matter how divided we can become on a variety issues, we can come back to the dining table to share what holds us together: humanity.

You don't have to be an easy-going social person (high-extrovert) to feel the need to be around other people for energy. Look at a professional football game. It would be easy (and probably a lot cheaper) to sit at home alone with a carryout meal from your favorite neighborhood restaurant, watching the game, and yelling at the T.V. about the bad call the referee just made. But we crave human synergy, camaraderie, and energy. That's why restaurants and bars get more business on game days — that's why football stadiums sell out with tens of thousands of raving fans. People amplify emotions.

YOU FEEL THE DESIRE TO GIVE

Think about what restaurants are at their essence: places to restore your soul. Don't think so? Take a trip back in time to Paris in the year 1765. There was a small tavern owner and soup maker named Monsieur Boulanger who thought it would be a great idea to be able to sell food to the public. However, back then the guilds (unions) controlled that and it wasn't allowed. Boulanger went to court and won his case due to the fact that there was no Soup-makers Guild.

He was a badass for going up against the guilds and fighting for his right to sell what he called "a restorative" to the masses. Basically, it was a bowl of sheep's feet in a white sauce (not cutting edge culinary by today's standard, but let's roll with it).

The sign above his door allegedly proclaimed, "*Boulanger débite des restaurants divins*," or "Boulanger sells restoratives fit for the gods." Restoratives, in this instance, refer to rich broths considered in the past to be capable of restoring one's health. "Restaurant," used in many languages today, comes from the French verb *restaurer*, meaning "to restore or refresh."

Next time you dig into your favorite dish made with a white sauce, look up and say thanks to a little rebel who went up against the establishment.

Back to giving to others. The trouble comes when you give and give to others without remembering that you also need to give to yourself. If your health has taken a turn or you find you're exhausted at the end of the day, you need to face the fact that you're not giving to yourself.

How can you give to others if you fail to maintain your peak performance levels? You can't.

This is when you start looking for the exit signs, but it's not time to get out. It's time to cowboy up and take care of yourself. Eat better (come on, you're surrounded by fresh ingredients). Sleep better (unplug your Xbox earlier or stop sending Snaps at two in the morning). Get some exercise (yes, you're on your feet all day in a restaurant), but that doesn't necessarily get your heart rate up and improve your cardiovascular capacity).

YOU LOVE THE CHAOS

Come on, deep down you love this industry! The excitement of the dinner rush can give you a buzz that you can't wait to recreate the next night. You might say you don't like it, even going out of your way to tell others. But when you're sitting there alone with your thoughts, you miss it. You crave it. You need it.

Of course, if your restaurant isn't run well, you might not have those warm, happy feelings about the service rush. However, if you've ever worked in a restaurant with a seasoned team that seems to move like a well-choreographed dance troupe, you know exactly the feeling of operating on the edge of being out of control yet remaining in control. Mario Andretti said it best: "If everything seems under control, you're just not going fast enough."

You live for this. The restaurant is your stage, and every night is a performance that allows you to participate in an event that elevates the human experience to a higher level. That's what restaurants truly do.

If you've been in the restaurant industry for any amount of time, and if you search your heart, you'll find that you don't want to leave this chaotic industry. It could be that you need to find a better leader.

The industry is flooded with bad and average restaurants that give our industry a terrible reputation. Conversely, there are amazing leaders in this industry. Maybe you're one of those great leaders. Maybe you've just forgotten to connect with *your why*?

Read this section again and see if you can reignite that spark you once had. When you do, take great care to fuel that fire every day and make a commitment to keep it burning inside.

How to Break Bad Habits in Your Restaurant

Change.

You know you should make those changes in your restaurant, so why don't you? Change is a fickle thing. While it calls to us on a deeper level, it's also quite resistant to being caught. Change is a hypocrite.

When you try to make changes in your life and your restaurant, change pushes back, sometimes rather harshly. Why? Because you're resistant to change yourself. A few bad habits you've developed make you more comfortable keeping things the same.

Your habits and the habits of your team run deep. It will take more than a memo or a one-hour workshop to overcome them. **Habits are at the foundation of change theory.** To conquer them, you must first understand why change is so hard to achieve.

Let's take a look at the three big reasons you don't—or won't—change.

1. FEAR

Know that fear, whether real or imagined, is a powerful enemy of change. Fear keeps us immobilized; stuck in situations that we know deep down we should change. Marketers know that too, and they use fear as a tool to get us to buy all kinds of things we don't need. The question is, will you allow fear to use you, or will you use fear to motivate yourself?

Fear of the unknown is ever-present and can be paralyzing if we allow it to be. Here's a common one: Why don't you train your team more? Fear says, "If I invest in training them more and they get better skills, they'll take those skills to another restaurant." That's a false assumption.

The only fear you should be harboring in the above situation is what will happen if you don't train your team. Fail to invest in the development of your staff, and you won't elevate your food, service, marketing, or leadership. You'll be stuck in a perpetual time loop. Your competition, meanwhile, will adapt and out-perform, out-sell, out-market, and out-train you. That's the cold, hard truth. Absorb it.

Fear is natural. It's a hard-wired human survival mechanism. **Fear needs to be acknowledged and respected; it doesn't need to be obeyed**. Face your fears, address them, and then do the opposite of whatever fear suggests. Run this thought through your grey matter, "Okay, I can see where investing in training the team is risky. There's a chance that some of the team will take their new skills to another restaurant. But those who stay will improve and elevate the entire brand."

2. COMFORT ZONE

Comfort is dangerous for restaurant owners and managers. The industry changes rapidly and if you don't or can't adapt to keep pace (or better yet, be innovative and stay ahead of the competition), you'll quickly find yourself displaced in your market.

Your comfort zone is where all your bad habits hang out. They're like old friends, and no one wants to get rid of an old friend, particularly if you've known them since childhood. Well, sometimes you must let go of old friends. If they're hurting you or keeping you from success, get rid of them.

So, what are some of the bad habits holding you hostage in your comfort zone? Let's take a peek…

Lack of follow-through: Remember when you said you were going to update your food cost spreadsheet and your pricing? You talked about it a few months ago, and you still haven't started on it. What happened? Good intentions don't build outstanding restaurants; actions and results do. And, seriously, what kind of message does this send to your team?

Inconsistency in marketing: You said you were going to ramp up your social media marketing. You get on Facebook and post regularly for a week. You get a little spike in business, then you get too busy and forget to post for another week or two. Your followers begin to tune out because your social media strategy is a little too unpredictable to follow. People like a consistent message sent across all your marketing. If you fail to deliver, don't be shocked to find your followers at your competition, getting their needs met.

Lack of a plan: You know you should make sales projections and establish budgets, so why don't you? Most likely, it's because it doesn't appeal to you as a fun activity. Most people who own and operate restaurants tend to be more on the "right-brain" side of things. They like the creative, visual, artistic, and organized chaos elements of the restaurant business. People who are "left-brain" dominant tend to gravitate toward analytical processes, systems, strategies, and details. To find a balance in your business, you need to make sure you have people on your team with complementary skills, and who can do the things that don't excite you. Not having a plan because you aren't very good at some tasks is a lame excuse. All outstanding restaurants make plans and then work those plans every single day.

POP QUIZ: are you right- or left-brain dominant?

Want to find out if you're right-brain or left-brain dominant quickly? Try this simple test: Put both your hands out in front of you. Now, clasp your hands in front of you, interlocking your fingers. Which thumb is on top? If your left thumb is on top, you're most likely right-brain dominant. If your right thumb is on top, you're most likely left-brain dominant. You can try clasping your hands and forcing the opposite thumb on top, but it usually feels pretty weird and unnatural.

---

3. FALSE EXPECTATIONS

Some people have what I call Fortune Teller Syndrome. They have preconceived notions that things won't work out. In other words, they're pessimists. You can usually tell if someone suffers from this syndrome by analyzing the language they use. If any of these statements sound familiar, honestly ask yourself the second question:

"We tried that before." (hmm, really) How many times did you try it?

"That won't work in our market." Do you have data and research to back that up?

"We've always done it like this." Have you considered that ***that*** might be the problem?

What I call Fortune Teller Syndrome is something I've explained previously: negativity bias. Some of the hardwiring that drives humans to survive and adapt isn't conducive to helping you grow your business. Negativity bias is when your mind reacts to bad things stronger than they do the good. Some people say it takes five positive comments to override every one negative comment. It's easy to see why sometimes when you don't get the results you want right away, you lean into beliefs that won't work.

The good news is that now you know about it. Having inside information about how your brain is wired is very helpful in creating change. When you're aware of something like negativity bias, you can make a choice. You can either choose to accept it and stay stuck or choose a different path and move forward.

That's the amazing thing about free will—you do have a choice.

Now that you understand some of the things holding you back from making the changes you need let's explore how to implement change in your life and your restaurant.

THE 3 PS OF REALIZING CHANGE

Purpose

Knowing your purpose, vision, mission, or why you need to change is powerful. If you know why the how is easy. The biggest obstacle you may face is failing to connect with a powerful enough WHY that will drive you to change. Your purpose must be connected to strong emotions. You can think of lots of logical reasons why you should change, but logic won't move you to take action.

Let's look at a common change many people struggle with: going to the gym. On the surface, you can think of a dozen reasons why you should go. You'll feel better. You'll have more energy. You'll be healthier. All great reasons. So why do most people not make the commitment and take action?

They may not have tapped into the positive emotions associated with going to the gym. Think about how you feel after working out. Confident. Happy. Calm. Love. Yes, love, because taking time to take care of yourself is love. **When you tap into emotions, you tap into your ultimate power source.**

Persistence

Remember that change will push back. That's the sweet soft voice of your comfort zone calling. You must commit to staying the course toward change. This is particularly difficult for restaurant owners and managers. You might be extremely committed and dedicated to making a change in your business, but other people on your team might not share your enthusiasm. Some team members will complain. They'll resist. They'll try to break your resolve. Now, *if you've tapped into a strong purpose and why, you'll be able to weather the storm.*

Persistence also means being adaptable and adjusting as needed. Of course, not everything is going to go as planned. You must expect obstacles to rise and challenge you. Thinking ahead and having contingency plans are the best ways to circumvent challenges.

In neuro-linguistic programming or NLP, there's a presupposition (guiding principle) that states: If something doesn't work, try something else. **If that doesn't work, try something else. If that doesn't work, try something else…** Do you get the hint? Too many times, we try to implement change and give up too easily.

Patience

Back in the 1950s, there was a plastic surgeon by the name of Maxwell Maltz. When he realized it took his patient about 21 days after surgery to get used to seeing their new face, he became fascinated by human behavior. This is where the famous "21 Days to Break a Habit" myth started.

The truth is that on average, it takes more than two months before a new habit or change becomes automatic. Sixty-six days, to be exact. Can you see why many people will give up when they don't see a change after just 21 days? For some people, it may take even longer than 66 days for a new habit to take hold. To make lasting positive change, you need to have patience.

Phillippa Lally and colleagues at the University College London published a study in the *European Journal of Social Psychology* that concluded it took anywhere from 18 days to 254 days for people to form a new habit (Lally et al., 2010). So, don't beat yourself up too badly when you don't see change happen as quickly as you would like.

Habits truly do make or break restaurants. Habits reflect the standards of the brand. It's in the things we see, like the way team members answer the phone, greet guests, serve drinks, plate entrées, treat each other, clean the bathrooms, present checks, and say goodbye.

It's also in the things we might not notice, like updating costs, managing budgets, training, team communication, hiring, and employee appreciation. Some habits are easy to start, like showing appreciation daily. It's as simple as walking up to someone on your team or a guest and saying just two words, "Thank you."

If you want your restaurant to stand out and excel, you must develop positive habits, which takes patience. As American writer and philosopher Will Durant said, *"We are what we repeatedly do. Excellence, then, is not an act, but a habit."*

Make positive changes to your new habits.

Are You Running Your Restaurant, or is it Running You?

#*WTSD*: **Without clear directions, your team will create their own.**

You must make it your mission as the owner or operator to discuss your core brand values and mission every day. If you don't, you'll get the same results as mentioned above: hit and miss.

You need to write your core values down and have a crystal-clear mission in mind that can be summed up in one sentence, one concise statement that you can bombard your team with every day to set the tone. Try to make it as short and powerful as possible. Use Six-Word Memoirs or a Tweet as an example. In Six-Words Memoirs you have—you guessed it—only six words. In old-school Twitter, you only had 140 characters to get your message across (now it's 280 characters). Use the old-school version. These exercises will force you to fine tune your mission down to a few powerful words.

Still stuck? Study the taglines used by some popular brands:
- Zappos: *Delivering Happiness*
- Mercedes: *The Best or Nothing*
- Dos Equis: *Keeping it Interesante*
- GoPro: *Be a Hero*
- Coca-Cola: *Open Happiness*

As the good book says, *"Where there is no vision, the people perish."*

YOUR MENU

Problem: When sales start to die, you become desperate and add items in a bid to get people to come back. By doing this, you dilute your brand identity. It may bring in a few new guests, but your message is now watered down, and your old guests will lose confidence in your brand. When there's no trust, guests go elsewhere.

Solution: Make sure your menu is a reflection of your brand. Great menus are:

Approachable

Your guests can relate to the familiar items on your menu. While it's great to have a few unique items that help you stand out in your market, too many can have a disastrous effect. You need items that trigger emotions in your guests. Too many menus are designed to serve an owner's or chef's ego and not with the guest in mind.

Containable

Your team needs to be able to execute the menu flawlessly and consistently. You can design the menu to be impractical from a culinary execution point of view, but here's the downside of that approach: most folks on your culinary team won't tell you they can't do it. They'll find a way to make it happen and sometimes that means they'll compromise standards, take shortcuts, and find an easier way.

Profitable

Let's not forget that you need to make a profit. Use tools like menu engineering spreadsheets to take emotions out of your menu programming process so you can determine whether your items are profitable and popular.

Your menu is your number one marketing and profitability tool—treat it with respect. It's essentially impossible to be everything to everyone. You're much better off filling a niche and excelling at a few great menu items than offering a lot of mediocre items. Do you see Shake Shack selling pizzas and burritos? There might be some logic to why they don't offer such things.

YOUR STAFF

Problem: You've made some bad hiring choices, usually when desperate to fill positions (known as panic hiring). These staff members bring along all kinds of bad habits, and now they've infected the rest of your team. You're stuck with poor performers who only care about themselves. Rather than fire anyone, you give into the fears of being short-staffed and hiring replacements that could be even worse. You'll use softeners to explain away your fear, like, "They're not that bad." Or you blame outside circumstances and make statements like,

"There are just no good workers out there," and, "These Millennials are all entitled and don't want to work."

Solution: Seek and you will find. If you think there are no good applicants out there, you won't find any. If your perception of Millennials is that they're difficult, that says more about your view of them than what's true. You need to understand Millennials so you can manage them properly. They're different, and using outdated management techniques don't work with them. Time to educate yourself about this new generation in the workforce.

Upgrade your team and get rid of the bad apples. You'll need to raise your standards first and never drop them. When you let the staff run your restaurant, it's like having the tail wag the dog: it just doesn't work. Neither will your restaurant until you take control.

You offset the replacement of bad team members by always recruiting. You must actively recruit new team members. I'm not talking about just posting a help wanted ad and hoping for applications to pour in—hope isn't a strategy. Recruiting means looking at resumes on job sites and business network sites like LinkedIn, and making the first move. It's simple: sit back and wait for top talent to come looking for you or **get after it and take action to ensure you attract the best**. Your choice.

YOURSELF

When the call for restaurant coaching comes in, I ask the owner to tell me the issues. Nine times out of 10, they tell me it's someone else on their team. If coaching could fix this "problematic" employee, they'd have the restaurant they wanted.

Problem: **It's you and your mindset.** You're too focused on outside circumstances instead of what's going on with you internally. Think of yourself as the source of water at the top of a mountain. Since you're the source, you're in control of the flow. You, not the people at the bottom of the mountain—they only get what you let flow down. That's how culture works. It starts at the top and flows down.

The chokehold on any restaurant is the mindset of the owner and operators. You are your problems, and you are your solutions. You can get out of this by shifting your mindset.

Solution: Get a coach or mentor to help you see through the story you've concocted about why you can't have the restaurant you want. It's not your staff. It might be the bad apples we discussed earlier that need to be tossed out. It's not the economy (a lot of restaurants are recording record sales and profits this year). **It's you.**

You must divorce your bullshit story and marry the truth. If your restaurant is running you, then today is your day to do something about it. Taking control won't be easy when you've allowed it to get away from you. It will resist and push back. You'll want to give in and go back to the easier way—*don't.*

Anything worth fighting for is worth the struggle and discomfort. The most successful restaurant operators are comfortable with being uncomfortable. Tony Robbins is the mind behind one of my favorite quotes, *"The quality of your life is in direct proportion to the amount of uncertainty you can comfortably deal with."*

Your restaurant is a living thing shaped by the level of energy you put into it. It thrives via the people you select to interact with your guests every day. It's your restaurant—don't waste another day not controlling how it's run.

Be the restaurant owner and leader you know you can be.

7 Rules for a
Kick-Ass Restaurant!

Do you want a better restaurant? Don't answer too fast; I want you to think about the deep implications of your answer. Lots of people want more; few are willing to step out of their comfort zones to get it. Your comfort zone is easy and, as the name makes clear, comfortable.

Nothing great ever happened in your comfort zone. Eating Doritos in a beanbag chair while drinking a soda and watching *Top Chef* might be the good life for some. But for the ambitious, the comfort zone is where dreams and potential slowly die.

So, if you want your restaurant to kick ass, you must be willing to go all-in. Over the years, I've learned to identify the patterns that lead to success and the traits that lead to failure. I've struggled myself whenever I deviate from my path. The seven rules below have been tested and are proven to provide the groundwork necessary to escape the cult of average and blast into the realm of outstanding.

I love that word. "Outstanding." To me, it means to stand out from the crowd, to surpass the ordinary, and to chart your path. Everyone can become outstanding—everyone. You have to be committed to these seven rules, do the work, and make adjustments. Make that commitment, and you'll get the results.

If you haven't been pushing yourself very hard, please don't expect overnight results. Even when you're doing all the right things, there will be a little "lag time" for the new habits and changes in thought to catch up and bypass the old habits keeping you where you are now. It's kinda like updating the operating system on your computer: be patient. *Keep at it and whatever you do, don't quit.*

#1. CULTURE FLOWS DOWN, NOT UP, AND IT STARTS WITH YOU.

This is my number one rule and for a simple reason: all business problems are people problems in disguise. Your restaurant's culture isn't an imaginary thing. It's real; it's tangible, it's the lifeblood of outstanding restaurants. Culture is created and fueled by the actions you take every day. **Culture can't be left to chance because it's a reflection of you.**

Think of culture like a pipe of energy that flows down to your team. The pipe runs straight up and down. You, as the energy source, are at the top and you control the flow. Your energy runs downward. Along the way, there are valves that have the potential to slow the flow. Those valves are the managers on your team. They can either increase the flow of culture, or they can impede it. Closed valves reduce the flow of energy to the team at the end of the pipe.

One of my primary tools for identifying where there are closed valves in the flow of culture is my 360 Leadership Evaluation™. I need to see how much of the culture you talk about really propagates to the team because that is what dictates how much energy gets to your guests. You might have the best intentions and vision, but if they don't flow down to the team that interacts with your guests, you're in trouble.

#2. ALWAYS MANAGE THE STATE OF YOUR RESTAURANT.

State management is the primary divider between the outstanding and the average. State is energy, and energy is everything. Let me repeat that: Energy is everything.

Energy creates atmosphere and is the hidden "it" factor that creates a great guest experience and then transforms it into exceptional! Here's the secret: people are energy. You're in control of the energy you bring into your restaurant.

Manage your state better with these tips:

Be aware
Your will world change when you become aware of your habits and patterns. Sadly, most people go through life like the walking dead, unaware of the things holding them back. Awareness precedes choice, choice precedes change—if you're willing to take action.

Thoughts become things
There's a fantastic line in William Shakespeare's *Hamlet* that will change your life once you understand it: "…there is nothing either good or bad, but thinking makes it so." **Nothing has meaning until you attach one to it**. A member of your team shows up 15 minutes late. Do you attach the meaning that they're irresponsible or disrespectful? Maybe they were just late, and it has nothing to do with you.

Hmmm... Life takes on a different view when we disassociate from negative viewpoints and become more open to other possibilities.

Watch your social orbit

Water seeks its own level, and we become like those with whom we associate. Hang out with losers and guess what you'll become. Hang out with highly-driven, focused, and successful people and odds are you'll mirror them. Your social orbit or peer group is more important than you realize. You'll need to rise to the level of a peer group to remain a part of it. Now, you might encounter internal conflict if you want to become better and reach a higher orbit, but keep a foot in your current one. Sometimes you have to let go of the things holding you down. That includes relationships that no longer serve you and your vision.

#3. MANAGERS MANAGE THE SHIFT; LEADERS LEAD THE VISION. BE THE LEADER THEY WANT.

Let's be brutally honest. There are very few true leaders in this industry. People love the title leader, yet few live up to it. The reality is that most people don't develop into leaders. Sure, there are natural leadership traits that help. Michael Jordan had incredible natural talent. What made him iconic was the work he put in to win 6 NBA championships.

Managers come to work and do enough of their jobs to get by. **Leaders learn to become better people.** They read, take online courses (shameless plug here for my program called The Restaurant Success Formula), they listen to audiobooks (*I use Audible, and it shows that I've listened to 605 books, which the equivalent of listening to audiobooks for 24 hours a day for 547 days or 13,128 hours*), and they seek out a mentor or coach. They're constantly improving their game.

Most managers cling to outdated management theories from the '70s! They still use carrots and sticks to get staff to comply. They abuse the power they have and create a culture of fear and intimidation. They hold the belief that they're irreplaceable. Now, let me assure you that *everyone* is replaceable. The replacement might not be the same—they might be better. It's the fear of being replaced due to lack of real leadership skills that causes most managers to overcompensate and behave like assholes. Humility is a sign of true leadership.

Managers run the shift like a game of checkers: pure reaction, not much strategy. Leaders lead through strategic vision like they're playing chess. They have figured out the variables for a variety of scenarios and play best-case and worst-case scenarios in their head to mitigate the downside. Special Operations Teams like the Navy SEALs, Army Green Berets, and Air Force Pararescue, spend more time training than they do performing missions. They keep their skills honed like a razor.

If you want to become a real leader, get out in front of your team and **lead**. It's that simple.

#4. YOU EITHER CONTROL TIME, OR IT CONTROLS YOU.

Time is a construct of the human mind. We created the concept of time and yet time controls so many of us. Time is always on our minds. Every day you're given 14,400 minutes to spend. The big difference between those who get what they want in life, and those who don't is how they invest their time.

The secret to time management is this: there's no such thing as time management! You can't control or manage time because it doesn't stop. There's no way you can stop time or press a pause button. What you *can* manage is your focus. Where you put your energy and focus is crucial to long-term success.

So, how can you manage your focus better?

Set reminders: If you have a smartphone (and I'm betting you do), you have one of the best tools available to help you: the alarm feature. Sometimes gentle nudges throughout the day are all you need to get back on the "focus track." I use this technique and I teach it in my **LevelUP!™ Peak Performance System**. I set my alarm for six reminders throughout the day at 9:00 a.m., 11:00 a.m., 1:00 p.m., 3:00 p.m., 5:00 p.m., and 8:00 p.m. (yeah, I tend to work late). This is a great way to help me draw my focus back on task and target.

Put a price on distractions: This is another tool taught in my LevelUP!™ System. You need to put a dollar amount on your time per hour. If you want to be worth $400 an hour, you need to act like it. Your words must be in congruence with your actions. Now, I don't have a problem with watching a movie or favorite T.V. show or spending some leisure time on social media. Just be aware that these platforms can become black holes that suck you in if you allow that to happen. The best way to control that is to think about how much you are worth per hour and imagine having to write a real check at the end of the week for the time you spent on those activities. Eight hours watching T.V., 8 hours on social media*, can add up rather quickly. If you're worth the aforementioned $400 an hour, then you would be writing a check for $6,400 for the week just in distractions. Ouch!

Research says that the average person spends about 2 hours a day on social media. That's scary!

#5. IT'S NOT THE PERSON YOU FAIL TO HIRE WHO DESTROYS YOUR RESTAURANT; *IT'S THE PERSON YOU FAIL TO FIRE.*

Who you allow on your team is probably one of the most important decisions you'll make as an owner or leader. Vetting people who want to join your team is crucial to long-term success. It's not just whether the person is a good fit for the job; it's also whether they're a good fit with the current team dynamics. Skills are important, but personality is everything!

The other side of the hiring coin is letting go of bad fits for the team. Listen, even if you ask all the right questions, do background checks, and have a candidate take a behavioral survey (which I recommend), and they seem like a great fit for the team, they might not work out due to team dynamics. Some people are very good at interviewing. They know what to say to get the job. It's only when you throw them in the mix, and they work with your current team that their true self emerges. Most people will be on their best behavior for about two weeks before their little quirks will start to appear. Everyone has quirks—they're what make us unique. You need to decide when someone's quirks start to appear whether they're going to be acceptable for the overall team dynamic.

My favorite motto is to **be slow to hire and quick to fire**. When you see behavior or a pattern that's a warning sign, cut them loose. Trust me; the behavior will only get worse as time goes on. Too many owners are afraid to discipline or let go of poor performers, so they allow them to stay. It wreaks havoc on the team and eventually will affect the guest experience.

If you have anyone on your team who you know you should let go, do it. If someone is unhappy on your team, you're holding them back from finding a restaurant at which they'll be happy and thrive. Not every restaurant is a good fit for everyone. Just like your restaurant won't fit a certain demographic, you might not be a good fit for some employees. Don't be selfish and hold onto people who aren't thriving in your organization, allow them the chance to find happiness. Just let them find it *somewhere else.*

#6. RESTAURANTS GET BETTER WHEN THE PEOPLE IN THEM BECOME BETTER.

School is never out for professionals. The old saying that "learners are earners" is true. The more you learn and grow, the more value you bring to the market. If you're a leader, the more you learn about communication, management theory, marketing, service, operations, team dynamics, and personal development, the more you are worth. But if you think that can all happen during your 40-50-hour work week, I have some sad news for you: that's not going to happen.

#WTSD: *Don't train until you get it right, train until you can't get it wrong!*

You must push past your comfort zone if you want to grow. As I've said many times, pushing past your comfort zone isn't as easy as people think. But hey, if it were easy everyone would do it. There are five key challenges you must contend with to break free of your comfort zone: authenticity, competence, resentment, likability, and morality. Sometimes you only hit a few of these challenges, and you might be able to work through them. Other times you're going to get slapped upside the head by all 5, and that feels like running into a brick wall. Coaching is an effective tool to lure people out of their comfort zones. To learn, you need to move beyond your comfort zone.

After you learn it, you need to train, train, and train some more to develop new behaviors or skills. Without enough training, you'll just slide back into your comfort zone. This is where most restaurants fail— not enough training. They train the team when they're brought on and maybe—just maybe—train them once in an infrequent while. Few restaurants make the effort to really become world-class at training. Whatever you think is a good amount of training is likely far below the level required. The best way to get the most out of your training is to shift your culture from a training culture to a learning culture!

Training cultures use the normal training curriculum that focuses on job skills. You train at the onboarding phase and maybe a class every six months. Perhaps you hand out a book for people to read. However, there's no discussion or agenda to extract the information and apply it to the business. Training cultures do the minimum needed, and that's why they're average.

Learning cultures focus on not just developing skills but enhancing them. Restaurants truly get better when you have better people working in them. Work on the real skillsets that hold people back: communication, social skills, body language, building rapport, organization, focus, and personal accountability. Honing these skills will elevate them to legendary status. Invest in developing your people, and they'll build your business. Most restaurant owners don't focus enough on the people they employ. Change that, and you'll change your business for the better.

#7. AWARENESS PRECEDES CHOICE; CHOICE PRECEDES CHANGE.

You're your biggest problem and your best solution. That starts with self-awareness. Awareness is freeing once you come to grips with it. The truth will set you free, right after it pisses you off.

After reading all of this, do you feel uncomfortable? Good. Being uncomfortable is a great place to start. Nothing will get better for you until you feel uncomfortable. If you want to push through to the point where you take action, you need to become upset.

"Upset? Hey, that's not very positive, coach!"

I know, I know. Stay with me here.

Your comfort zone can be a blind spot for you. Even when you start to realize something might not be right, and you feel uncomfortable, that's not enough to make changes. You're going to need to dig deep and write down what it will cost you if you don't change. That can be a dark and brutal exercise, but you need to use the pain it may cause to move you to take action.

You need to turn your "shoulds" into "musts." You should fire that poor performer; you should train your team, you should be marketing more on social media, you should take better care of yourself... Shoulds don't happen very often. Only when shoulds become musts do they happen and motivate you to take action.

You are your biggest obstacle to getting more from your restaurant and yourself.

Now you have some tools to make that happen, but only if you make it a must and take action — now.

The 80/20 Restaurant

I've received quite a few emails from managers asking about the Pareto Principle and how it can be applied to their restaurants.

As a reminder, the Pareto Principle is named after Vilfredo Pareto, an Italian economist. In 1906, he discovered that 80 percent of Italy's land was owned by 20 percent of the population (this was true in other countries, too). Soon after, he observed that 20 percent of the peapods in his garden was producing 80 percent of his peas.

The 80/20 concept has since been shown to be applicable in a variety of situations (and eventually was named for Pareto).

Wikipedia's definition, "...for many events, roughly 80% of the effects come from 20% of the causes."

That definition works well enough for me. Another name for this idea is, "the law of the vital few and trivial many." It sounds terrible at first when you realize that it's often being applied to actual human beings, but economists do like to deal with numbers more than people.

- *The Pareto Principle can be applied to a restaurant in a few ways.*
- Roughly 80 percent of your business comes from 20 percent of your customers. I've discussed the importance of converting your customers into raving fans.
- About 80 percent of your headaches will come from 20 percent of your customers or staff.
- Approximately 20 percent of your time and effort is responsible for 80 percent of your results.

While it's not necessarily as easy to use this principle in a restaurant as it is to use it in sales, the idea that 20 percent of causes are responsible for 80 percent of results can still provide savvy operators with plenty of insights.

As far as customers go, you want to identify the 20 percent who are making you money, and the 20 percent who are bumming you out. You want to nurture and grow the good 20 percent, and ruthlessly weed out the bad 20 percent. Okay, maybe not ruthlessly, but you get the idea.

Most of the problems originating from your staff are likely to stem from a core group of people. You need to get rid of those employees.

To varying degrees, a big chunk of your menu is dead weight. I've talked about menu engineering, menu innovation, and the life cycle of menu items before. Constantly evaluate your menu's performance and periodically review it to identify poor performers. It is likely true that a smaller percentage of your menu items are responsible for most of your sales.

Finally, while not related to the Pareto Principle at all, Vilfredo Pareto also famously noted that human behavior is driven far more by sentiment than logic. Which, it turns out, is also totally true. With that in mind—and knowing how much "stuff" you're dealing with in your day-to-day life—it's important to be smart about allocating your time, energy, and resources to the aspects of your restaurant that is going to perform.

Wasting 80 percent of your energy on something trivial as far as the bigger picture is concerned is, well, a waste. I see it all the time with owners doing tasks that they should delegate to others. Do you need to write the schedule if you're an owner with two or three competent managers? The answer is no.

HOW TO WIN PLAYING THE 80/20 PRINCIPLE

Develop Your Strengths

You hear this all the time: work on your weakness. It's a common idea in business that one needs to focus much of their time and energy, identifying and correcting weaknesses. More time and energy are often *misspent* mitigating flaws than spent on **developing strengths**.

By working on your weaknesses (which, to be fair, seems to be born of common sense), people don't realize that they're creating a glass ceiling for themselves. When you spend too much time minimizing flaws, you can't spend enough time on the things that can make you great. As a result, you're limiting your growth. And let's be honest with ourselves here: most people don't do business with an organization because they're pretty good in several areas—they do business with them because they're great in one.

So, the idea here is that you spend 80 percent of your energy on the things that you do well, and 20 percent of your energy on everything else.

This ensures that you continue to grow your strengths and, subsequently, the unique brand identity that sets you apart from your competitors. Marcus Buckingham, author of *Go Put Your Strengths to Work*, is a globally recognized thought leader of playing to your strengths. I have applied his principles when working with restaurant teams to amazing success.

Employ Your Strengths

Everyone knows (or should know) that they're good at some things and not so great at others. This is why it's amazing to me that some people spend so much time seemingly banging their head against the wall doing things at which they're just average or terrible.

Example: Not everyone is cut out to keep the books. I know I'm not. While as an operator you should understand the books, if you're terrible at keeping them, you need to outsource that task. That could mean hiring someone specifically to do that for you, finding better computer software to help manage finances, or contracting a third-party to take care of it for you.

Repeatedly banging your head against the wall only distracts you from more productive uses of your time and will both burn you out and hold you back in the long run.

Leverage the Principle

One of the best ways I can think of for using the 80/20 Rule is on your menu. In a lot of restaurants, there seems to be a very wide net being cast. That is, the menu is all over the place, or what I call the Mega Menu. I've talked about the idea of less being more with your menu items before, and my point stands. Eighty percent of your menu innovation energy should be spent identifying, developing, and leveraging your menu's strengths, not trying to account for what you think someone might like.

Restaurant Coach Key Point: You can't be all things to all people. You can be one thing to some people, though, and having a cohesive menu identity helps you focus on your strengths. That, in turn, helps you put your best foot forward with customers and diverts attention from shortcomings.

The moral of the story here is not to limit yourself, your restaurant, and your brand by overly focusing on correcting your flaws. **Most of your attention should be focused on leveraging your strengths because those are what sets you apart and speaks to your guests**.

That is how you become outstanding!

Why Thinking Outside the Box is WRONG!

Thinking outside the box is a cliché that has been around for decades. It's so overused in business that it has lost all meaning. The box implies rigid, constrained, and unimaginative thinking. Back in the '70s and '80s, management consultants loved to pull out a little test called the "nine dots puzzle."

The goal is to link all nine dots using four or fewer continuous straight lines without lifting the pen or tracing the same line more than once. The trick is that it can only be done when you take the line *outside the box.*

Thinking outside the box can be a dangerous trap. Problems arise when we want to innovate just for the sake of innovation. Many people want to do the new thing; few want to do the *right* thing. If you want to be the best at what you do, make sure everything is in order inside the box before you venture outside it.

So, before you shuffle off to the next project, idea, or menu, let's make sure you have everything in order. Here's a checklist of the things you should have in order before taking the trip "outside the box."

Have you updated your current menu costs within the last month?

That includes having a written recipe for everything you make in the kitchen. Yes, that goes for all the culinary professionals who like to create new dishes yet fail to cost them out to determine whether they're profitable. Coming up with new, innovative items to wow your guests is fun. Coming up with new, innovative items that wow the guests **and make a profit**, that's the challenge.

Have you run a menu analysis in the last three months?

Do you know the stars, plow horses, puzzles, and dogs on your menu? What's your action plan for the items that don't make a profit, and/or customers aren't buying?

Have you done a market analysis of restaurants within a mile of your location in the last three months?

You might be shocked to discover a few new restaurants have opened around yours without you noticing.

If you updated your menu recently, have you also updated those changes online?

Websites like Yelp, Trip Advisor, and Google Places will need to be updated with your current menu.

Have you held a training class with your team within the last month?

Training consistently is what separates outstanding restaurants from the mediocre. Think of it like going to the gym; consistency yields results (outstanding!). You're mediocre if you think going to the gym for one week will get you in shape, and you'll never need to go back. It's sad that many operators approach their training programs with that same mindset (once and done; next).

Have you cleaned and organized your back storeroom?

You know the one: the place in your restaurant that becomes a catchall for anything and everything you're not using currently. You think sizzling fajita plates are going to be popular again? Good luck.

Have you used social media to engage with your guests and not just talk about yourself?

Here's the not so subtle secret about social media: it's about being social. The 80/20 Rule is a good one to follow. 80 percent of your social media posts and activities should be about your guests and their interests. 20 percent should be about your restaurant. There are many unwritten rules for conduct on social media. Reciprocity is king.

Are you using other social media platforms in addition to Facebook?

Yes, it's hard to believe that there are other venues out there for staying in touch with customers. Twitter, Instagram, Pinterest, LinkedIn, YouTube, Snapchat…. It's a big, crazy, internet-connected world out there, and if you're not in the game, your restaurant will be sitting on the sidelines watching as the competition slowly takes away your market share.

Do you have an active recruiting plan for new staff?

Please don't tell me you only advertise for help when you have a job opening. Are you unaware that there's a war over talent being viciously fought today? If you're only advertising when you need someone your chances of finding top talent are slim. Hiring staff can be a passive or an active process. You can sit back and wait, or you can use tools like LinkedIn to actively search for applicants in your market. Just remember that in today's economy, it's an employee's market. There are a lot of restaurants trying to attract an ever-shrinking labor pool. If you want to attract top talent, you must make sure your restaurant is the employer of choice.

If you have all the above items in order within your box (a.k.a., your restaurant), congratulations, you're one of the few.

Thinking outside the box is easy. It's fun to break away from the same routine and focus on something new and shiny. The problem is that thinking outside the box distracts you from putting your focus where it needs to be. Think inside the box. Make sure your brand, culture, decor, service, menu, food, beverage, restrooms, staff, and guests are all taken care of first.

The devil is in the details. Get used to it.

YOUR RESTAURANT *STILL* SUCKS

The 7 Habits of Successful Restaurateurs

There is inspiration all around if you choose to open your eyes and take it in. Becoming a better leader, owner, or chef is not bestowed upon a few chosen few. There is no such thing as a born leader. Everyone can lead if they truly deeply desire to step up and take control of the wheel of their restaurant and their life. Most would rather sit in the back seat and be a spectator. Life is not a spectator sport.

Success and failure leave clues behind. If you are wise enough to take the lessons from the failures and the blessings of the successes, you have a great chance to not only reach the top, you can stay there.

When you study restaurant success (and failure) as I do, you start to see the puzzle of what makes a success restauranteur. Carefully put the pieces together, and you have a winning recipe to get exactly what you want in life (both professionally and personally). There is a better way and it does not involve beating your head against the wall just hoping things will get better next week. Things never get better on their own. They get better when you step up and take some damn action to ensure your success.

Successful restauranteurs are not lucky or born under a certain Zodiac sign. They come from all races and walks of life. They might speak your language, maybe not. Success is not a thing. Success is feeling. True success is a combination of your three hearts (the head, the soul, and the gut). When in alignment you'll find that the outside noise of the world stops for a brief second and you can hear for the first time the beauty of everything around you.

How do you get there? How do you reach this success nirvana? Just adopt these seven habits of the most successful restauranteurs into your daily life and you'll find what you seek.

1. SELF-CARE

The hospitality industry is one of giving. We give, give, and give to our team, our guests, our craft, and our families. What about giving to yourself? What about you? Who recharges you?

If you don't make time to recharge yourself, you'll be moving closer and closer to that condition called burnout. It's like going to work with your smartphone only charged at 25% and expect it to last all day with being recharged. When you run out of energy, your emotional self takes the reins to get you through the day (it's a survival mechanism). You become snippy and short with people.

Now, you don't have to go overboard and spend 2-3 hours at the gym. You need to take some time for yourself to recharge your internal battery. That could be some gym time, or it might be:

- A hike
- A walk
- Yoga at home
- Mediation
- A bike ride
- Making breakfast for someone you care about
- Reading
- Journaling
- Talking to a positive friend

There are so many things you can do for yourself. You need to get past the negative self-talk that taking time for yourself is being selfish. Taking care of yourself is required to reach the top. Successful restauranteurs know this, and they block off time on their calendar for self-care.

2. KAIZEN

After World War II, Japan was slowly trying to recover from the economic devastation that follows such events. To build their economy, they knew they had to provide products that created value and that the world would want.

To help Japan, they enlisted the help of an American by the name of Dr. Frederick Deming to help get their quality control systems in line. Through this process, they found the formation of a word which now is a philosophy of life: *Kaizen*. In its raw translation it means **constant and never-ending improvement**.

The Japanese take this concept seriously, and it is adopted into all forms of their life. You are always looking for ways to make it better. Ways to improve.

Things that have a lasting impact. Not just today, but every damn day! Kaizen is not a word just to be used; it is a way of thinking that can improve not only your restaurant but your personal life as well.

3. QUALITY QUESTIONS

Your brain is amazing! It truly is. When you ask it questions, it quickly searches the database in your head to give you an answer. Think of it as a lot like Siri on your phone. Ask, and you shall receive.

The downside of that is that when you ask bad questions, your brain gives you bad answers. Garbage in, garbage out. If you ask yourself why your staff doesn't do what you ask them to do, your brain returns the answer, "they don't care!" Maybe. Most likely, it's not true. You focus on the negative, and your brain gives you more of the same.

How do you stop this gloom and doom merry-go-round? Start asking better questions. In coaching, I do this all the time. When someone asks a disempowering question, I give them a nudge in a different direction by throwing out: "You need to ask a better question."

Instead of, "Why doesn't my staff do what I tell them?" Reframe that question to one you probably should be asking, "Have I been the leader they need and shown them exactly what I expect?" One sure way to tell if you are asking better questions is the general tone they take.

Bad questions have a tone that is whiny, powerless, blame, and shameful. They come out as being a victim of circumstances. They shut people down because they break people down.

Quality questions have a tone of confidence that is powerful, sure, commanding, and inspiring. They come out as being in control of circumstances. They get people to follow you because they elicit trust in you as a leader.

4. PROACTIVE

You have two ways to deal with things when they pop up: you can be reactive or proactive.

Reaction is how most respond to situations. It's primal and emotional. It also is volatile hard to control. When you react, you show people you don't have control and that erodes trust among your team. Once you lose trust, you've lost your ability to lead a team effectively. Now can trust be rebuilt? Yes. Will it take time? Depending on how many times you keep breaking down the trust circle. The more reactionary you are, the harder it is to come back.

The most successful restauranteurs adopt a mindset to be proactive. They play out scenarios and train for a variety of situations. Training and preparation are their primary tools. Will you always be ready for all the situations that pop up? Of course not, because there are too many variables. Being proactive allows you to gain confidence and certainty that you can handle whatever comes your way. Proactive is more mental than anything else. It's calming your mind to look for solutions.

Reactionary mindset looks to solve the problem now. It's not concerned about anything except fixing what's broken at the moment. Reactionary managers are firefighters. They are going from problem to problem to put out the fire. Here's the downside of that mindset: when there are no fires to put out, the firefighter sometimes starts the fire.

Proactive mindsets look to prevent problems before they start. Think of these leaders more like Smokey the Bear. They look ahead to see potential issues. They train their team and communicate the expectations of the standards. Reactive managers are playing checkers. Proactive leaders are thinking far ahead like in a chess game.

5. OTHERS ORIENTED

Egocentric personalities permeate the industry. The most successful restauranteurs have a healthy ego of confidence that doesn't overshadow the people around them. They know that to accomplish great things, it takes a team effort.

When leaders put the team and the guests in front of their desires, amazing things happen. People know you care about them, and there is no more powerful force in society than knowing someone else cares about you. It's a human need to be needed.

There is an epic quote by the great Zig Ziglar that captures the essence of this mindset: "You can have everything you want in life if you just help enough other people get what they want." Successful restauranteurs embody this in everything they do. They ask better questions. Most managers ask the question: *"What's in it for me?"* The successful ask: *"What can I do for them?"*

6. PRODUCTIVE

Time management is always a struggle for many managers. Successful restauranteurs know that time management is a myth. They focus more on getting results by managing their attention and controlling their calendar.

Throughout the day you will have a lot of things vying for your attention. From your staff, the guests, your friends, your family, and of course that 24/7 stream from social media. So many ways to go and not enough of you to go around. You don't have to be a slave to time. You can control it by carefully making choices of how you spend it. That involves saying "no" at times and making sure to put it on your calendar.

Your calendar is the holy grail of being productive. If you think about it, it's a dream. When you start taking about it, it starts to become possible. However, when you schedule it on your calendar, it become reality! Use your calendar to block off time to work on projects that move your business or career forward. You can't just expect opportunities to work on your stuff to happen by chance or when you get a moment. Successful restauranteurs don't wait for luck; they make their own by controlling their calendar. Having little white space on your calendar is a sign of a productive person.

7. BALANCED

You can work 80-90 hours a week, but there is a point where the extra hours stop being productive and you lose control of your emotional state. When you lose control of your emotions, you lose control of your brand.

Working long hours in a restaurant is not a badge of honor *(as I've mentioned before)*, it's just stupid. It's facing the truth that you don't have control of your business and that you think throwing more hours at the problem is the solution. **It's not.**

There comes a time where you need to focus on work that returns more results. That means stop wasting time with activities that do not play your strength and that others on your team can do. Here we get into that mindset many have of "they must do everything themselves." **You don't.**

Taking away the opportunity from others on your team to grow is a sure way to increase your turnover. With the labor pool in the restaurant industry struggling as it is, the last thing you want to do is add to the problem. People need growth like they need appreciation.

Seeking balance is never easy. It takes discipline to say no to requests. It takes courage to trust. It takes a real leader to step up and lead by example. Successful restauranteurs empower, train, and trust their team to do the right things in their absence. Hate to be the bearer of bad news, however, there is more to life than spending every waking hour at your restaurant. It's a big world out there. *You should check it out.*

They say if you are tired of the same old story, then you need to turn the pages (insight courtesy of REO Speedwagon). It's true. Adopting these seven habits into your life will change the way you see yourself and the role you play in your organization. **When you change, your business will change.**

Stop looking outside for the answers to the problems you can solve by becoming a better person.

Last Call

"You're dangerous," he says.

"Why?"

"Because you make me believe in the impossible."

—Simone Elkeles, Rules of Attraction

Why Restaurants Fail

There's only one reason why _your_ restaurant will fail.
First, let me tell you all the reasons it _won't fail._

It's not your business partners.

It's not your staff.

It's not your market.

It's not the economy.

It's not your significant other.

It's not your competition.

It's not your price point.

It's not even who is the current President.

The only reason your restaurant will fail is because of _you_, the restaurant owner.

I've spent the last nearly four decades working in the restaurant industry. I've owned restaurants. I had the honor of working with celebrity chef Wolfgang Puck for five years. I've had successes, and I've had failures. I've come to terms with owning all of it, good and bad. And I'm here to tell you that if you can't own your successes _and_ your failures, you can't move forward. Moving forward with gusto requires a coach.

Are you still with me?

Great! Because what I want to do is offer you some advice on how to select the best restaurant coach for your restaurant.

WHAT DO YOU WANT TO LOOK FOR IN A RESTAURANT COACH?

The first thing you need to understand is the difference between advice and opinion. Everybody has an opinion. Advice is different because it's usually information given firsthand from someone who has been there. I see so many restaurant coaches in the market today who have never actually owned a restaurant.

Would you trust a skinny chef? **No.**

Would you hire an overweight person to be your personal trainer? **No, of course not.**

So why would you take restaurant advice from someone who has <u>never owned</u> *a restaurant?*

Taking that even further, is the coach you're considering willing—eager, even—to tell you about their failures, what they learned from them, and how they became successful afterward? Failures are your biggest capital—they're the source of most of our learning. If you're going to take advice from someone and know that it's not just opinion, make sure it's from someone who's been there.

In all my years, I have distilled my experiences down to three keys that make outstanding restaurants. The first one is fundamental to all restaurants: the **systems** required to operate a restaurant. Every great business coach understands systems, and that's what most of them teach. Ninety percent of restaurant coaches focus on systems. What do I mean by that? It's your menu; it's your marketing, it's your checklists, it's your training, it's your budgets, it's your procedures; it's all the fundamental elements that are needed to manage day-to-day operations.

Don't get me wrong; systems are very important. I would go so far as to say they're the framework to restaurant success. There are some great restaurant coaches out there who are awesome at teaching systems. However, the problem is that they only focus on systems. **You can have the best systems in the world, but if you don't have a plan to use those systems strategically, you're going to fail because you have no direction.**

The second area is understanding **strategy**. What is a great business strategy? It's asking better questions. *Why are you in business in the first place? Why do customers drive to your restaurant? What are your core values? Why does your business exist? What are your overall strategic objectives guiding your restaurant?*

There are probably a dozen restaurant coaches out there who understand strategy at a high level. Strategy is the difference between playing chess and playing checkers. Most restaurant owners run their restaurants based on reaction, just like someone playing checkers. The market does this; they counter with that. When you start running your restaurant with a strategic plan, you consider all the moving pieces and develop a plan to use each one for its strengths.

The challenge with strategy is it requires a deeper level of thinking. Most restaurant owners get too caught up in the day-to-day operations to come up with a strategic plan to move their businesses forward, and that's why they struggle. Probably 10 percent of restaurant coaches out there understand restaurant-specific strategic planning well enough and can help a restaurant owner move forward. You must understand that if your strategy isn't driving your systems, you're screwed!

However, systems and strategy, while crucial elements for a restaurant, only make up **20 percent** of its success. **Yes, that's right only 20%!** There's a third area that almost all restaurant coaches ignore, likely because most aren't qualified to talk about and coach it. That's unfortunate because this third area is responsible for **80 percent of restaurant success. I'm talking about** <u>psychology and the mindset</u> **of the business owner.** As a restaurant owner, you can learn all you need to about systems and strategy, but what makes you and your restaurant outstanding is **how you apply them.**

Many behaviors of restaurant owners are *unconscious*; so, how can you be aware of them without a knowledgeable coach identifying and pointing out your blind spots? If you'd like to learn more about systems, strategy, and the **mindset** of successful restaurant owners, I invite you to take a look at my program called **The Restaurant Success Formula**™.

It's one clear 9-step roadmap to double-digit profits in 90-days without sacrificing your life to your restaurant. *Say it can't be done?* I have used this for eight years with thousands of restaurants to get results. Success often isn't just about doing the right things; <u>it also requires proper sequence and proper focus.</u>

So many of the "restaurant experts" out there are selling you **just a part of the solution** to achieve success. **The Restaurant Success Formula**™ is the first program that will set you up for long-term success by focusing on the *right things in the right order.* This program has been proven to get results for those that are willing to follow the roadmap and implement the three-phase process.

- **Foundation** - When you are building a house, a solid foundation is not just a nice thing to have...it's a requirement. Here we focus on the foundational building block of branding - *you.* Understanding *your* strengths, *your* core values, and the story behind *your* brand.
- **Framework** - Once you have a solid brand foundation, we can start to build the structure for restaurant success. This comes down to systems, hiring/training, creating a menu that amplifies your brand message AND <u>makes money!</u>
- **Functionality** – Finally, it's time to dial in the winning strategies that make the difference between restaurants that thrive and those that survive. Time to accelerate your marketing, implement a strong strategic plan, and maximize your P&L so you **finally can run your restaurant** (*not letting it run you*)!

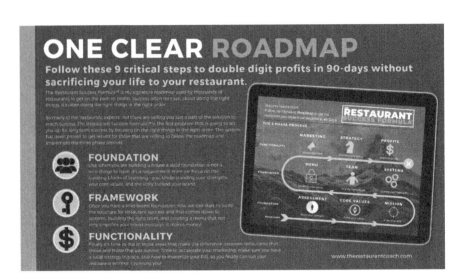

ONE CLEAR ROADMAP

Follow these 9 critical steps to double digit profits in 90-days without sacrificing your life to your restaurant.

The Restaurant Success Formula™ is my signature roadmap used by thousands of restaurants to get on the path to profits. Success often isn't just about doing the right things, it's often doing the right things in the right order.

So many of the "restaurant experts" out there are selling you just a part of the solution to reach success. The Restaurant Success Formula™ is the first program that is going to set you up for long term success by focusing on the right things in the right order. This system has been proven to get results for those that are willing to follow the roadmap and implement the three phase process.

FOUNDATION
Like when you are building a house a solid foundation is not a nice things to have, it's a requirement. Here we focus on the building blocks of branding - you. Understanding your strengths, your core values, and the story behind your brand.

FRAMEWORK
Once you have a solid brand foundation, now we can start to build the structure for restaurant success and that comes down to systems, building the right team, and creating a menu that not only simplifies your brand message, it makes money!

FUNCTIONALITY
Finally it's time to dial in those areas that make the difference between restaurants that thrive and those that just survive. Time to accelerate your marketing, make sure you have a solid strategy in place, and how to maximize your P&L so you finally can run your restaurant without it running you!

Time to Take Action!

I was going to call this chapter *"Stop Bitching About Your Life!"* but my editor thought it was a bit much. *(See how I still got my original title in there, though?)*

Don't tell me you got through this entire book and thought I wasn't going to throw a little shade your way one last time? If so, you haven't gotten to know me very well. If you're not taking some action today to change yourself, then seriously—<u>what the fuck are you waiting for?</u>

Sitting on the sidelines and making excuses isn't going to get you anything except more negative energy and shitty results. Throughout this book (and my first book, *Your Restaurant Sucks!*) I've given you tons of tools that can change your restaurant and your life. You need to apply them and apply them consistently.

It all comes down to <u>A.C.T.I.O.N.</u>

> **A = Attention:** distractions steal time from you.
>
> **C = Consistency:** you have to work at it every single day.
>
> **T = Tenacity:** you're going to want to quit. Don't.
>
> **I = Immediate:** make the right things a priority.
>
> **O = Obsession:** you're going to need to develop a healthy obsession.
>
> **N = Now:** the time to start your journey toward becoming outstanding!

I can't say it enough: focus and attention are the real currency today. You must understand and embrace that time is attention. How you focus your attention, spend your time, and who you give it to is precious.

Life, of course, isn't that easy and it will try to rob you of your attention by throwing all sorts of things in your path and keeping you from getting what you want. That Facebook notification, the staff who wants to rant about their bad day, the small talk that keeps you from getting back to a project... **They're all stealing your attention.** You can't multitask (even if you think you can). Humans aren't designed for multitasking, so stop lying to yourself. Instead, control small blocks of time to focus and move your agenda forward—it's the only way.

OWN YOUR DAY AND YOUR CALENDAR!

If there's one superpower you need, it's **consistency**! Habits only change through constant repetition and reinforcement. You can't do something once or twice and think that's it. Nope—you have to work at it until it becomes unconscious, automatic. If you need to think about it, it's not wired deeply enough to your neural network (your brain) to become second nature. True success comes when your bad habits are replaced with positive habits. They make or break restaurants and people. Look at people who get by, stuck in survival mode, and you'll see that they're besieged by bad habits. To break free from the past and get away from being average, you need to ditch your bad habits.

When you start to make changes and develop new habits, you'll find that you need a dose of tenacity to make them stick. The funny thing about change is that it doesn't want to materialize. We tend to want others to change so we can stay the same. Has anyone ever suggested that you change and explained that they're fine just the way they are? I'm sure you have. Hypocrisy runs rampant in the world. Don't succumb to it. Rise above it and be willing to fight for what you want in life.

There will be times when you want to stop. **Don't.**

There will be moments when you second guess yourself. **Don't.**

Your comfort zone will beckon you. **Don't go.**

To change and reach your goals you need to not only have the right priorities; you have to put them in the correct order. Success is like a combination lock: if you don't enter the digits (priorities) in the right order, you'll never open it (reach your potential). Getting things done is important—getting *important* things done is crucial to your success. You must be able to prioritize things, much like a triage situation. Not everything that comes at you during the day is a priority. You must intentionally focus on the tasks that yield a significant return on your attention investment.

You must also become obsessed with changing and taking action if you want long-term success. Obsession is the only way to build the restaurant and life you truly want. The word gets a bad reputation, but not all obsessions are unhealthy. A healthy obsession is one that's an internal fire driving you when you need it.

Finally, you need to tap into the power of the present, which is **NOW**! You can't go back and change yesterday (I'm still trying to convert a DeLorean into a time machine) and tomorrow is just a dream. The only thing you have control of is ***this*** *moment.* Taking action **now** is the cure for procrastination!

You just need to get your ass moving in the right direction and let momentum help you achieve your goals. Success breeds more success, and once your high-achieving, badass self gets a taste of it, you'll want even more. My favorite saying to clients is, "**When would <u>NOW</u> be a good time?**". Write that down and put it in a few places that can serve as a constant and gentle reminder to take action **now**!

You have the tools you need right here in this book. All you need to do is apply them to finally get the restaurant and life you deserve. Stop bitching about your life. *Isn't it time to drop the stories, the excuses, the drama, all the bullshit and just get what you want?*

I think you're ready. The next move is up to you.

Sign up for one of my programs, enter my world, and play the game at my level.

What's Next?

Start with my booklet, "Outstanding Mindset." It is a step-by-step guide to having an Outstanding Day! **This booklet is exclusively available on Amazon.** Plus, I included several bonuses in this informative booklet!

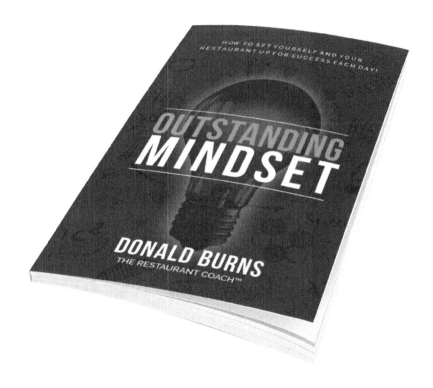

School is never out for the true professional. People who have applied the principles outlined in this booklet have experienced fantastic results. The beautiful thing about getting a taste of success is you'll want more!

Welcome to **The Outstanding Mindset Club**! Once you get the booklet, you can join the **private Facebook group — Outstanding Mindset Booklet —** for like-minded people such as yourself who have absorbed the content of this booklet and want to network with others who want more from themselves and their restaurants. You're the result of the people you associate with regularly. The Facebook group is your place to find peers who will lift you up to become your best!

You'll also get access to the mini **Outstanding Mindset Online Course** plus some bonus materials as well, including my **Outstanding Mindset Daily Planner**!

Hey, it's free to become a member when you get this booklet. ***When opportunity knocks, you must do your part and open the damn door.***

You need to do the work and apply the principles in this booklet to get results. Many will get this booklet, read it once, and not do one thing new to obtain the life they want. I'm betting you're not like that. I believe you'll take action and get results. Just make sure to create new habits and keep pushing yourself to change. Change is never easy. If it were, everyone would have the life and restaurant they want…**and** *we know that most don't.*

THE RESTAURANT COACH™ PODCAST

This is a *free* resource. Subscribe, so you never miss an episode. It's fully loaded with interviews with leading restaurant experts, tools, and tips to get you the restaurant and life you want.

THE RESTAURANT COACH™ (TRC) NATION

"A lot of people put pressure on themselves and think it will be way too hard for them to live out their dreams. Mentors are there to say, 'Look, it's not that tough. It's not as hard as you think. Here are some guidelines and things I have gone through to get to where I am in my career.'" — Joe Jonas

I started **TRC Nation** as a place where **sisters and brothers** from the restaurant industry could gather to get solutions to real issues they face every day. Not a place to bitch and complain about how much the industry sucks, but a place where positive attitudes prevail. I truly love this industry with all my heart, and if you become a member of TRC Nation, you do too, even if you might have fallen out of love with it.

The spirit of hospitality is what drives us, and I wanted to help bring that back to the restaurant world. To do that I wanted to **start** a <u>mentoring program</u> for restaurant leaders (at all levels) **to start** the revolution to bring back the core values that the restaurant world once had: respect, integrity, compassion, humility, and service to others.

TRC Nation is honored to have a growing list of world-class industry experts (mentors) that are willing to donate some time each week (for an 8-week program) to help others rekindle that spark and find direction in a turbulent industry.

Each mentor has been hand-picked by me for the experience they offer and the value they bring every day to raise the standards in the restaurant industry.

How do you get a mentor? It's easy. First, apply to join **TRC Nation on Facebook** and then apply to get a mentor from the post talking about the program! Just hit **'Sign Up'** and the road to getting everything you want begins! See you inside TRC Nation!

https://www.facebook.com/groups/135011193999569/mentorship_application/

RESTAURANT MASTERMINDS™

What a mastermind?
I learned early in life, you become like the people you associate with. I was fortunate to surround myself with people who wanted to be the best. It's those people who bring value to your life and challenge you to push beyond normal limits that produce a change in your mindset. When you change the way you look at the world, your world truly does change.

Success is about synergy. You can only get to a certain level by yourself. As an entrepreneur, I have pushed myself to higher levels and once reached, I would plateau. So, I sought out mentors and coaches that helped me push through those challenging plateaus to reach the next level. I am always pushing the edge to drive me higher.

A fellow restaurant consultant mentioned he was starting a mastermind group and asked if I wanted to be a part of it. That one decision has forever changed the trajectory of my business! Honestly, I was a little skeptical about being in a group of other business professionals. I never realized just how powerful being in a group with other high achievers could be. No bullshit. I cannot put into words the energy shift a mastermind can give you and your restaurant.

You have a fire inside that you feed every day. That's why you do this! That's why you get up after being knocked down. In a mastermind group, you have others that will also feed that internal fire that you have been doing alone for years.

You see, you are not alone in a mastermind group. You are part of something bigger than yourself and your restaurant. The mastermind group enables you to become a better person, and when you become better, your restaurant will become better too.

SUCCESS IS JUST ONE-DEGREE

I've been thinking lately about how little things make a big difference. Consider this: if you're going somewhere and you're off course by just one-degree, after one foot, you miss your target by 0.2 inches. Trivial, right? Not so fast. What happens when you get farther out?

- After 100 yards you'll be off course by 5.2 feet. Not huge, but noticeable.
- After a mile, you'll be off by 92.2 feet. One-degree is starting to make a difference.
- Traveling from San Francisco to Los Angeles, you'll be off by 6 miles.
- If you are trying to get from San Francisco to Washington DC, you'll end up on the other side of Baltimore, 42.6 miles away.

Over time, a mere one-degree error in course makes a huge difference!

The same is true in your restaurant. That's why you can't run your restaurant on autopilot. If you don't set the course correctly in the beginning atop a solid foundation, the odds of getting off course quickly escalate. That is why you must always monitor your results and make constant course corrections. How much better could your restaurant be if you made even just a one-degree effort to improve something about yourself or your restaurant, every day? It doesn't even have to be anything hard. **You have to do something and do it consistently.**

Pick something to do one-degree better today, and then never stop doing it. I promise this will change your life.

Restaurant Masterminds™ was created to give you that one-degree edge.

WHY DID I START RESTAURANT MASTERMINDS™?

People have asked me to do this. High performers need to be around each other. We are drawn to people like us like a magnet. We know that it's easy to fall into our success traps and routines if we were not constantly learning, talking with mentors, and challenging ourselves. Hell, when I was young, I thought I didn't need anyone to push me. That was the arrogance of youth talking. Over the last five years, I have had substantial business growth. That growth <u>EXPLODED</u> when I joined an elite mastermind group.

You join a mastermind for one of three reasons:
1. **You need a new perspective.** You *know* that what got you here won't take you to the next level. Masterminds broaden your view and open your mind to more advanced levels of thinking.
2. **You need new strategies and tools.** There's so much amazing insight available from other high-performing people, inside and outside the restaurant industry. Industry experts and thought leaders from a variety of other fields have been invited, including tech experts, marketers, Fortune 100 executives, retired military members (USAF Pararescue & Navy SEALS), accountants, restaurant real estate experts, architects, nutritionists, and sports psychologists. *I'll bring in the experts needed to help you raise your game.*
3. **You want the good stuff.** Masterminds are the place where people speak freely and share gold nuggets to success in business and life. Even when you're on a call listening to someone describe the challenges they're going through, you'll see how the group pulls together to offer creative solutions to seemingly insurmountable problems. Also, the masterminds are where I beta test a lot of new programs, strategies, and workshops. *You get a front row seat to it all!*

WHY JOIN?

As the restaurant industry gets more competitive, the time is right for you to join **Restaurant Masterminds™**. It's a safe way to get closer to coaching, without jumping into the deep end of the pool. It's time to break free from mediocrity and fulfill your restaurant's potential.

Don't Settle for Mediocrity

If you're ready to face the truth and explore the real reasons why you and your restaurant are in the state they're in, then you belong in

Restaurant Masterminds™. You will raise your game as you spend more time in the company of other like-minded restauranteurs. We become the average of those we associate with. That's why I'm very selective regarding who is allowed into this mastermind group. When you commit to the group, the group will commit all their resources to get you the restaurant and life you crave. **Fair warning**: we get down to business during our meetings. At times it will be brutally honest, however never disrespectful. The mastermind group will keep you accountable. I tell you that so that you go in with your eyes wide open. At the end of each meeting you will have an action plan, objectives you need to achieve before the next meeting - which the group will hold you to. It takes real discipline to succeed in any endeavor. Being held to your word by your mastermind colleagues ensures you maintain the **disciplined behavior** necessary to succeed in your restaurant and your life.

*You can get more info at **www.therestaurantcoach.com** or join us at our Restaurant Masterminds™ Annual event: **The Restaurant Success Summit**™ www.restaurant-successsummit.com*

GO ALL IN WITH AN ACCOUNTABILITY PARTNER...
THAT MEANS HIRE ME AS YOUR COACH!

Do you have a coach?
If not, you could be limiting your restaurant's success. That's because coaches help you identify and focus on what's important, which accelerates your success.

Great coaches:
- **Create a safe environment in which people see themselves more clearly;**
- **Identify gaps between where the client is and where the client needs or wants to be;**
- **Ask for more intentional thought, action, and behavior changes than the client would have asked of him/herself;**
- **Guide the building of the structure, accountability, and support necessary to ensure sustained commitment.**

Successful athletes understand the power of coaching. The United Kingdom Coaching Strategy describes the role of the sports coach as one that *"enables the athlete to achieve levels of performance to the degree that may not have been possible if left to his/her own endeavors."*

Innovative restaurant brands understand that coaching can help their leadership team increase their performance at work. They invest in coaching for their senior leaders and high-potential employees.

Coaching also has an impact on an organization's financial performance. According to an International

Coaching Federation study, 60 percent of respondents from organizations with strong coaching cultures report their revenues to be above average compared to their peer group. When applied, coaching pays for itself.

If you are starting a restaurant and want to set yourself up for success right from the start, or if you're an existing restaurant owner who wants more, coaching is the ultimate tool.

Is coaching for everyone? **Of course not**. Visit my website at www.therestaurantcoach.com to learn more and take The Restaurant CheckUp™ for FREE.

Warning: Restaurant coaching is <u>not</u> for everyone.

Side effects include: increased profits, better staff, happier guests, stronger brand identity, reduced stress, improved relationships, and quality sleep.

*Talk to The Restaurant Coach™ to see if coaching is right for you.

About db

Donald Burns is The Restaurant Coach™, named one of **The Definitive Restaurant Experts to Follow** and **One of 23 Inspiring Hospitality Experts to Follow on Twitter**.

A restaurant consultant for a $4.2-billion-dollar company, he is the leading authority, speaker, author, and international coach on how restaurant owners, operators, and culinary professionals go from *just* **good** to **outstanding.** A former **USAF Pararescueman** (PJ), restaurant owner, and Executive Chef with Wolfgang Puck, he has the unique skills to break restaurants free from average and skyrocket them to peak performance.

He works with independent restaurants that want to **build their brand**, **strengthen their team**, and **increase their profits** *without* sacrificing their lives to their business.

His first book: **Your Restaurant Sucks!** *Embrace the suck. Unleash your restaurant. Become outstanding.* is an international best seller and received the ***2019 Industry Book & Author of the Year Award*** *by Nightclub & Bar.*

Pick up your copy at Amazon! ***Available in Kindle and Paperback Formats.***

Acknowledgments

I must thank a few people who have made this book possible.

Reece Regalado & Darren Palehorse – Two men who on **September 27, 2018**, brought me back from being dead by giving me CPR when I went into **cardiac arrest**. They gave me a second chance to live. There are not enough words to show my appreciation and gratitude. *If they were not at the right place at the right time (with the right skills), you would not be reading this book.*

David Klemt – My editor and friend who takes the rawness of my words and sculpts them into what you're reading now.

Doug Crowe – Author, mentor, and friend who turns manuscripts into best sellers. You started me down the path of being an award-winning author, and for that, I am eternally grateful.

Drayton Boylston – my business & mindfulness coach. Thanks for introducing me to executive coaching and to be more present in life.

My Business Colleges and Mentors Who Inspire me to Become Better - Bruce Irving, Mike Ganino, Andrew Carlson, Yigal Adato, Chloe DiVita, Kelley Jones, Brian Duncan, David Cantu, Dan Carroll, Andrew Freeman, Eva Ballarin, Manel Morillo Prieto, Manuel Balanzino, Ramon Dios, Doug Radkey, Ed Mugnani, Tony Robbins, Grant Cardone, Brendon Burchard, Brain Johnson, and Gary Vaynerchuk.

To my friends at **Shamrock Foods** that allow me to do what I do and change the industry…*one restaurant at a time*: Thax Turner, Kelly Musselman, Kelley DeFraia, Chef Kelli Welby, Rodney Barton, Matthew Griste, Starson Roy, Ryan Hallum, Bill Focke, Rick Robinson, Ron "Bo" Bryant, and John Maier.

Donna Turner – Keeps me in check and makes sure I live between the dirt and the clouds.

To members of my elite mastermind group: The Level 7 Syndicate – you inspire me to become a better man.

To my fellow **Pararescue Brothers** – A group of men who live by a code of honor that nothing could ever break. The bonds of brotherhood never fade. **That Others May Live**. *HooYah!*

References

Dvorak, N. and Kruse, W.E. (2016). "Managing Employee Risk Requires a Culture of Compliance."

Lally, P., van Jaarsveld, C.H.M., Potts, H.W.W., and Wardle, J. (2009). "How are habits formed: Modelling habit formation in the real world." *European Journal of Social Psychology*. 40(6): 998-1009.

Mehrabian, A. (1972). Nonverbal Communication. New Brunswick: Aldine Transaction.

PostBeyond™. (2018). "2018, the Year of Social Advocacy in the Workplace." *Post Beyond Inc.*, Toronto, Ontario. https://www.postbeyond.com/employee-advocacy-guide/. (last accessed February 1, 2019).

Yang, S.S., Kimes, S.E., and Sessarego, M.M. (2009). "Menu price presentation influences on consumer purchase behavior in restaurants." *International Journal of Hospitality Management*, 28(1): 157-160. https://scholarship.sha.cornell.edu/cgi/viewcontent.cgi?article=1752&context=articles. (last accessed February 7, 2019).